Josephine Egan

A Century of Service in Wales

The Honourable Augusta Charlotte Elizabeth Herbert,
by permission of Llyfrgell Genedlaethol Cymru /
The National Library of Wales

A Century of Service in Wales

The Story
of the
Daughters
of the Holy Spirit
1902–2002

JOSEPHINE
EGAN
DHS

P³P

Published in Great Britain 2005
THREE PEAKS PRESS
9 Croesonen Road
Abergavenny,
Monmouthshire NP7 6AE
mail@p3p.org   http://p3p.org

The illustration on the front cover is reproduced
courtesy of Dom Dyfrig Harris OSB,
Belmont Abbey, Herefordshire

Designed & set in Fournier at Three Peaks Press

Printed in Wales at Gwasg Dinefwr, Llandybie

A CIP record for this publication
is available from the British Library

ISBN   1—902093—11—9

Preface

ACENTENARY IS A TIME TO TAKE STOCK OF EVENTS, AND TO REMEMBER the people involved in weaving the web of history. The Congregation of the Daughters of the Holy Spirit has given just over a century of service in Wales; mainly in education, but also in social care and in ecumenical endeavour. It is appropriate, therefore, to reflect on the story of the religious foundations that the sisters, as exiles from their native Brittany, set up and ran in Wales over the past hundred years.

The anti-clerical laws in France at the beginning of the twentieth century were part of a long struggle between church and state, which led to the separation of the two. The fear that the government of that time would bring about the dissolution of the congregation, either directly or through unfavourable legislation, was acute; for many years the Congregation of the Daughters of the Holy Spirit fought a fierce battle for survival.

However, with the enforced closure of so many schools owned or run by the sisters, it was decided that a number of them should emigrate and seek to live their vocation in more friendly countries, in Europe and beyond. It is for this reason that the Daughters of the Holy Spirit arrived as exiles in Wales, a country which shared a common Celtic origin with their own native Brittany.

My thanks are due to the many people who made this book possible. The primary sources used in this book are all written in French, and I owe a deep debt of gratitude to Anne Marie Davies DHS, provincial archivist, who has spent years translating all the sources relating to the foundations established by the congregation in Wales and England. My thanks, too, go to the following people, who contributed in various ways to the final outcome: to the Reverend Dr David H. Williams of Aberystwyth who designed the map of Wales on page 9, showing the location of the foundations, and who read the script and offered perceptive criticisms; to David Haswell, B.Arch (Hons), RIBA, for help with preparing the images for publication; to Dom Dyfrig Harris OSB, of Belmont Abbey,

Herefordshire, for the front cover illustration, and to the staff of the Archives, Maison Mère des Filles du Saint Esprit, Saint Brieuc.

I gratefully acknowledge the grants made by the following towards the publication of this book: CADW—Civic Initiative (Heritage) Grant Scheme; Monmouthshire County Council:Welsh Church Fund, and The James Pantyfedwen Foundation Aberystwyth. Finally, I wish to thank Three Peaks Press, Abergavenny, for the publication of the book.

The book is dedicated to all the benefactors and benefactresses of the Daughters of the Holy Spirit in Wales, who helped the sisters in their time of need: chief among these is the Honourable Mrs Augusta Charlotte Elizabeth Herbert of Llanover, whose wish it was to have a foundation of the Daughters of the Holy Spirit in every town in Wales, and who initiated negotiations for the establishment of so many of the foundations; Miss Abadam and Dr Johnson of Carmarthen; Miss James of Tenby, and the many others whose names are not even recorded in the sources. It is also dedicated to the sisters who pioneered the foundations, and to all the sisters who have carried out their apostolic ministry in Wales, over the past hundred years.

JOSEPHINE EGAN DHS
Abergavenny
Candlemas Day, 2005

Contents

Foreword	David H. Williams	8
Maps	The Location of the Foundations Made in Wales	9
	The Key Locations in Brittany	10
One	Landmarks in French Education	11
Two	The Founding of the Congregation of the Daughters of the Holy Spirit	14
Three	Persecution during the French Revolution and its Consequences	20
	Persecution and Exile	25
Four	1902: The Daughters Come to Wales	34
	The First Foundation:	
	St Mary's Convent, Monmouth	36
Five	1903: More Foundations in South East Wales	46
	St Joseph's Convent, Usk	46
	St David's Convent, Brecon	55
	St Alban's Convent, Pontypool	66
Six	1903: Foundations in West Wales	86
	St Winefride's Convent, Carmarthen	86
	St Margaret's Convent, Tenby	96
	St Padarn's Convent, Aberystwyth	107
Seven	Expansion: Foundations in 1904	126
	St Anne's Convent, Llanrwst	126
	St Mary's Convent, Pembroke Dock	145
	St Joseph's Convent, Pwllheli	159
	St Helen's Convent, Caernarvon	175
Eight	1906: The Twelfth Foundation in Wales	202
	St Michael's Convent, Abergavenny	202
Nine	The Golden Jubilee of the Province	233
	The State of the Congregation in the 1950s	237
Ten	The Second Vatican Council & its Aftermath	252
	Re-organisation, Change and Renewal	252
	The Last Foundation in Wales: Blaenafon	256
	New Ministries; the Growth of the Associate Movement	260
Eleven	Conclusion	263
	Bibliography	266
	List of Illustrations	268

Foreword

Reverend Dr David H. Williams, FSA

ANY GOOD HISTORY OF THE RELIGIOUS LIFE CAN MAKE STIMULATING reading. In this carefully researched and lucidly written volume, Sister Josephine Egan DHS has accomplished that, and much more. She traces quite vividly the trials and triumphs of her Congregation during the past three hundred years of its history and, more particularly, its last century of service here in Wales.

Reading the pages of this book, the impartial observer might feel that, on occasion, certain decisions of the general superior (as regards the opening and closing of communities and the transfer of sisters) were at times unwise, or at least difficult to understand. The extant documentation rarely, however, reveals the reasoning behind such decisions and, of course, the superiors were often the victims of very difficult circumstances in their day. Now, as Sister Josephine points out, times have changed, and (largely as a result of Vatican Council II) any such decisions would be less autocratic, and would result from much broader consultation and agreement.

To-day, few sisters of the order still reside and work in Wales, but the Congregation has left in several corners of the Principality an enduring legacy, not least in the field of education. In this respect, much is owed to the sisters. Their congregation was raised up by Almighty God to fill specific needs in the Church of earlier times. This the sisters did superbly well.

Now that, for the most part, the torch borne by the Daughters of the Holy Spirit has passed into other hands, especially an educated laity, the debt owed to them in Wales by people of all denominations should not be forgotten, and Sister Josephine's fine work ensures that it will be remembered for generations to come.

Aberystwyth
Feast of the Epiphany, 2005

MAP OF WALES

*Showing the location of the Foundations
made by the Daughters of the Holy Spirit*

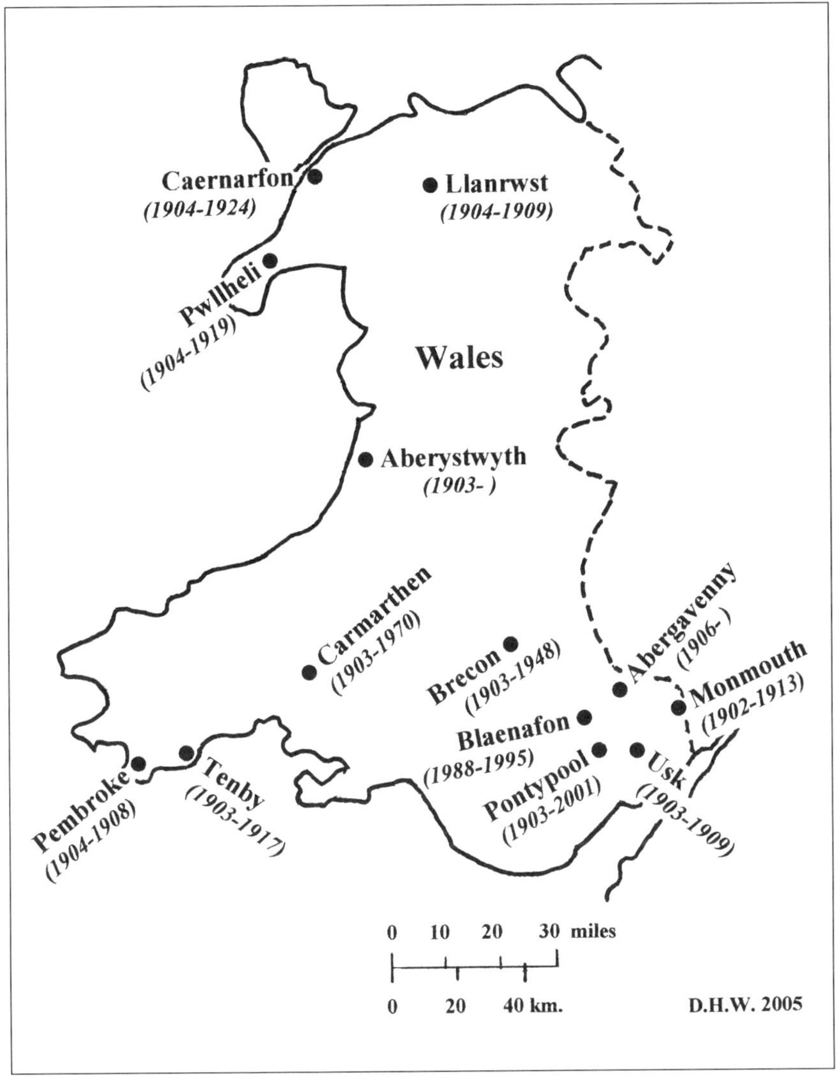

MAP OF BRITTANY

*Showing key locations associated
with the Daughters of the Holy Spirit*

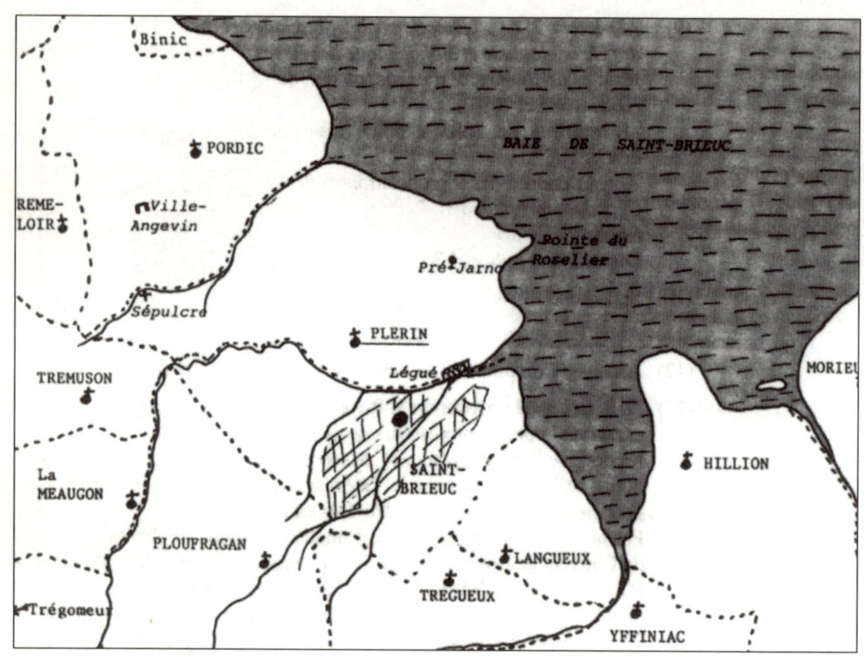

CHAPTER ONE
Landmarks in French Education

FROM EARLIEST TIMES, CHRISTIAN EDUCATION IN FRANCE WAS THE responsibility of the church. Up till the French Revolution, at the end of the eighteenth century, it was accepted that the control of education at all levels should be in the hands of the church. From the beginning of the second and third centuries when schools and libraries began to appear side by side with the churches, it was the bishops and the clergy who had taken the initiative in providing instruction in both religious and secular subjects. During the fourth and fifth centuries, small country schools began to be founded for the education of the common people, and there was a move towards universal education as early as 700 AD. The Council of Rouen, for example, ordered all Christians to send their children to school, a fact which pre-supposes the existence of numerous schools, at least in that diocese.

Under Charlemagne (769-814), the French bishops made efforts to provide universal education. In 797 Theodulf, Bishop of Orléans, ordered

> that priests should set up schools in the villages and towns and that no fee should be exacted from the children in return for their service. (Hilary Dale, 1963).

The great cathedrals and abbeys all controlled schools that provided more advanced instruction and some of these schools, such as the schools at Corbie, Saint-Wandrille, Tours and, above all, the Palatine School at Aix, were famous all over Europe.

By the twelfth century, most of the larger centres of population were provided with schools. By the beginning of the fifteenth century however, Jean Gerson, the Chancellor of the University of Paris, found it necessary to ask the bishops to make a point, during their pastoral visits, of ensuring that every parish should have its own school. "In every parish", he wrote

> let special care be taken in accordance with the sacred canons, to provide instruction for the children and especially moral instruction which must be based on the principles of our religion [Ibid].

In 1560, a royal ordinance decreed that parents should be forced, under penalty of fine, to send their children, both boys and girls, to school.

By the seventeenth century, there was a move to provide funds from ecclesiastical revenues to support a schoolmaster in every town and village, to give free instruction to children in the Christian religion and in other necessary areas of knowledge and good manners. Again, in 1598, a decree of King Henry IV repeated the command that parents were to send their children to school. For the most part, however, these regulations went unheeded. The difficulty of providing sufficient funds to finance such a large educational project, the low esteem in which the office of the elementary school teacher was held, and the lack of enthusiasm with which many parents of the poorer classes greeted the proposal of compulsory education for their children prevented any widespread enforcement of the law. Despite the frequent exhortations of the hierarchy, the establishment of widespread primary education was a slow process.

A genuine attempt was made during the seventeenth century to establish schools, and to render more efficient those schools which already existed. The most usual type of elementary school was known as the *petite école*. These schools were under the control of the bishop of the diocese, who exercised his authority in their regard through a dignitary known as the 'scholastic', the clergyman responsible for all the *petites écoles* in each diocese. He issued the teaching licence of the schoolmasters and mistresses and inspected the schools twice a year. No one was permitted to teach without a licence. One of the reasons for this ruling was the anxiety of the bishops to ensure that all those who taught in these schools were orthodox in their beliefs.

After the Wars of Religion, it was realized that the school more than any other institution was the most effective instrument for combating the heresies of the reformers; hence the interest in elementary education at that period. Laws were issued forbidding anyone suspected of protestant sympathies to set up a school or teach. During the reign of Louis XIV, watchfulness against unorthodoxy among members of the teaching profession was renewed on account of the Huguenot heresy. The Huguenots, who were forbidden to run schools of their own in the larger towns of France, resorted to *écoles buissonières* (hedge schools) held secretly in the woods or open countryside, and although attendance at such schools was made a punishable offence, it was not an uncommon practice. In order then that the church should closely supervise the establishment of schools, any candidate for a teaching post in a *petite école* was requested to find three respectable persons who would join with the parish priest in attesting to his orthodoxy and good morals. Only then would the scholastic provide him or her with a teaching licence, which was renewed yearly on a given day at the scholastic's office.

The majority of the *petites écoles* were maintained by endowments and legacies bequeathed by benefactors. These revenues were, however, rarely sufficient for the upkeep of the schools and teachers, so it was customary to charge a small school fee of three or four *sous* for learning to read, with an extra charge for writing and arithmetic. Children who could not afford even this small fee were admitted free. The fee-payers sat apart from the free pupils, lest the rich, ordinarily regarded as cleaner than the poor children, should be infected with vermin from the poor children. To increase their small income, the teachers were sometimes authorized by the scholastic to take some pupils as boarders. Such teachers were called *permissionaires*.

The *petites écoles* were usually held in a private house, the schoolroom on the ground floor often serving at the same time as the schoolmaster's living room and kitchen. Seated on wooden benches, the children were taught christian doctrine and reading, and sometimes writing and arithmetic. The first lessons in reading were generally taken from Latin books, of which the children understood nothing; this was because the Latin spelling was more phonetical than the vernacular, which the pupils were permitted only when some progress had been made. The books were almost exclusively religious. Some pupils were invited to bring family documents such as leases and wills, to give them some practice in deciphering manuscripts.

Even in the eighteenth century, education was by no means accessible to all, owing to the unequal distribution of schools, and the difficulty of finding teachers. As great an obstacle as any to the development of elementary education was the necessity of charging fees, and the clergy made efforts to found free schools, sometimes with the parish priest or his curate acting as schoolmaster. Other free schools were run by religious orders of both men and women.

CHAPTER TWO

The Founding of the Congregation of the Daughters of the Holy Spirit

THE FOREGOING WAS THE GENERAL STATE OF EDUCATION IN FRANCE at the beginning of the eighteenth century when the Congregation of the Daughters of the Holy Spirit was founded in Brittany in 1706 (See map 2, p.10). In the Diocese of Saint Brieuc, where the congregation was founded, there were *petites écoles* or charity schools in existence in many villages and hamlets, but these were mainly for boys. There were, in addition, small schools run by priests who lived at home in their families. Having no parish, while they waited for the patronage of the aristocracy to provide one, they spent their time teaching Latin to the sons of farmers and small landowners whose parents wished to send them on to the college in Saint Brieuc.

The scholastic who was appointed in 1690 in the Diocese of Saint Brieuc was Dom Jean Leuduger **(Plate 1)**, who inspired the founding of the Daughters of the Holy Spirit as a religious congregation of women dedicated to the education of youth and the care of the sick. Jean Leuduger was the son of a farmer in the parish of Plérin, a small town not far from Saint Brieuc. "His parents were a good-living christian couple, reasonably well off." (Ropartz, 1857). It is on record that his mother, Louise Quinio, was a woman of such deep piety that when the time came for the birth of her son, she arranged for the birth to take place in a stable so that from the time of his birth, the baby should have as close a resemblance as possible to the Christ child. Jean Leuduger, the fifth child of Jean Leuduger and his wife, was born on 9 November 1649. He was baptised the same day in the church at Plérin, and as soon as his mother held him in her arms, she offered him to God with the prayer that he would one day be a priest.

Of his childhood we know nothing, until the day in his eighth year when he was sent to the *petite école* at La Ville-Hervy, kept by a certain Edmé Duval, who did not keep him long.

> The child had a quick intelligence, a ready understanding, and an excellent memory; by nature he was serious and industrious. The village school master had nothing more to teach him. (Ropartz, 1857)

His next teacher, Jean Ruellan, was probably a priest. From him Jean learnt the rudiments of Latin, and he made such rapid progress that in 1661 his parents sent him to the College in Saint Brieuc, known in those days as *L'Hôtel du Paradis*. After four years at the college, where he learned to speak fluent Latin and to understand Greek, he persuaded his parents to send him, at considerable sacrifice to themselves, to the Jesuit College in Rennes, where he had the privilege of studying logic under a certain Père François, who as a young priest counted Descartes among his pupils. During his time at Rennes he was uncertain about the direction his life should take. To help him decide, he set out alone and on foot on a pilgrimage to Rome, in the hope of resolving his difficulties at the tomb of St Peter. After an absence of twenty-eight months, he returned and placed himself under the direction of the Dominican Fathers at Rennes and studied theology as an immediate preparation for entering the seminary of *La Grande Grenouillière*, at Saint Brieuc.

His mother's wish was fulfilled when Jean was ordained at the end of 1674. He celebrated his first Mass in his native Plérin on New Year's Day 1675. From the early days of his priesthood, he interested himself in the religious education of the young, the most important part of his apostolic work. Although he always took an active interest in the promotion of christian education throughout the diocese as canon scholastic, his attention was particularly drawn towards the children of Le Légué, a small fishing port in the estuary of the River Gouët, in the parish of Plérin. There was no school there, and the children were left to run wild about the countryside while their parents were busy with the fishing boats or small farms. As soon as Jean Leuduger became scholastic of the diocese he was determined to remedy the situation and, as no benefactors could be found to build a school, he decided to start one on his own initiative.

With this plan in mind he persuaded a young kinswoman, Renée Burel, to abandon the idea of entering the Ursuline Convent in Saint Brieuc, and to devote her life instead to the education of the poor. And so together with Marie Balavenne, an older woman and the widow of a sailor, he set up a charity school at Le Légué, sometime between 1698 and 1705. Renée Burel had money of her own and, augmented by Jean Leuduger's, used this to build the school **(Plate 2)**, the foundation stone of which was laid in 1705 by Mgr Frétat de Boissieux, the Bishop of Saint Brieuc.

> This obscure village school was to prove the cradle of the great religious family of the White Sisters. Its beginnings could not have been more humble, and that seems to be the rule of all religious families, and a rule moreover that admits of no exception, ever since the seed of the Catholic Church itself was planted in the Heart of a Baby in a wayside stable. (*The White Sisters*, p.21)

At this time the bishop approved the simple rule of life which Jean Leuduger had drawn up for the two women. There was no idea of setting up a new religious congregation, and for the first months of their life, Marie Balavenne and Renée Burel regarded themselves simply as regular members of the Third Order of Holy Love, a pious society which had existed in the parish of Plérin for some fifty years, for the purpose of providing religious instruction for the children of the district.

The life lived by the two schoolmistresses was a regular one, divided between prayer, teaching in the school and visiting the poor and sick of the parish. As time passed, however, they felt an increased desire to consecrate themselves more fully to God by binding themselves to Him by the vows of poverty, chastity and obedience. Through Jean Leuduger, they approached the Bishop of Saint Brieuc and obtained the necessary permission, and on 8 December 1706 they made their religious profession in the little chapel of Le Légué. From then on, the sisters adopted as their religious habit the ordinary costume of the women of Plérin, but dressed in white, in honour of Our Lady's Immaculate Conception, a feast which is kept with special solemnity to this day and is second in importance to the Feast of Pentecost, the patronal feast of the congregation.

The new congregation had, as yet, no official name. The sisters were known as the *Filles* or the *Soeurs Blanches* (White Sisters) or the *Filles de la Charité de Plérin* (Daughters of Charity of Plérin). Jean Leuduger had a great devotion to the Holy Spirit, as had Monsieur Allenou de la Ville-Angevin who came to Plérin as curate in 1710, and who was largely responsible for the development of the congregation. He had studied for the priesthood at the Seminary of the Holy Spirit in Paris. It was decided then that the sisters should be known as the *Filles du Saint Esprit* (Daughters of the Holy Spirit), a title that was confirmed by the Bishop of Saint Brieuc when he approved Monsieur de la Ville-Angevin's completion of the Rule in 1733.

The Rule directed that while the first concern of the Congregation of the Daughters of the Holy Spirit was to be the adoration of the Blessed Trinity "and most especially the Third Person, the Holy Spirit, who is the love of the Father and the Son," (*Rule of Life*, 1733) they were to care for the poor and the sick, visiting them and assisting in every way possible and "to keep a school for the little girls of the parish, teaching them their prayers, the catechism, reading, writing, counting, sewing etc…"

In 1710 another girl from Plérin, Charlotte Corbel, came to join the community; others soon followed. The little school at Le Légué grew rapidly. Although there were rarely more than thirty pupils on weekdays, every Sunday brought as many as two hundred older girls who were kept at home during the week to help with the work of the house or farm. In 1720 the sisters moved to a larger school in Plérin **(Plate 3)**, and the number of pupils was soon doubled. In 1723, the school was said to be the best set up in all the country.

The greatest desire of the sisters who taught in the school was to help their pupils to grow up into honourable Christian women. The training of the children in the natural and supernatural virtues, the duty of correcting their faults and the instructions of the Rule on this subject were precise:

> When a Sister is obliged to correct the children of God, whom he has confided to her, she shall remember first of all that they are the children of God. Secondly, she must remember that they are more pleasing to God than she is herself, as they are more innocent, and that God whose place she holds never punishes his children but by love.

They were never to punish their pupils through anger or impatience and they were "never to strike a child." They were not to inflict a punishment without making clear the reason for which it was being imposed. The children were to learn to observe the rule of Christian courtesy on entering and leaving the classroom. The sisters taught their pupils household crafts of marking linen, hemming, knitting, spinning and weaving.

The sisters were to be strictly impartial in their relations with their pupils. If any had a right on their preference, it was the most poor, and they were to consider themselves fortunate in having a great number of the poor among their pupils, convinced that it was these who were most capable of drawing down God's blessing on their house. They were instructed to inspire in their pupils a great love for the poor, and this was to remain one of the most cherished characteristics of the Daughters of the Holy Spirit. The first sisters guided by their Rule realized that the best way of gaining the confidence of the poor and directing it to God was to share their poverty.

The simplicity and poverty of the life of the first Daughters of the Holy Spirit is part of the history of the congregation, which tells a moving story. In their little school, they had few books and little paper. The children's first writing lessons probably consisted, as in other schools of the period, in tracing in sand with their forefingers the letters written on the board by the schoolmistress or monitress. Once the alphabet was mastered in this way the pupils were promoted to the use of a slate on which they wrote with a sharp stone, washing off their work when the slate had been filled.

Lessons lasted six hours a day. Each lesson began and ended with a prayer, and every half hour a pupil in each class, appointed by the sister, called upon her companions 'to raise their hearts to God.' The Rule further directed that whenever the school was within a reasonable distance of the parish church, the sisters were to take the children there every morning for a brief period of private prayer, taking care to make them walk 'two by two'. As they made their way to and from school along the narrow Breton lanes, the little girls were to recite the rosary.

Every evening when lessons were over and the children had been dismissed, the sisters left the convent and spent the rest of the day visiting the poor and sick of Plérin and its outlying hamlets. Dom Jean Leuduger had written a letter to the sisters in which he had this to say:

> Should a destitute person call at the house during meal time, share your food with him; do the same also with neighbours whom you know to be in difficulties, put aside a portion for them also. (*The White Sisters*, p.28)

Their visits to the poor and the destitute, which entailed both actual nursing and the distribution of alms which had been entrusted to them by charitable people, enabled the sisters to extend the religious influence which they exercised in the school, and to maintain a close contact with the families of their pupils. It was in connection with this side of their work that they extended their mission to nursing and, thanks to the generosity of Count Claude de la Garaye, a hospital was opened at Taden on 16 June 1730, although at that time the congregation numbered only ten sisters. In addition to the premises, the Count granted them a hundred pounds a year to meet the expenses of the dressings and remedies, which they would need in their work among the sick.

The work of the sisters at Taden gave many other landowners the idea of founding convents in their parishes in order, as one of them put it:

... to obtain some comfort for their tenants, help for the sick and useful christian education for the children.

In nearly every case the conditions under which the foundation was made were the same as those at Taden, the landlord providing and endowing the convent and the sisters agreeing to undertake the works stipulated by the benefactors.

In 1722 Jean Leuduger died, worn out by his apostolic labours and by the extreme voluntary poverty in which he lived. He left the young congregation in the hands of Monsieur de la Ville Angevin, who was by now parish priest of Plérin.

In 1720 the latter, with the approval of Jean Leuduger, had transferred the sisters' school from Le Légué to a larger house, which he had bought in Plérin itself. This house was subsequently to become the first mother house of the Congregation of the Daughters of the Holy Spirit. Fourteen years after its foundation, the congregation was firmly established in Brittany, the land of its birth.

CHAPTER THREE

Persecution during the French Revolution, and its Consequences

ON TWO OCCASIONS IN ITS HISTORY, THE CONGREGATION OF THE Daughters of the Holy Spirit had to face persecution in their native Brittany. At the outbreak of the French Revolution, there were nineteen convents of the congregation all over Brittany. These were situated in remoter areas, for during the first century of its existence the congregation was insistent in restricting its exterior works to the service and education of the poor in the country districts, and avoiding the larger towns where other charitable institutions were already established. The later development of the congregation, and the demands of bishops and parish priests, were to make it impossible to refuse the undertaking of work in urban districts.

In the eighteenth century, France was teeming with new ideas which since the seventeenth century had been spreading all over Europe. Philosophers were advocating a society in which each citizen would enjoy equal dignity and equal rights, a democratic society freed from the absolute power of the monarchy and of the church, often too closely linked with the nobility. Little by little, these ideas gained ground. In 1789, the Revolution broke out. It proclaimed the motto of the Republic: 'Liberty, Equality and Fraternity.' Unfortunately, it brought in its train devastating violence. In the name of republican liberty, the legislative assembly of 1792 abolished all the corporations, the secular congregations or congregations of women dedicated to the service and relief of the sick either in hospitals or in their homes.

Sister Marie Allenou de Grandchamp (1743-1779), who had succeeded Marie Balavenne, the foundress, as superior-general in 1743 died thirty-six years later on 25 November 1779. It was her successor, Catherine Briand (1779-1804), who had the task of guiding the congregation of seventy-three years' existence through the tumult of the French Revolution. The convent at Plérin, the mother house of the congregation, was invaded by the revolutionaries for the first time on 19 August 1791, but the superior received them with such calm authority that they left without requisitioning any of the convent property. The mayor of Plérin protested in the name of the inhabitants, against this violation of a religious enclosure, but the authorities of the Saint Brieuc district paid little heed to his letter.

A few weeks later, however, the dowries of the sisters, which brought in a total of five hundred and seventy pounds a year, the congregation's sole source of revenue, were seized. On 18 November 1792, an inventory of the convent at Plérin by a government official was made, and on 2 January 1793, the sisters were ordered not only to surrender their few altar vessels, but to pay a fine equal to their monetary value. A further fine of three thousand francs was imposed, because

> in defiance of the law, these women continue to wear a forbidden uniform and scattered about the countryside, are encouraging fanaticism and propagating the most dangerous of prejudices and because their house at Plérin is the nursery of the communities of the same order. (Hilary Dale, 1963)

Other insults followed and finally on 18 January 1793, the district commissioners came to the convent and informed Catherine Briand and the sisters that they were given seven days in which to evacuate this and the other eighteen convents of the congregation and return to their families. The superior-general was now well over seventy years of age, but she received this announcement calmly, and read in a firm voice the protest, which she had hastily written on receiving news of the commissioners' approach:

> Our principal aim in Plérin and all our other houses established within the Province of Brittany are charitable institutions in which the sisters devote themselves to works of charity and endeavour to go daily to the assistance of the sick in the poverty-stricken villages. The article of the law of 18 August 1792, which prescribes the suppression of religious congregations, makes a formal exception for charitable institutions such as ours. Humanity, compassion for the suffering of the peasantry is even stronger recommendations for our conservation. (Archives, Saint Brieuc).

The commissioners listened to the protest; then they collected the paper on which it was written and declared they would pay no heed to it. They seized all the articles listed on the inventory of 15 November 1792, but left everything except the contents of the chapel and the pharmacy, on condition that it should all be distributed between the sisters as personal dowry legally due to each of the expelled sisters.

The mayor of Plérin and the municipal council pleaded for the sisters to remain, but to no avail. All he could do was to claim the convent as municipal property, and keep it for the sisters till their return at the end of the French Revolution. On 23 January 1793, most of the sisters left the convent; six remained, but they were driven out by force five months later.

In 1794, the town council of Plérin received orders to denounce the Sisters of the Holy Spirit who persisted in living in the parish. On the contrary, however, the mayor spoke on their behalf. "In spite of their irregular position," he said,

> these women, twenty in number, to whom we should add three nuns from enclosed communities who are living in the town, can only be said to be very useful in taking care of defenders of our country who have returned home in bad health, as well as those who have contracted illnesses through nursing them. They live a very retired life and cause no trouble. (Hilary Dale, 1963)

Still most of them had to disperse. Those who returned to their families carried on as far as possible their former works of charity and some sought to teach the children of the village. The Christian education of children had no place in the programme of the Revolution, but the authorities found that they had made a mistake in thinking that they could do without the services of the sisters completely. At Quimper, for example, Sister Marie Claude Bodet who had been imprisoned for refusing to take the constitutional oath was released every day to visit the sick and dying in their homes, o n condition that she returned to the prison before nightfall. The sisters at St Paul de Léon were released for the same purpose, and in several districts the sisters were gradually able to resume their work.

Other sisters were less fortunate. The sisters of Saint Herblon and Derval were imprisoned at Nantes. Despite the petition of the public that two of them be released, the revolutionary committee refused the request. This prison was filthy, unaired and full of disease. One sister died there on 29 May 1794; many of her companions died shortly after their release.

For the most part, the arrest and expulsion of the sisters was greeted on all sides with indignation and dismay. There is on record just one instance where the sisters were denounced to the revolutionaries. This was in the town parishes of Ploeuc and Plaintel, which were the property of the

Marquis de Lafayette, in both of which the sisters had schools. The disaffection of the Marquis de Lafayette from the revolutionary party must have caused a bitter reaction against the church and the aristocracy in at least his Breton domains.

A thousand citizens willing to swear against the sisters came forward to denounce them. On 25 October 1792, the following letter was addressed to the head of the French Republic. They wrote:

> We the undersigned citizens, denounce the White Sisters as enemies of the Republic. They render no service, they maintain contact with bad citizens both émigrés and others, who have remained in France, and they live in houses belonging to the nobleman, Lafayette, well known as a traitor to the country. By their poisonous suggestions, they are sowing discord and division among all the citizens, saying that the constitutional priests and the district and departmental administrators offer sacrifices to the devil and have dealings with him. They go about preaching the counter-revolution in all the houses. The undersigned beg you to deliver them from the terrible scourge of the aforesaid sisters of Plaintel and Ploeuc; moreover, as the law prescribes that the houses and belongings should be sold for the profit of the nation, they being the property of an émigré. They exhort you to dispossess the aforesaid sisters immediately and expel them from the department…(*Vie de Jean Leuduger*, Author unnamed).

In these and similar ways, the sisters suffered the trials of the Revolution.

When the French Revolution finally came to an end in 1800, the sisters began to return to the mother house, which the loyal mayor of Plérin had prevented from being sold as national property. The number of the sisters was considerably diminished by now. Several had died during the Revolution, while others could not bring themselves to leave the works of charity they had begun during their enforced absence from the convent. But those who returned resumed their former life with fervour, and many new prospective members began to arrive to take the place of the missing members of the congregation.

One of the first concerns of Napoleon's government was educational reform. The Revolutionary Assembly had held lofty ideas of their duty to educate the people, but had done little about it. On the contrary the education system, which had until then been the responsibility of the church, was almost completely destroyed. The nation-wide enquiry made in 1800-1801 showed that primary education, especially, was in an alarming state. Jean Portalis, one of the authors of Napoleon's civil code and the future minister of public worship, expressed the need for a return to religious beliefs and practices. "It is time," he said,

> for theories to give way to action. There can be no education without moral and religious training. For the past ten years, education has been non-existent; it must be based on religion…and so the whole of France calls religion to the moral rescue of society.

Portalis suggested that the only way to remedy the state of affairs was to appeal to the religious orders to take charge once more of the primary education of the nation's children.

In a report to Napoleon, he recalled that the plans specified in the revolutionary decree of 30 May 1873, for an efficient but entirely secular system for primary education had failed for lack of funds and lack of teachers. "Once we see" he concluded,

> that primary education must be based on the principles of religion, we can easily realise that for this purpose, as for the case of the sick, the religious societies are not only the most suitable for the education of both boys and girls, but that these societies must even be regarded as indispensable.

Napoleon's views on the subject were in agreement with those of Portalis. Permission had already been given for the religious orders to resume community life, and they were now invited to take up their works in the primary schools, which they had been forced to abandon on 1792.

In 1804, Sister Yvonne Blec'h was elected superior-general of the Daughters of the Holy Spirit. The outstanding event of her term of office, which ended in 1813, was the official recognition of the congregation by the state. An Imperial Decree of Napoleon dated 13 November 1810 approved the statutes of the Congregation of the Daughters of the Holy Spirit. Its goal is set out as the care of the poor, the sick and the running of small schools, especially in the rural areas. Article 2 of the statutes extended the field of action. "The Daughters of the Holy Spirit may carry out their tasks in the towns and may run hospices, welfare centres at the request of the local authority and with our authorisation" (Article 6). The fact that this decree recognised the congregation as a teaching order and sanctioned its "running of small schools" was to be the congregation's safeguard throughout all the storms over Christian education, which surfaced again at the beginning of the twentieth century.

Persecution and Exile

THE CONGREGATION of the Daughters of the Holy Spirit survived the horrors of the French Revolution. The congregation was, however, faced with persecution for the second time in its history a century later, in the struggle between church and state over the question of education. which was a long and bitter one. The congregation, which by now had grown and flourished within Brittany, was faced with an even greater challenge which resulted in exile for many members of the congregation to Holland, Belgium, Great Britain and the United States of America.

The conflict between the church and state over the future of education in France continued throughout the nineteenth century, and a brief outline of the growing rift between church and state will help to illustrate the unexpected developments within the Congregation of the Daughters of the Holy Spirit. In March 1880, soon after a new government was formed under Jules Grevy, a new law was passed, to exclude clergy from the university boards, and attacking the liberty of the secondary schools. The clause read:

> No one may be allowed to direct an establishment of any kind, nor to teach in such an establishment if he belongs to a non-authorised religious congregation.

All congregations were henceforth to be approved by the state. This was rejected by the senate by 148 votes to 129. The government replied to its rejection with two other decrees issued on 29 March 1880. One suppressed the Society of Jesus (Jesuits), giving it three months to leave the country; the other ordered all non-authorised congregations of men to ask the government for recognition within the same limit. When petitions were made for recognition, they were not granted and despite the efforts of the Holy See, the French bishops and the superiors in question, the government succeeded in closing 261 establishments and expelling 5,643 religious. Owing to the public indignation which these measures aroused, the government did not dare to extend its application to the congregations of women at that time.

In 1882, a law was passed forbidding ministers of religion from entering nursery or primary schools for the purpose of inspecting, supervising or directing them, and more grave still, forbidding the giving of religious instruction on the schools' premises, even outside school hours. Religious instruction was to be replaced in the curriculum by "civic instruction." A law of 28 July 1882, forbade nursery teachers to teach their pupils their prayers, or to speak to them of God, and another circular of 2 September 1882 ordered that religious emblems and pictures should be gradually removed from all nursery and primary schools, all of which was naturally ignored by the teaching religious congregations whose sole aim was the Christian education of youth. The final and most drastic law of all was passed on 30 and 31 October 1886, announcing that public schools of all grades were to be staffed exclusively by secular teachers trained in the state training colleges, from which the chaplains had been removed since 1882. This change was to be effected in boys' schools within five years of the promulgation of the law; in girls' schools it could take place more gradually, with the death or retirement of the existing religious staff.

After the law of 1886 proclaiming the secularisation of the state schools, government opposition to the teaching orders steadily increased. At the same time, the nation began to see more clearly what was happening, and there grew up a strong feeling of resentment against the government's policy, a feeling which in many places was translated into action.

One incident among many will help to illustrate how these anti-clerical measures affected the congregation. The girls' school at Pordic in the Côtes-du-Nord had been under the direction of the Daughters of the Holy Spirit since 1881, when a convent and school had been endowed by the parish priest and several local families. According to Article 18 of the law of 1881, which directed that no more religious should be appointed to posts in state schools, the death of the headmistress, Sister St Omer in 1892, might easily have been the occasion for the secularisation of that school. But the prefect of the Côtes-du-Nord at the time would not take such a step and it was under his successor, a supporter of the anti-clerical laws party, that orders were given for the school at Pordic to be placed under the direction of the secular staff. On the morning of the secularisation, 21 June 1892, the sisters found to their joy that not one of the pupils had abandoned them. On the contrary, all the children with their parents were waiting outside the class-rooms which one or two families had provided for them in other premises, until they could build their own school, the *école libre*, as it was henceforth to be called, to distinguish this type of school from the secularised schools.

To justify its policy before the public, the government had asserted that the loyalties of a great number of Catholics were for the royalist parties and this was opposed to the republic. The church protested, and on 16 January 1892, a collective letter was published by five French cardinals enumerating the acts of oppression which the republic had sanctioned against the church. On 10 February, Pope Leo XIII in his encyclical *Inter Innumeras Sollicitudines* asked French Catholics not to judge the republic by the irreligious character of its government, and explained that a distinction must be made between the form of government which ought to be accepted and its laws, which ought to be improved.

Anti-clericalism grew, and there was new legislation formulated against religious congregations by the Waldeck-Rousseau Ministry of 1889-1902. Taxes were levied on all religious institutions, and the Daughters of the Holy Spirit were obliged to sell some real estate to pay these exorbitant taxes. Fifteen properties were put up for sale in order to meet the sum required. The decision of the congregation was as follows:

> Today, 25 February, 1901, the Congregation of the Daughters of the Holy Spirit can no longer delay and is obliged, in order to satisfy the demands of *enregistrement* (registration of institutions by the state) to offer certain of its properties for sale... According to the fundamental principles of our law, taxation should be the same for all. It is in this way that the ruin of convents will be gradually brought about. Little by little, they will be effaced under the merciless fiscal laws and the laws of education.

The law of Association, as it was called, was also passed during the Waldeck-Rousseau ministry. It stated:

> In addition, every existing establishment of an authorised congregation must apply for authorisation to the Council of State if it does not already possess the special authorisation exacted by the law of 24 May, 1825.

During Monsieur Waldeck-Rousseau's ministry the law of association was not fully imposed, and when the general election of 1902 returned him to office, he handed over premiership to Monsieur Emile Combes. The latter applied this law as soon as he came into power. Three months were given for application to the Council of State and this would expire in October 1902. The Holy See left each superior-general free to determine the line of conduct best suited to saving the honour and the interests of each congregation. Two hundred and fifty congregations decided on dispersion and exile, and all through the month of September there was a continuous exodus of religious from France. About 615 other congregations applied to the council of state for a decree of authorisation but all their applications were refused.

A further law of 1 July 1901 had stated:

> No religious congregation may be formed without an authorisation,
> granted through a law which shall determine the conditions of its
> functions. It shall found no new establishment except by virtue of a
> decree of the Council of State. The dissolution of the congregation, or
> the closure of any of its establishments, may be effected by a decree
> formulated by the Council of Ministers.

On 9 July 1901, in a simple ministerial circular, Monsieur Emile Combes ordered the closure of 2500 *écoles libres* (Catholic controlled schools as opposed to state-controlled schools), all of which had been founded before the July edict. Among the 2500 condemned schools throughout the whole of France, 125 were established by the Daughters of the Holy Spirit. The ministerial circular was conveyed to the mother house of the congregation in Saint Brieuc, and to the headmistresses of the schools concerned on 11 and 12 July 1901, just two days after its promulgation. A week was given for the 625 Daughters of the Holy Spirit teaching in these schools to return to the mother house in Saint Brieuc where they might apply for the authorization for their schools, exacted by the government. The instructions sent out by the superior-general and her council were as follows: the sisters were to have everything ready for their departure, but in protest against the injustice of the minister's circular, they were not to leave their schools until forced to do so. For the next thirteen years up till the outbreak of the First World War, there began a fierce struggle for the schools run by the Daughters of the Holy Spirit.

Meanwhile all over France protests were raised against the closure of schools. To the voice of the French bishops was added that of a large number of politicians. Meetings of protest were held in all parts of Paris and the provinces. Faced with widespread opposition, Monsieur Combes granted a delay to those establishments, which possessed what were known as the *Décrits de Tutelle* on condition that they applied immediately for the authorisation. Forty-seven establishments of the Daughters of the Holy Spirit benefited by this decision.

The tension and unrest increased daily, however, especially in Brittany, where the measures were considered as a direct attack on the beliefs and principles of the people. In the towns and villages of Morbihan, Finistère and the Côtes du Nord, preparations were made not only to protest against the closure of the schools, but also to prevent the government order from being carried out. Most of the schools run by religious orders which had been ordered to close, did so, but the Daughters of the Holy Spirit, unflinching in the attitude they had adopted from the beginning, decided to remain in their convents until they were driven out. The Bretons who protected them day and night in their convents were even more anxious to keep the sisters than the latter were to remain. Finistère, where 140 schools had been affected by Monsieur Combes' circular, was the department in which resistance to the law against Catholic schools had been the most systematically organised. Men and women of all classes and occupations united to organise resistance, and guards were set up round the convents to see that no one entered to expel the sisters, and that the sisters themselves did not attempt to leave the schools.

Then came the expulsions in August 1902. On 7 August, twenty-five sisters were expelled from the Pensionnat St Julien in Landerneau, Finistère. Until 1893 the sisters had directed the communal school. When this had been secularised, they had started the Pensionnat St Julien; by 1902 it counted six hundred pupils and was staffed by twenty eight sisters. A detachment of mounted policemen and two companies of the nineteenth infantry regiment arrived at Landerneau to be greeted by about three thousand local inhabitants who had assembled, on hearing of their advance, to protect the sisters. There was an order for a cavalry charge and also an infantry charge, but so great was the opposition of the people that the battle lasted five hours. The sisters were eventually driven out.

Threats increased in intensity and severity. Monsieur Combes sent this warning letter to the superior-general:

> The Council of Ministers has decided that the Superior General should be officially warned through the intermediaries of the diocesan authorities that if she does not order the members of the Congregation to leave these establishments unconditionally, and if the order is not executed, the whole Congregation will be held responsible according to the law of 1 July 1901.

The situation was now very grave, but faced with the untiring vigilance and fierce resistance of the Bretons, the council of the Congregation of the Daughters of the Holy Spirit felt that to order the sisters to leave their convents, on which an unceasing watch was kept by the local people, would only give rise to more serious disorders, and would put the sisters in the position of receiving an order which their defenders would make it impossible to obey. In her letter to Monsieur Combes, the superior-general wrote:

> I got in touch with our defenders in Finistère. I met with strong resistance from the owners and founders of the schools and especially

from the townspeople by whom the houses occupied by the Sisters are constantly surrounded.

She continued:

As for making the entire Congregation responsible for the failure of my efforts, I venture to hope that your sense of justice will prevent you from taking such a measure. To do so would be to multiply by 300 houses a disturbance which I am doing my best to allay, and which at the Mother House where more than 100 sick and invalid Sisters are confined to their beds, would take on proportions against which it is impossible to provide. (Archives, Maison Mère, Saint Brieuc).

On the same day, 8 August, the Prefect of the Côtes du Nord wrote to the Vicar General of the Diocese: "May I impress on you how important it is that she (the Superior General) should recall her sisters from Finistère by tomorrow, Saturday. If she delays any longer, it will be too late." On 10 August 1902, the superior-general wrote to Monsieur Combes stating that she was ordering the sisters in Finistère to disperse but that she had no power over the public who would probably prevent the order being carried out.

In a decree 27 June 1902, the government ordered the immediate closure of 125 religious establishments opened without authorisation since 1 July 1901, in the year of Combes' edict. Most of the schools belonged not to the congregation, whose members taught in them, but to private individuals. The Daughters of the Holy Spirit staffed five of them. At one of these, the school at Missiriac, the expulsion of the sisters, which took place on Sunday 9 June, was immediate and merciless. It was conducted by the Sub-Prefect from Plomek, accompanied by the deputy commissioner of police, the Justice of the Peace, the recording officer and a detachment of armed police. The sisters were given an hour to gather their possessions and as soon as they had left the house, government seals were placed on the door. At Juan-les-Pins, where the sisters had charge of an orphanage and school for only eight months, the expulsion took place on 30 June. Given only an hour in which to pack up their belongings, the sisters had to leave the convent between two rows of armed police officers. They were provided with pauper tickets, and sent off by train to Saint Brieuc, to the mother house, and were subjected to police inspection at every stopping place on the way.

Meanwhile the newspapers, which supported Monsieur Combes, asked for the dissolution of the congregation. The national newspaper *Le Petit Parisien* went so far as to announce in bold headlines that the decree of dissolution had been pronounced. The newspaper *Le Radical* also announced on 14 August that the decree of dissolution was ready for the signature of the president. The *Aurore,* the *Siècle*, the *Petite Republique*, the *Rappel,* which supported the policy of Monsieur Combes, all called for the dissolution of the congregation.

The expulsion continued with speed and severity. On 8 August 1902, seven convents were closed; on 11 August, twelve communities were expelled and nine others on the 12, 13 and 14th of the same month. The prefect of Finistère appealed to the people:

> If you were good citizens, you would not say: 'I am first and foremost a Christian, but 'I am first and foremost a Frenchman'.

This was greeted by an uproar from his hearers.

> We are first of all Christians. We want the Sisters, long live freedom. We will resist to the death. We would rather die than lose our Sisters.

On 16 August there were five more expulsions, after a prolonged battle in which the whole population, men and women together, opposed the attackers.

Scenes similar to these were enacted during the next few days in towns and villages all over Brittany. On the outskirts of the parish where the sisters awaited expulsion a watch was kept from some vantage point and, at the first sign of the approach of the government forces, the inhabitants were called together by bugles and church bells. Resistance to the troops usually lasted two or three hours, and then, before serious injury to life could be given, the Breton leaders would call a halt and the soldiers would proceed to break into the convent. If the lock could not be removed quickly enough, an axe was used to break down the door, at the other side of which the superior of the convent with the parish priest and a local deputy, would be found waiting to read a formal protest before yielding to the order of expulsion. The struggle always ended with a procession to the church.

In Le Fulgoët, a place of popular pilgrimage, and in Ploudaniel and Saint Méen parishes, the harvest had been neglected in order that a constant guard might be kept on the convents, and preparations made for their defence. The weeks of waiting by which the government hoped to weary the Bretons of their vigilance, had served only to strengthen their resolve to defend the schools, and to defend them if need be with their lives. There was no excitement or hysteria in their attitude, which was one of clear determination to do their duty to the church and their children, no matter what the price might be. "What we prize above all else," said one farmer at

Saint Méen to a Paris reporter "is our religion, and we mean to keep it and hand it on to our children." Their resistance was to remain within the limits of the law. "The defence of the Sisters is being undertaken in earnest," wrote the parish priest of Saint Méen, "but understand, our protest will be what it should be …legal. There will be no shooting, no pitch-forks, but the whole village will be round to the Sisters' door, necessitating the use of force on the part of the authorities." Inside the convents, the sisters quietly waited, continuing their life of prayer and work, as if there were no threat hanging over their school and their way of life.

The newspaper *Liberté* wrote of the situation at Saint Méen:

> It is a miracle that this day has ended without bloodshed. The most violent demonstrations in Paris are nothing compared with the revolt of these Bretons wounded in their faith and who, far from avoiding the blows of their opponents, seemed to go to meet them as if to their martyrdom.

Only the splintered doors, the broken walls, the trampled gardens and the seals on the convent doors showed what had taken place in the parishes.

The situation continued in this way. More and more frequently, Daughters of the Holy Spirit appeared in court charged with continuing to direct a school, which had been ordered to close, or with re-establishing a religious community, which had been ordered to disperse. Some magistrates acquitted the sisters, others condemned them for the same "crime." Sometimes the headmistress was charged alone, sometimes the whole community was inculpated, and often the owner of the school as well. The sisters, who were condemned on charges connected with teaching, always appealed against the sentence. Although their appeal was seldom successful, it gained time and enabled them to continue to teach for as long as their sentence was on suspension, especially if the case was carried as far as the Court of Appeal in Rennes.

Of those who had been expelled and were therefore excluded from teaching in France, about five hundred of the youngest and most robust were to be sent to establishments in Belgium from 1901, and to England and the USA from 1902. The sisters who remained in France were too numerous to be given accommodation in the mother house of the congregation where every available place was taken. They therefore remained in the neighbourhood of their former convents, depending for their food and lodgings on the charity of various families of the parish.

Although the members of the congregation would have gladly gone to prison in the cause of Catholic education, only one actually suffered such a penalty. This was Sister St Valentinien, the headmistress of the village school at Penquesten in Morbihan. On 8 March 1912, two policemen arrived at the village, with a warrant to arrest Sister St Valentinien. The news quickly circulated and all the inhabitants armed with sticks and umbrellas, came to the defence. The police officers were forced to go back to headquarters without the sister, but early in the morning of 29 July, they returned, this time in a motor car escorted by eight mounted policemen, and seized her as she left church after Mass. She was pushed into the car and taken straight to the prison in Lorient. There she refused to exchange her religious habit for the prison uniform. She settled down quite happily in her cell, glad to have forty days before her for prayer and reflection.

The superior-general, Mère St Georges **(Plate 4)**, wrote to the whole congregation on 15 December 1902:

> This year 1902 is coming to an end, leaving deplorable ruins in its wake. On I July 1902, the storm, which had been predicted, erupted, and the first blow destroyed five of our houses. This year during the month of August, after the brutal expulsions of which many of you were victims, more than one hundred of our houses fell. From the start of the first closings to the expulsions and laicisation, 132 houses are actually closed. It had taken the terrible shock caused by the application of the law of 1901 to bring us to decide to emigrate to foreign lands. Born in Brittany, we wanted to remain here and devote ourselves exclusively to Brittany. One hundred of our sisters have been dispersed in different countries: Belgium, England and the United States of America. They are establishing works there whose beginnings are necessarily difficult: poverty, destitution is at the base of these nascent works, but isn't that a good sign?

And she encouraged her sisters to have faith and trust in the midst of adversity.

> May our dear exiles not lose hope, may they ardently ask God to give them, in its fullness, the special grace of their beautiful mission, and full of faith and trust in his divine goodness may they surrender themselves courageously and devotedly to the work of our beloved congregation.

The situation continued in this way till the outbreak of the First World War in 1914, but we now turn our attention to the fortunes of those sisters who left France as exiles to settle in a foreign land, where they continued in very different circumstances and with much suffering, to carry out the mission of the congregation. By the time that exile was forced upon the sisters, the congregation had been in existence almost two hundred years.

CHAPTER FOUR
1902: The Daughters Come to Wales

IT WAS IN THE CONTEXT OF THIS ACCOUNT OF THE STRUGGLE FOR THE future of the Catholic schools in France and of the future existence of the congregation itself that the first exiles set out across the Channel for Britain on 10 March 1902 **(Plate 5)**. The first three foundations were in England, however: one in Hertfordshire at High Wycombe, one in Buckinghamshire at Olney, and one in Devon, at Ingsdon Manor, Newton Abbot.

The account of the departure of the first three sisters who were to found the convent at High Wycombe is a moving one and these pioneers have left us a vivid account of their departure from their native Brittany. This account would probably find a resonance in the hearts of all those sisters who crossed the Channel driven from their native land. The sisters were accompanied by a representative of the superior-general of the congregation, Sister Marie Théodose, and also by the ecclesiastical superior of the congregation, Monsignor Jules Morelle from the diocese of Saint Brieuc.

> With these two persons as our guardians and protectors, we set out on our journey into exile...

writes the chronicler. When the train on which they were travelling stopped at Rennes, sisters from the communities there came to the station to bid them farewell. In Paris, where they had to stay overnight, they received hospitality from the sisters of another congregation, and on the following day 11 March, they set off from the Gare du Nord by train for Boulogne, the port of departure for England. At Amiens, sisters were also at the station to bid them farewell.

On arrival at Boulogne, they embarked on the South-Eastern Chatham Railway Steamship, which was to take them into exile from their beloved Brittany. As one of them wrote:

If our aim had been to attract attention, we could not have been more successful in doing so. Everyone stared at our white habits, which had not been seen in those parts before. On land and on the sea, we remained the object of many curious glances.

One gentleman was heard to remark: "These are more French Sisters going into exile." They set sail under a clear and cloudless sky and a calm sea. One can only imagine their feelings when the signal was given for the vessel to set out to sea. One of the sisters notes:

> We sat on a bench a little on one side, and we prayed the rosary. With our eyes turned towards France, we watched its dear coastline recede into the distance and at this moment felt more keenly than ever the pain of separation. At Folkestone, we took the train for London, again 'eyed by curious onlookers' and arrived at Charing Cross Station, London, after two hours. (Archives, Saint Brieuc).

The parish priest of High Wycombe, Father Flint, met them in London and accompanied them to High Wycombe, where the first foundation of the Daughters of the Holy Spirit was to be made in England.

Many of the French religious orders which sought refuge in England during the Combes regime chose to settle in the northern and more Catholic counties, where they would easily find pupils for their schools.

The Congregation of the Daughters of the Holy Spirit, however, was moved in the choice of localities by a feeling of religious gratitude towards the early evangelisers of Brittany. Remembering Brioc, Cadoc, Samson and many other Welsh saints who had left their native land so many centuries before to carry the news of the gospel to Brittany, the superiors of the congregation decided to repay the debt in some small measure by bringing back the Catholic faith to the towns and villages of Wales.

Added to this, the Honourable Mrs Herbert **(Frontispiece)** of Llanover, Abergavenny, played a considerable part in enabling the sisters to establish so many foundations in Wales over a short period of four years. This lady, Augusta Charlotte Elizabeth Hall, in 1846 married John Jones, whose name was later changed to Herbert, and became a Catholic. She devoted her life to good works and was a generous benefactor of the Daughters of the Holy Spirit in Wales. Her husband's aunt Apollonia had married a Monsieur Rio from Brittany and undoubtedly the Honourable Mrs Herbert, who travelled extensively in Europe, would have known the Daughters of the Holy Spirit from her visits to Brittany. She certainly was their great patron, and they called her their "foundress," a title which, though strictly uncanonical, illustrates the very high esteem in which she was held by the sisters.

Between 1902 and 1906, twelve Convents were opened in Wales at Monmouth (1902), Carmarthen (1903); Usk (1903); Pontypool (1903); Brecon (1903); Aberystwyth (1903); Llanrwst (1903); Pwllheli (1904); Caernarfon (1904); Pembroke Dock (1904); Tenby (1904) and Abergavenny (1906). Only one small foundation was made in Wales at the end of the twentieth century, at Blaenafon in 1987.

It is to the establishment of these foundations, with all the difficulties, hardships and sufferings involved, that we now turn our attention.

To prepare the exiles for their work in Wales, courses in Welsh were added to the English classes at the mother house in Brittany and as most of the sisters were already Breton-speaking, Welsh came more easily to them than English, given the similarities between the Welsh and the Breton languages. Schools were opened, if one did not already exist, wherever the sisters established a convent, or at least that was the aim of the sisters. As the Catholic population of Wales was at that time very small, the bishops encouraged the sisters to admit Protestants as well as Catholics to their schools in order to have enough pupils on their register to obtain official recognition. This policy brought the sisters into contact with children and adults of the other christian denominations and they hoped that by their example and charity they would break down the prejudices, which had grown up against the Catholic church in non-conformist Wales. Further contacts were made by means of the private lessons in needlework, art, music and French, which were for many years their chief, and sometimes their sole means of livelihood. In many of their foundations, too, the sisters were glad to have domestic work since they spoke little English at the beginning, and laundries were opened in a number of foundations.

The First Foundation:
St Mary's Convent, Monmouth 1902-1913

It was in the county of Monmouthshire, in the border country between England and Wales, in the county town of Monmouth, that the first foundation in Wales, and the fourth foundation in Britain, was made. At that time, Monmouth was part of the Diocese of Newport, which had been established six years earlier in 1896. The Rt Rev Cuthbert Hedley OSB was the bishop of the diocese, and Father Sidney Nicholls was the priest in charge of the Monmouth mission.

A brief outline of each foundation with all the difficulties and problems encountered shows a rich missionary endeavour on the part of the first sisters. We are fortunate in having many of the original documents for tracing the history of these foundations, which are extant in the correspondence between the superiors of the foundations and the major superiors of the congregation in Brittany. In some of the foundations, a detailed account of the day-to-day life of the sisters is also preserved for us in the Annals of the community, or in the official bulletin of the congregation entitled *La Colombe*. There are fortunately some primary sources for tracing the history of the foundation at Monmouth, but there are no extant Annals, if such were ever written. The principal sources, therefore, for the foundation at Monmouth are the letters exchanged between the three sisters who succeeded one another as superior of the community, and Sister Marie Théodose and Sister Marie Angélina, and the major superiors of the congregation in France. These letters provide a vivid account of those early days.

One of the earliest letters dated 13 May 1902, is from a Lincoln's Inn solicitor, Mr Dudley Leathley, undoubtedly acting for the Honourable Mrs Herbert, to Sister Marie Théodose, who was responsible for setting up the communities in England and Wales. In this letter the solicitor quotes from a letter he had received from Father Nicholls, the priest in Monmouth.

> I should be very glad to welcome the Sisters you write about, provided of course that everything was satisfactory. With regard to a house, I have one on my hands at present, which I think would suit them. It is mission property and adjoins the presbytery, but the locality, unfortunately, is not all that could be desired, although it is not a slum. The rent is £19 (nearly £1,000 in today's currency) a year, exclusive of rates and taxes. There is no Catholic school here, so the few Catholics there are attend the Protestant school, coming to me for catechism during the week. The schools here are all under the Board of Education and in good working order, whether the Sisters later would be able to get their school similarly placed, I cannot say. I would think there would be a fair opening for lessons in French, music, etc... (File 12G4, Archives, Saint Brieuc).

On 15 July, 1902, Monsignor Morelle wrote to Bishop Hedley from Ingsdon Convent in Devon, as follows: "Through Mr Leathley (the solicitor) I hear that the priest at Monmouth has a house to rent to the sisters." He then asks the bishop whether he would be willing to have the sisters in his diocese. The reply, dated 17 July, 1902, was addressed by Bishop Hedley to Monsignor Morelle. In his letter, he stated that he would have no objection to the sisters residing at Monmouth but that he did not think it would be possible for them to open a primary school as the Catholic body would find it difficult to provide buildings that would meet the requirements of the law. There were only one hundred and ten Catholics in Monmouth including twenty-three children who attended the state school. Bishop Hedley also wrote to Mr Leathley stating that he wished to give every help in his power to the sisters expelled from their convents in Brittany. He also reiterated that he did not think it would be possible to open a school in a town where there were so few Catholics. He suggested that the sisters could help the priest with the religious instruction of the children and adults. He wanted to know how the sisters intended to earn a living before he could agree to the foundation. He pointed out that orphanages, convalescent homes and hospices were already sufficient in numbers in the area, and that these institutions were expensive to establish. Finally, the bishop requested a meeting with the sisters to find out what financial backing they had, if they could speak English, and what work they were prepared to do. (Archives, Saint Brieuc, File 12G4)

There was further correspondence during the following months. In a letter dated 5 October, 1902, Sister Marie Angélina, the general bursar, writing from the convent in Olney, Buckinghamshire, to the superior-general, spoke of a meeting with the bishop in Llanishen, Cardiff. She said that the bishop was very much in favour of the sisters coming to his diocese. He offered them exile in Wales, and she promised that the sisters would learn Welsh. She quotes the bishop as saying: "As soon as you have sisters, let me know. I shall do all I can for you." Father Sidney Nicholls also wrote to Sister Marie Angélina on 21 October saying that he would be glad to welcome the sisters to Monmouth.

Sister Thérèse du Saint Esprit who was to be the first superior of the proposed foundation at Monmouth wrote from the convent in High Wycombe to the superior-general on 19 November 1902. She voiced her misgivings about her responsibility. She outlined some of the problems they would be facing. She said that they would have almost no money; she wondered who would teach the lessons that were being proposed; she asked whether books could be sent from Brittany where so many schools had been closed down because of the anti-clerical laws in that country. To give some reassurance to the sisters, we learn from a letter of 29 November written by Father Nicholls that the furniture had arrived for the house. There were thirty parcels in all and, in addition to this, there was a piano. He said that the remainder of the furniture was due to arrive the following week. He added that he was eagerly awaiting the arrival of the sisters.

Once the decision to open a house in Monmouth had been taken, three sisters were sent there in December 1902. The three sisters who formed the new community at Monmouth were Sister Thérèse du St Esprit Queoron, Sister Amélie Le Bihan and Sister Marie Terlet. There is on record an account of their arrival (*La Colombe, 1903*).

> Monday 8 December 1902, Feast of the Immaculate Conception: Snow fell throughout the night blanketing the streets and houses in white. A cold wind is blowing, nevertheless the three exiles venture out of doors in the early morning to go to the Catholic Church. Wrapped in their cloaks, which do not really protect them from the cold, they bravely make their way to the place where Jesus dwells in the Blessed Sacrament. They are going to ask him for the comfort and strength needed for the mission he has assigned to them in this strange and foreign country.

After Mass they returned to The Parade where a certain Miss Weetman had for two days given them hospitality. After breakfast, they took their leave of this kind lady who provided them with a small basket of provisions. Frozen with the cold they arrived at their future convent, 28 St Mary Street **(Plate 7)** which like the Catholic mission was called St Mary's, and opened the door. What did they find? They answer is recorded in the same article *in La Colombe:*

> Piled pell-mell, packing cases, items of furniture, iron bedsteads, trunks, empty rooms with bare walls and a kitchen in which there is no fire lit. And they lament that it is a special feast of the Congregation of the Daughters of the Holy Spirit and this is the way they are to celebrate it, therefore, aliens in a foreign land, in an unfurnished premises and experiencing the bleakness of the wintry weather.

Such was their introduction to Wales.

Two workmen sent by the parish priest arrived to help move the cupboards and bedsteads, and the sisters busied themselves emptying the packing cases, making beds and putting away the household linen. The sisters made themselves more or less understood by the workmen who left when they had completed their task. Then the sisters heated water on the primus stove to make three cups of coffee, which Miss Weetman had given them together with bread, butter, and milk. It must not be imagined that their meal was a sad one, quite the contrary. They even managed to laugh and when the hot coffee and bread so charitably given by Miss Weetman had restored their energies, the sisters set off again to the church (**Plate 8**) which was just one door away from the convent, where they spent the rest of the day in the Eucharistic presence of Jesus. There, close to Him and His Blessed Mother, whose feast it was, they found the rest and relaxation, which their hearts as well as their bodies needed.

On 12 January 1903, just over a month after their arrival in Monmouth, Sister Thérèse addressed a letter to the superior-general. She spoke about a visit to the Honourable Mrs Augusta Charlotte Elizabeth Herbert in Llanover. She was warmly welcomed by Mrs Herbert, who spoke of her desire to open convents for the sisters all over Wales. She provided them with a box of provisions, as she did so many times in those early days, even sending boxes of provisions from London when she stayed in her residence in Mayfair. On this occasion, she also gave the sisters £2 for their rail fare from Monmouth to Nantyderry railway station. The sisters had not long been in Monmouth when Mrs Herbert published an advertisement in the *Monmouthshire Beacon,* the local newspaper:

> A community of French Catholic Sisters have just arrived from Brittany and settled in Monmouth, 28 St Mary Street. They will visit the poor and the sick and are anxious to find pupils for French, Music and Painting, Drawing and Embroidery among the non-Catholic inhabitants of the neighbourhood. Their terms will be very moderate and they are accustomed to tuition.

This advertisement, however, gave offence to some, and an anonymous letter to the *Beacon* questioned the intentions of the sisters.

A certain John Matthews sprang to their defence the following week assuring the people of Monmouth that the Sisters would not wish to offend anyone, and that the doubt over the wording of the advertisement was entirely the consequence of their limited command of English. He also remonstrated with the previous correspondent for wanting to question the offer of the sisters to visit non-Catholic sick and poor (David Powell, *St Mary's Catholic Church, Monmouth 1793-1993).*

Elsewhere the sisters had a positive response to the advertisement, for in a letter to the superior-general, written by Sister Marie Théodose on 28 January, 1903, she said: "The Monmouth community is going well. People are asking for French lessons, music lessons etc.", and she ends by saying that the people of Monmouth revere the sisters, and this less than two months after their arrival. Since, however, circumstances did not allow them to pursue the congregation's traditional works of teaching and nursing, they were content at the beginning to give private lessons in French, music, painting, and embroidery, and the Sunday catechism classes for the children of the parish.

Almost from the start, Sister Thérèse who was the superior of the community found that a considerable amount of her time was taken by the Honourable Mrs Herbert of Llanover, "a notable and wealthy Catholic who very soon after the Sisters' arrival in Monmouth constituted herself their patron and benefactress, urging them to make numerous foundations in Wales and thereby help to bring the people back to the Catholic faith of their forebears." (*La Colombe*, 1903)

The private lessons are described by Sister Paul, who joined the community in January 1903, in a letter she wrote to Monsignor Morelle in 27 June 1903:

> By God's grace we have begun our apostolate: Sister Amélie has started her needlework classes which are attended by sixteen ladies for an hour on Tuesdays and an hour on Wednesdays. I think it is to Mrs Caffrey who is so helpful that we owe these lessons. Another lady is eager to arrange lessons in French conversation. Sister Marie Thomasine has six students for music and art lessons and wishes she had more. Sister Marie would very much like to have started an infant's class but the parish hasn't a room that would be suitable, so she has to wait and keep on hoping.

Other glimpses of the sisters' early contacts can be gleaned from *La Colombe*. On 9 October, 1903, we read:

> Mabel Edwards came at three o'clock for her French and Needlework lessons. She told us that she had been to tea with Lord and Lady Llangattock and that the Lady not knowing that Mabel came to us for tuition, had said to her: "Mind that the Sisters do not turn you into a Roman Catholic." To which Mabel replied: "Never fear that; the Sisters do not speak about religion unless we want them to." Lady Llangattock countenanced this with: "But they are so nice that I fear they will fascinate all the young ladies in Monmouth."

This type of remark helps to illustrate both the impact the sisters had, and the nature of the misunderstanding which the sisters' religious affiliation would lead them to experience in those early days in Wales.

Another glimpse of their relation with the people of Monmouth is found in the same number of *La Colombe:*

> Yesterday evening, four little protestant girls came and knocked on our door. When we opened it to them, they said: "Sister, we like your church." To which I replied, "Very good, what is it that you want?" "We want to belong to your church." I enquired in a few words about their

parents' religion and concluded from the children's answers that the parents had no religion. So the Sister referred them to Father Nicholls, the priest of the mission. The Sister added: "Then we'll see when you can come to the convent."

For the little community of exiles at Monmouth the highlight of the first year was a visit from the superior-general Mère St Georges, and Mgr Morelle, the ecclesiastical superior of the congregation, on 7 October 1903. A detailed description of the visit is given in *La Colombe*, which expresses their excitement at the news, and the days of waiting for the visit.

> How long the hours seem when one is waiting and especially when those awaited are so dearly loved… Midday, the sound of the carriage was heard outside. It brought the visitors whom Sister Marie and the superior had gone to meet at the station. They came, with complete self-forgetfulness and disregard for personal comfort, in inclement weather, solely to give pleasure to exiles and to bring them a ray of happiness.

An account of their departure is equally moving:

> The jubilation that marked the day our guests arrived has given way to an indefinable sadness…

And a reflection on their farewell message entitled 'France at Monmouth, for two days' asked:

> Who could have said a year ago when the storms of persecution that drove us from our convent was at its height that in our land of exile we would soon be the object of the esteem, sympathy and affection of a people who are as generous as they are hospitable?

And again:

> Emboldened by your goodness and intrepidity I dare hope that in this Welsh soil on which you first set foot fifteen days ago, you will walk again when you come to visit, not just a few small as yet fragile foundations, but numerous and flourishing schools where the pupils are instructed in the truth, where Jesus and his church are revered. Such is our dearest wish. May Jesus grant that we see it realised.

Exactly one year after they settled in Monmouth on the Feast of the Immaculate Conception, things were somewhat different at St Mary's Convent. There were ten sisters present to celebrate the feast: the future superiors of the foundation at Pembroke Dock, and of Llanarth where proposals were in hand to open a convent, the three sisters destined for the foundation at Brecon and two sisters from Pontypool which had been founded just two months earlier. "This day which marked the first anniversary of the founding of St Mary's was truly delightful, as well as being in marked contrast to it."

Bishop Hedley visited Monmouth for confirmation and praised the work of the sisters in preparing the children for the sacraments, and the following day Bishop Hedley paid a visit to the sisters. Their wish to have a school was pursued, a topic which was presumably discussed with the bishop. The general bursar of the congregation visited the community on 26 October 1904, after Sister Thérèse wrote to the superior-general, telling her that there was a large empty property for sale in Monmouth: it was called Cartref and had been a hospice. The general bursar thought it would be very suitable as providing more space for the community and the possibility of starting a boarding school. About a year later, the superior of Monmouth wrote to the superior-general after her enquiries about leasing or obtaining Cartref **(Plate 9)** and asked what she should do. The answer was: "Find the money needed; get a loan."

In the middle of the negotiations, however, Sister Thérèse was sent on 17 April 1906 as the new superior of the community founded at Abergavenny. She was sad at the thought of leaving Monmouth. Sister Paul, her successor as superior, continued the negotiations and in November 1906 she wrote to the superior-general to say that she had secured a lease for six years from the owner, Mr Albert Lewis of Priory Farm. So a convent school was opened in 1907, even before the move to the new premises.

In 1908, the sisters left the mission house at 28 St Mary's Street, and moved to Cartref in St James Square. There were five sisters in the community at this time. Sister Paul asked the superior-general to send a suitably qualified sister to teach the pupils who were to prepare for examinations. Her request was not granted, for in September 1908 she wrote:

> The number of pupils is increasing and they want to be prepared for their exams but I have no one to do this. Could you send us a Sister who is suitably qualified?

Three weeks later, Sister Paul wrote again:

> We now have thirty pupils, yet for want of suitably qualified teachers, we are unable to provide the standard of teaching that the parents expect. I am afraid that they will soon start to withdraw their children.

To add to the difficulties, Sister Paul who had undertaken the negotiations for the opening of the school when Sister Thérèse left there for Abergavenny in 1906, was herself transferred to Carmarthen, and replaced by Sister Marie Thomasine as superior of the community. This need to transfer sisters from one foundation to another was undoubtedly problematic for the success of the school, for the new sisters who arrived would not be sufficently up-to-date with the negotiations. Yet this practice of moving sisters from one foundation to another as needs dictated continued, despite any undesirable consequences.

In January 1911, Sister Marie Thomasine wrote to the superior-general saying that five of the twenty-six pupils were leaving at the end of the term. At that time there is mention of two boarders in the school, one from Port Talbot and the other a French girl, a relative of the superior. This state of affairs was beginning to indicate that the future of the school was not a certainty, and when in 1913, a general councillor of the congregation made a canonical visitation of the communities in Wales, she wrote to the superior-general:

> I'm sure we could close our house in Monmouth where there is nothing more to be hoped for.

In support of her view, she reported that there were only one hundred Catholics in Monmouth and the number was always decreasing as Catholic families moved away on account of the difficulty of finding employment in the town where jobs were scarce. "There is little scope for our work," she wrote,

> only ten children attend Sunday catechism classes. There are only two Catholics at our private school. Also there are plenty of schools in the town to choose from. The school is the community's only source of income apart from needlework classes of Sister Bernard. In a word there is no apostolate for us in Monmouth. (Archives, Dossier 12G4)

So negotiations for their departure began to take shape. They decided they could leave before the expiry of their lease on their house by paying the proprietor a small indemnity, and this was agreed. The reaction was to be expected. The superior wrote:

> The news of our leaving Monmouth has caused quite a sensation, Catholics and Non-Catholics alike have come to say how sorry they are.

Father Nicholls, the parish priest, was also saddened by the decision and wrote to the superior-general to try to reverse it. "The Sisters will be greatly missed," he wrote,

> and if only you could alter your decision it would give me much pleasure. I have promised the Sisters a house adjoining the presbytery as a Catholic School.

The people of Monmouth also drew up a petition with ninety signatures, to try to keep the sisters there. It read:

> This petition is to ask the Reverend Mother if she would be so kind as
> to allow 'The White Sisters' to remain in Monmouth. Their good works
> both in church and school have gained them popularity; and their
> removal from Monmouth would not only be a grief, but a loss to all.
> Signed: 30 July 1913 (The list of signatures follows).

Unfortunately, the decision to close the foundation at Monmouth was maintained.

On 22 July, 1913, the superior-general wrote to the bishop saying that she regretted to have to inform him that she found it necessary to recall the sisters from Monmouth, and she thanked him for his support during their years there. Father Nicholls also wrote on 28 July, 1913, to the superior-general, telling her of his great sorrow at the painful news of the departure of the sisters from Monmouth. The sisters left Monmouth at the beginning of August 1913. Before their departure, they published a letter of farewell in the *Monmouthshire Beacon*. It read:

> The Mother Superior and the Sisters of St Mary's Convent, Monmouth,
> wish to give their best thanks to all the kind people who have
> sympathised with them in their heartfelt sorrow at being ordered to
> leave Monmouth. They are particularly grateful to all those who have
> signed a petition towards them staying on in this place. The Reverend
> Mother General has kindly heard their petition but as matters have
> already gone too far, she is compelled to maintain her decision.
> (Archives, Saint Brieuc).

The general tenor of the extant correspondence which deals with the life and work of the sisters at Monmouth was one of optimism, courage, and a determination to make a success of their apostolate there. The superiors obviously had not paid sufficient attention to all the advice they had received in the beginning from those who did not favour the setting up of a school in a town like Monmouth where there were so few Catholics, and where the system of education with two renowned public schools allowed of no competition. As the first foundation in Wales to open, where so many sisters arrived from Brittany and stayed while waiting for the foundation for which they were destined, we can imagine that the sisters regarded St Mary's Convent, Monmouth, as the most important community in those early years.

When the convent closed in August 1913, after almost eleven years of existence, the furniture was sent to Caernarfon in North Wales where a foundation had been opened in 1904.

CHAPTER FIVE

1903: *More Foundations in South East Wales*

TWO OF THE SIX FOUNDATIONS MADE IN WALES IN THE YEAR 1903 were made in March of that year. One was St Winefride's Convent, Carmarthen, opened on 26 March, and two days later St Joseph's Convent, Usk, was opened in the small market town of Usk in Monmouthshire. While the community at Carmarthen flourished for many years (sixty seven years), the one at Usk had a very short history, a mere six years.

St Joseph's Convent, Usk 1903 - 1909

AN ENTRY in the Usk parish register of the Catholic church made by Father Heneka, the parish priest, summarises the community's brief history.

> St Joseph's Convent—Daughters of the Holy Spirit. There was a convent of five nuns in Usk from 28 March 1903 till 14 January 1909. They lived in a house in Mill Street, Usk, for which they had to pay £30 rent a year. They found it impossible to make a living there, since there was no Catholic School in Usk. They were well received in Usk and well favoured, even by protestants. They left the town in great sorrow on 14 January 1909. They would have greatly desired to remain, if there had been a better prospect of making a living.

From the correspondence exchanged between the superior-general and Sister Thérèse, superior at St Mary's Convent, Monmouth, it became apparent that it was the Honourable Mrs Herbert of Llanover who urged, as she had done at Monmouth, that a foundation should be made at Usk, and who later put Father Heneka, the priest at Usk, in touch with Sister Thérèse.

Several extant letters give us an idea of the negotiations for this foundation. In a letter dated 30 January, 1903, Father Heneka wrote:

> I shall be happy for you to come and see me any day next week…I do hope that it will be possible to have one of your convents in this pretty little town.

Two weeks later, he wrote to Sister Thérèse again:

> The bishop has given his consent for the foundation, and awaits a letter from your superior general or the ecclesiastical superior.

He went on to advise that the service of a qualified lay teacher should be secured from the outset.

In his next letter, dated 16 February, Father Heneka informed Sister Thérèse that he had found a pretty little house called Castle Cottage, for renting at £30.00 (£1,500 in modern equivalent) a year, with a view to opening a school at Usk. There was no time to be lost if it was really wanted for the sisters. If this cottage is the house which the sisters rented, it was situated in Castle Parade, and not in Mill Street. There is no indication in the sources that the sisters lived in two different rented houses during their time at Usk. Having received a letter from Sister Thérèse notifying him that the superior-general had authorized a foundation at Usk, Father Heneka took steps to secure the house in question; and on 25 February wrote to tell Sister Thérèse of this. "Everyone," he added, "is delighted at the prospect of Sisters coming to Usk." (Dossier 12 G6, Archives, Maison Mère, Saint Brieuc).

The Annals of St Joseph's Convent, Usk, (if ever they were written) have not been preserved. The only source, therefore, available for an account of its short history of six years are the thirty seven letters written by the superior, Sister Aline, to the superiors-general, Mère St Georges (1903-1908), and to Mère Marie Alvarez (1908-1909), which provide a fairly full picture of its history. Some of these originals exist only in the edited form printed in the official bulletin of the congregation, *La Colombe*.

The first letter dated 6 April 1903, (printed in *La Colombe* 1903), recounts the sisters' arrival in Usk and their first days there.

> I am pleased to be able to tell you that the three Sisters (Sister Aline, Sister Anne and Sister Claire) have arrived.

They were accompanied by a maid, presumably a French girl, Marie Trottin, whom they had brought with them from Brittany. They had a good journey and were keeping well. They found their way to Monmouth without difficulty and were happy to see the sisters there.

From the moment we arrived they showered us with kindness. The following morning, 27 February, we were blessed in being able to hear Mass and to receive our dear Lord in Holy Communion for the first time in this foreign land. On Saturday we had to make our way to Usk. The good Father Heneka having sent us a telegram, we could not linger in Monmouth. We arrived at Usk as the parish mission was about to end and Father Heneka told us that our coming to Usk was its crowning point... He comforted us by saying he was sure that we would succeed, and that our presence would contribute a great deal to the work of conversion. And I believe him, because he appears to be such a holy man.

On the following Sunday, the sisters were present for the instruction given by the missioner and for the ending of the mission at 7 o'clock in the evening. During benediction there was a renewal of baptismal vows, with lighted candles. The account continued:

> A lady sent her eight-year-old girl to get candles for the sisters. I must admit, this moved me to tears, tears of tenderness and joy as I sensed that already we were loved by these people who scarcely knew us.

Of the 1,430 inhabitants in Usk, only one hundred were Catholics, and this was likely once again to prejudice their great desire to have a school in Usk. However, they settled in, under the patronage of St Joseph. In her next letter to the superior-general, dated 31 May, about a month after their arrival in Usk, Sister Aline tells her that the community has taken in a lady boarder, a Mrs Twomey, and that they are very pleased with her, but she regrets that the lessons they hoped for are not yet very plentiful.

In May 1903, the assistant superior-general, and the general bursar of the congregation came to visit the recently founded communities and to see about those projected for the near future. The sisters in Usk were only too delighted to welcome them, and Father Heneka was glad to make their acquaintance, so much so that on 3 June he wrote to the superior-general expressing his joy at meeting them. He wrote:

> No doubt you have already heard a great deal about Usk from the two visitors. How pleased I was to see the two heroines, the saintly women who are helping you to protect your congregation in these perilous times. Continue the struggle, God will himself give you the victory. Our Sisters are doing well. For the first time they celebrated your congregation's great feast (Pentecost) in exile but they celebrated it in a spirit that does credit to your congregation.

He went on to praise their efforts in the cleaning and decorating of the church for special feast days, and Sister Anne, the organist, for training the choir to sing at the High Mass. "The children love them," he wrote,

"...Protestants admire them. The beginnings are hard, as we know, but the Sisters are not losing hope. They remain calm in the face of difficulties. They are starting to have pupils from Protestant families in particular..." (Archives, Maison Mère, Saint Brieuc, File 12G6).

Three months after their arrival, Sister Aline wrote a long letter to Monsignor Morelle speaking of their happiness in Usk.

The three of us keep marvellously well. I think that the air of Usk must really suit us. Pupils are beginning to come. Sister Clare gives seven hour long lessons in French a week and will probably have more in September. She is becoming known for the quality of her lessons and is a friendly person. Sister Anne, whom you will be seeing shortly, plays the organ in church; so far she has only three pupils for music, but is promised more on her return from Saint Brieuc. The people of Usk would be inconsolable should she not come back (In fact she did not return to Usk but was sent to the USA.) There is no shortage of demand for needlework lessons, so there will be enough of them to occupy a sister full time. So as you see, our beginnings in Usk are not too hard. The people are very friendly. We also visit the Catholics who are ill.

The other day we went to see a good man of eighty-five years of age who is coming to the end of his life. With tears in his eyes he said: 'Now that I have seen the Sisters, I can die happy,' a reminder of the words of Simeon in the temple when the child Jesus was offered there. We visit him every day and as we take our leave, he says a heartfelt 'God bless you.' I am not really able to speak the language, and have no time to study it. Once I am able to make myself understood, I shall be quite happy in exile.

In his capacity as editor of *La Colombe*, Mgr Morelle added the following lines to Sister Aline's letter which was published in the year 1904:

This letter fills us with hope for the future of the work at Usk. We trust that our dear sisters, with the fatherly encouragement and support of the good Father Heneka, will have a fruitful apostolate in this mission. The convent has been placed under the patronage of St Joseph, as can be seen in the photograph which Father Heneka has sent us (**Plate 10**).

The group photograph shows Father Heneka, the three sisters and a number of children, together with two women, probably Marie Trottin, the little maid, and Mrs Twomey, the lady boarder.

After this very promising beginning of the foundation at Usk, where the sisters settled in so quickly and were very happy, difficulties unfortunately began to make their presence felt. As mentioned Sister Anne, who was the parish organist, left Usk for the USA. Sister Angélique was sent to replace her, but she was an artist rather than a musician so she could not give music lessons or play the organ as Sister Anne had done. This was an unfortunate move, since it hindered the smooth running of the work which the sisters had undertaken. It is understandable, however, in the context of the development of the congregation at that time when foundations even as far away as the USA had to be staffed with the sisters who were sent into exile. To meet the growing demand for needlework lessons, Sister Elie was sent to join the community. However, her talent was for embroidery not dressmaking, so the hope for income from music lessons and dressmaking did not materialise. In a letter to the superior-general on 23 August, 1903, Sister Aline thanks her for the "alms" she sent, and goes on to say that she fears the community will not be able to meet its expenses for very much longer. She writes:

> The little boarders we were hoping to have are not going to come after all; their mother finds that that our house is not suitable. There is a house near the church that we would dearly love to have, but we are poor. We have no adequate building and no teachers.

In October 1903, they received a short visit from the superior-general Mère St Georges and Monsignor Morelle, who were making a canonical visitation of all the foundations in England and Wales. The visit was short because they had first to go to Llanover to see the Honourable Mrs Herbert who wanted to discuss with them the interests of the congregation in Wales. Monsignor Morelle mentions this visit in *La Colombe*, (1904, No.1). It appears that Mrs Herbert insisted on them going by coach to Pontypool to meet Father Degan, the parish priest at Pontypool to view a house intended for a new community to be opened at Pontypool. He notes that from Pontypool to Usk the journey proved somewhat traumatic. The River Usk, swollen by recent heavy rains, had overflowed its banks and made the road into a swirling torrent. The water reached to the horses' chests and came in under the coach doors, but providence saw to it that the travellers came to no harm, and reached their destination safe and sound.

Sister Aline's last letter to the superior-general for 1903 is dated 28 December. She mentions her own illness as an excuse for the delay in writing. She says that for the community's first Christmas they received gifts from the poor as well as the rich. In this letter she also mentions that with a view to increasing their meagre resources, the sisters had circulated a leaflet advertising French conversation lessons, as had happened at the convent in Monmouth when the sisters arrived there.

Sister Aline's first letter in 1904, 17 January, was linked with the sending of the community accounts for 1903 to the mother house in Saint Brieuc, a practice that existed for all the communities established abroad as well as in France. These accounts showed the record, no doubt, of their poverty rather than of anything that might be termed their "financial situation". She also tells the superior-general that, owing to the illness of Sister Elie, they are finding it difficult to keep up with all the sewing to be done. Five weeks later, on 18 February, she wrote to the superior-general saying that she had to buy a sewing machine so as to be able to keep up with all the orders received, and that she was given money towards the cost of it. She mentions that Sister Elie is ill again. She also told the superior-general that the lease of the house would expire on 1 March, and asked if it should be renewed. The little school which they had started was obviously not succeeding, as she wrote:

> We have fewer pupils this year, but we have some consolation in our exile as we are able to teach the children to know God. We have catechism classes twice a week, we are making garments for the poor children, and we visit the sick.

In the autumn of 1904, the general bursar, Sister Marie Angélina, came again on business to Wales and visited the sisters at Usk. Writing again to the superior-general on 12 November, Sister Aline tells how pleased they were with the visit. She mentions that the number of private lessons is diminishing, but that there was plenty of sewing to be done. Sister Anne Emmanuel (newly arrived in the community) seemed to be managing with the sewing. In her last letter of the year, dated 24 December, she says, "We have a lot of orders for sewing at present, but Sister Anne Emmanuel is no good at cutting out." She also said that they received a number of gifts at Christmas, which helped to make ends meet.

The following year, however, the tone changes. In 1905, Sister Aline writes

> The number of private lessons is forever fluctuating, even the orders for sewing are fewer at present; however, this allows us a bit more time for going out and for tidying up the house. There is great excitement in Usk: Colonel Herbert who stood as a Liberal candidate in the election has won a seat in parliament.

(There were plans to have another foundation at Llanarth, but it never materialised). There are three letters extant for the year 1906. In the earliest, dated 22 April, Sister Aline wrote to the superior-general that Sister Claire had been very ill with pneumonia, but adds that the danger point had passed. She also said that every Wednesday a group of ladies came to the convent to work (sew) for the poor. In August, Sister Aline wrote to the superior-general to thank her for the money which had been sent from France to help them in their poverty, saying that she feels "embarrassed to be always receiving." The need was not only for money but also for personnel. Sister Elie who did needlework in the community was transferred to Pwllheli and another sister was needed for needlework. Sister Claire was convalescing in the convent at Monmouth. In her last letter for 1906, dated 11 November, Sister Aline gave news of the health of the sisters and ended on an uncharacteristically disheartened note:

> There is now no hope of ever having a school in Usk; the town is so small; it has no trade; no manufacturing industry, nothing. Our landlord wants to sell the house we rent from him, so what are we to do?

On 6 June 1907, Sister Aline says: "The Sisters are keeping fairly well except for Sister Armand who is complaining of chest pains but the doctor finds nothing wrong with her." Once again she asks for a sister who can cut out patterns and another one for all the embroidery and fancy work to be done. In her letter of 21 September 1907, she submits for approval the project of transferring the Usk community to Barry Docks "since" as she writes, "the house we now occupy is to be sold in the more or less distant future." The superior-general must have agreed that she should explore further the Barry project. On 24 October, in her letter to the superior-general, she speaks of a meeting between Sister Thérèse and Bishop Hedley in Cardiff. "He wanted us to go to Barry and look for a house that very day." But she told the bishop she would have to write to the authorities in the congregation for authorisation. From her subsequent letter of 16 November, the superior-general and her council must have decided against the move to Barry. Sister Aline writes:

> I submit to your decision but let me for the sake of my conscience, acquaint you with our situation here in Usk (as compared with Barry) where there is such hope of being able to do good. If you decide otherwise, may God's will be done.

However, having read her letter of 16 November, it appears that the superior-general reconsidered her original decision and authorised Sister Aline to explore the project further, that is a foundation at Barry Docks.

Father Byrne, the priest in charge at Barry Docks, was anxious to have them in his parish. In January 1908, two members of the general council of the congregation came from France to look at properties in Barry Docks, but nothing remains in writing to indicate what they thought of them as possible locations for a community. Preparations were obviously well advanced, for the sisters had intended to leave for Barry in June 1908.

When Sister Aline wrote on 20 September she expressed fresh hopes for the community in Usk. "Father Heneka," she wrote, "is thinking of opening a parish school and of obtaining a salary for a Sister who would teach in it, by voluntary subscriptions. Will you fix the sum to be asked for? We still have an abundance of needlework to be done." Father Heneka, however, did not succeed in his plan to open a school.

In October 1908, Sister Aline writes of another unexpected request from Father Morrall OSB in Bridgend, asking the sisters to go there. He wrote that he would be pleased to entrust the two schools in Bridgend to the sisters. The raising and then the dashing of these various hopes cannot but have generated feelings of insecurity and anxiety about the future, which is probably the reason why, as seems to have been the case, the superior-general instructed Sister Aline to cease negotiating about Barry or Bridgend and to be prepared to close the house at Usk. In her reply, Sister Aline acknowledges the letter received with these instructions and says:

> I am disposed to do all I can to obey you... Father Heneka is pleading with us to remain here for Christmas so that the dear Catholics, who will soon be losing us for good, may have a sung midnight Mass just once more. Sister Jeanne has been practising with the choir for a long time now.

On 28 February, Sister Aline wrote to the superior-general saying that "nothing has been settled about the house in Barry Docks." In this letter she also says that there was in the Usk newspapers a notice saying that the house occupied by the sisters was to be let. Father Heneka was sad at the thought of them leaving Usk, but he understood there was no future in Usk for them. She wrote again in March saying that the house in Barry seemed suitable and that they would need to move there in June "otherwise we will find ourselves without a roof over our heads." In this letter, she asks if they may rent a house in Usk on a month-to-month basis, so as to be able to leave for Barry in June. No further letters were sent between April and September because there was a change of superior-general; Mère Marie Alvarez succeeded Mère St Georges. The feeling of uncertainty and insecurity for the future, since the house they occupied was to be let, must have been a great trial for the sisters, which is probably the reason why the superior-general instructed Sister Aline to cease negotiating about a foundation in Barry Docks, and to prepare for the closure of the house in Usk.

The hard work to survive went on. The sisters had to work until 11 o'clock at night in order to finish all the needlework that had been ordered. In her next letter in December, she said that the sisters' last Christmas had been marked by the great generosity of friends and parishioners; by the beautiful Midnight Mass, at which "there were far more communicants than when we first arrived." Moving to practicalities, she wrote: "How are we going to manage to pack up in this weather, the snow is lying thick on the ground?" In mentioning each sister by name, she says: "I shall miss every one of them."

The last letter to be written from Usk prior to its closure was dated 11 January 1909, and read:

> I have received your invitation to return to France, which is the culmination of a sacrifice I am being asked to make, for I love England dearly. I have met with so much kindness here and have had to struggle so hard to learn the language…I would not have believed that it would cost me so much to leave Usk. But do we not have to bless God for everything? Were it to mean death, I would still repeat: 'Blessed be God.'

The sisters appear to have been very happy in Usk despite the difficulties, and eleven sisters passed through the community in just under the six years of its existence. Sister Aline herself returned to France, and the two other remaining sisters at the time of the closure were assigned to other convents of the congregation in Wales or England.

The departure of the sisters from Usk was a sad moment in the history of the congregation in Wales. The sisters had settled there; the people loved them, and if they had been able to earn their livelihood, they would certainly have remained. It is significant that seventy one years later, in 1980, there was an invitation to the sisters to "Come back to Usk." It happened in this way. The parish priest in Usk, Father Keegan SJ, on coming across the entry in the parish registers made by Father Heneka, in 1909, was prompted to write to one of the sisters that he knew, asking her to try and find out from the provincial archives the number of the house in Mill Street, where the sisters lived from 1903 till 1909. He then went on to say:

There is still no Catholic school in Usk and I would like to start an independent primary school. Most of the Catholics with very young children here are tolerably well off. Usk is a growing town: there is a new housing estate for executives' houses. The area is now largely a dormitory district for professional people. An independent primary school would easily be self-supporting. It would attract many non-Catholics. There is also a detention centre and a borstal to attract those who do not realise that it is the rich whose spiritual need is the greatest.

Regrettably, Father Keegan's hopes that the Daughters of the Holy Spirit would return to Usk remained unfulfilled. The provincial government at the time did not have the means to re-found a convent in Usk.

St David's Convent, Brecon 1903-1948

THE CONGREGATION already had several foundations in England and Wales when negotiations began between Sister Marie Théodose and Father Griffiths, the parish priest of Brecon, who was anxious to have helpers in his small mission in the town. He offered to find a place for the sisters to live, and to make all the necessary preparations for their arrival in Brecon. Sister Marie Théodose visited Bishop Mostyn, bishop of the Diocese of Menevia, in May 1903, with a view to setting up other foundations in his diocese. The bishop invited her to try the parishes of Brecon and Llanelli which were possible places of mission, and he informed the priests of these two parishes of the possibility of such a foundation. He asked Sister Marie Théodose to report back to him after her visits. Brecon was chosen, and the bishop in a letter to Sister Marie Théodose said he hoped they would find their livelihood in Brecon. In his opinion, Llanelli would have been a better proposition, and he would have liked them to go there.

On 7 July, 1903, three sisters arrived from Carmarthen, where there was already a foundation established, and where they had been for several days waiting for their new foundation. The countryside through which they travelled reminded them of their native Brittany. Still they were fearful and anxious for their future, and from their hearts rose the silent prayer: "Lord, bless our efforts and grant that our sacrifices may serve the spread of your kingdom." Father Griffiths met them at the station and accompanied them to their rented property, called 'the Woodlands' (Plate 11), a quarter of an hour's drive from the town centre. He had arranged for a meal to be ready for the sisters and despite the fatigue of the journey they enjoyed it. Then they unpacked as much of the furniture as would be needed for the night.

From the moment of their arrival, the Catholics welcomed the sisters. Special mention should be made of Mr Llewellyn Williams and his sister, Miss Blanche Williams, whose daily kindness and helpful information did much to lessen their difficulties in those early days. Miss Williams, who spoke French fluently, often served as an interpreter for the sisters, and there was great need of such an interpreter in those early days, when the sisters could only speak a little English. There had been a Catholic presence in Brecon since 1642, and a Catholic church, St Michael's, since 1851. In this case, however, the sisters did not name their foundation after the name of the church, but chose St David, the patron saint of Wales, as the patron of this new foundation.

In the small town of Brecon, mostly Protestant, knowledge of the religious life was limited. Great was the astonishment, not to say apprehension, caused in Brecon by the appearance of these strangely-dressed women of whom nothing was known. In the minds of them all was the question: what was the sisters' purpose in coming to Brecon? No doubt, they felt it was to convert all the inhabitants to the Catholic faith. For this reason many resolved never to cross the convent threshold. The warm welcome that the sisters had received on their arrival in Monmouth and Usk did not seem to be replicated on their arrival in Brecon, although as time went on, the people of Brecon too grew to love and respect the sisters.

The stationmaster of Brecon approached Sister Marie Théodose one day and asked if the intention of the sisters was to convert the people of Brecon to Catholicism. She replied that the sisters respected everyone's religious convictions. Their intention was to give private lessons in various subjects and they hoped to open a school. "If that is really so," he replied, "I can tell you that you will succeed in Brecon and you will have many pupils. My work puts me in touch with many people and I shall make a point of dispelling the fears many of these have with regard to you."

Thereafter many ladies, among them Miss Morgan, an influential and very important woman, braved public opinion and came to welcome the sisters openly. Despite the stationmaster's predictions, however, very few pupils turned up at first, and it was difficult to procure a livelihood for the community. The Annals for these early days record:

> More than once we had to have recourse to the mother house in France to be able to meet the expenses of keeping house. (Annals pp. 2-3, Archives, Saint Brieuc).

Three months after the foundation of the convent, which had been placed under the patronage of the patron saint of Wales, St David, the superior-general and Monsignor Morelle visited the new foundation. One of the sisters wrote an account of this visit, which was published in *La Colombe* (1904, No.1 pp.164-165):

> During the month of September, we heard that our dear Mother General was in Belgium and that from there she would come, with our good Father Superior, to visit all the communities in England and Wales. How delighted we were to receive this news! And how eagerly we counted the days, which must pass before the happy event! 'We will arrive at 3 o'clock' was the message conveyed by the telegram, which Father Superior sent us on 4 October. At about half past two, we went to the station. Nature itself was in festive mood; the mists had cleared, the sun shone brightly. The train pulled into the station. Who could describe our emotion when among the passengers getting off the train, we recognised our venerable Mother and Father Superior? Had it not been for the English greetings spoken all around us, we could have thought that we were at a station in France. A few minutes later, we were back at St David's Convent. After a short rest, our travellers went to visit Father Griffiths, the parish priest, and then the family of our devoted benefactress, Miss Williams. Next day, Father Griffiths during the evening service at the parish church arranged for a hymn to be sung to the tune of a French hymn 'Unis aux concerts des Anges,' a well-known melody, which transported us in spirit to one of our churches in France.

The end of the visit was as sad as the excitement of its beginning.

> Every medal has its reverse side: the very next day our well-loved visitors had to leave us. Nature seemed to share our sadness, and seemed to weep with us, once they had left us to go to the foundation in Usk. That was the moment when we experienced again the pain of separation. The thought that God would reward us for this sacrifice gave us courage to be generous in making it.

The visits, which the sisters received from their superior-general and Mgr Morelle in those early days of their exile, were always a source of great joy, comfort and encouragement to them. No doubt, they were occasions too when they received news of their families, especially during the period of the two world wars.

The sisters set to work to find out how they might earn a livelihood in this new foundation. The Annals for the year 1904 record their early experiences. A few families had ventured to send their children for lessons in needlework and art; several ladies also had asked for lessons. These slow and painful beginnings notwithstanding, the sisters had hopes for the future and resolved to leave their small house for a larger one, near the church and the town centre. "This larger house separated from the street by an iron railing, with a garden behind it surrounded by a high wall seemed purpose-built to serve as a convent" **(Plate 12)**. The owner, Councillor Jones Williams, was in no hurry to rent his house to nuns. He seemed to doubt the honesty of these strange would-be tenants, or rather he had his suspicions, well founded as it happened, about their financial situation. The account in the Annals continues:

> He did not know however, that the poor of God never go in want. The lease was agreed, and the sisters sub-let the Woodlands, which had been leased to them for three years. In the month of October they took up their abode in Glamorgan Street.

Once they had moved into this large house with its spacious rooms, the sisters were keener than ever to have more pupils and made numerous novenas for that purpose. Before long they were able to start a small class **(Plate 13)**. Among these were several Catholic children, so they could give them religious education lessons. They gave catechism lessons on Sunday, as well as preparing the church linen, and decorating the altar. In addition they visited the Catholics in the parish who had ceased to practice their faith. In this way, they felt that they had established themselves at Brecon. They had started a small school, had private lessons in art and needlework and, what was most precious to them at all times, they were able to visit the people in the parish and the sick in the neighbourhood.

On 20 August, the little convent chapel was blessed. As noted in the Annals: "Great was the joy of the community and its confidence in the future was strengthened." It was decided that the children who were ready to do so, would make their First Holy Communion in the convent chapel, at Christmas 1905. The day before this arrived, two of the boys came, sad-faced, to tell the sisters that they would not be there because their parents were about to leave Brecon. It was decided that for these two boys the date of their First Holy Communion would be brought forward, and the sisters had the happiness of seeing their parents follow their sons to the altar to receive Holy Communion. Having listened to their sons' pleading, they had returned after a time of lapsation, to the practice of their faith. And the ceremony was followed by a festive breakfast for the communicants. Father Griffiths paid for this meal.

The sisters continued with their needlework lessons as one form of providing their livelihood. In an attempt to increase their meagre income, they accepted orders for trousseaus as well as for other fancy items. Times were difficult in those early years, but the sisters struggled on with courage and determination to succeed. Three years later, 1908, when the superior-general and the general bursar came from France to visit the community, their income was still inadequate for their needs. There were only eleven pupils in the school when the canonical visitation took place. The number of pupils would rise a little and then fall so suddenly that the school fees could not be relied upon as a means of livelihood. So a more lucrative way than sewing was decided upon as a means of supplementing the income from school fees. This was to be the setting up of a small laundry, though very discreetly, because it was feared that if word of this were to spread, it would prejudice the future of the school. So rather than take in washing for the town, an attempt was made to find a notable family in the area willing to have its linen laundered by the sisters, at an advantageous price. The superior of the Abergavenny convent succeeded in finding a family whose life-style produced the amount of laundry that the sisters could manage, and arrangements were made to undertake this work.

It was as if providence had awaited this fresh proof of devotedness on the part of the sisters before bestowing a blessing on their establishment and making their work fruitful. There was a significant rise in the number of pupils and soon the community was able to meet its expenses. Now that the sisters were giving more time to teaching, they were not able to give enough time to the laundry work. Mère Marie Angélina, the general bursar, who visited the community in June of that year, arranged to send three or four girls in their teens from Brittany, probably from one of their orphanages, to help with the laundry work. Once these had been initiated into the work, they proved a great help to the sisters who, for their part, trained them in orderliness and the love of work well done, as well as continuing their Christian instruction, thereby preparing them for the future.

On the educational front, things began to improve. In June 1909, the sisters had the satisfaction of recording the first successes of their pupils in their music exams. In December of that year, another source of joy was the arrival of their first little boarder who was soon followed by a second. Another mark of progress is noted in the Annals, where it is stated:

> At Christmas time we had our first prize-giving, held in St Michael's Hall. To mark the occasion, our pupils gave a little performance and some of their work was put on display. Parents and well-wishers, as well as the curious, came to swell the audience. The event was presided over

by Miss Morgan Jones, a former member of the municipal council and the historian of Breconshire. In words that were simple but very convincing, she praised our little school, and then went on to say how she had welcomed the sisters' arrival in Brecon, adding that by their lives of prayer and self-sacrifice they could not fail to draw down God's blessing on the whole town. Father Griffiths, the parish priest, thanked her for her gracious words and voiced the sisters' gratitude to the audience for the interest in the convent, which their presence showed. This first performance, which was to become an annual event, resulted in our having several new pupils for the school as well as for art classes. (Annals, pp. 6-7).

The early years of difficulties and struggle were coming to an end as the school began to grow and develop. In April 1910, when Mother Marie Dominique, the sister in charge of the English and Welsh communities, came to visit the community, the number of pupils had risen to thirty instead of the eleven at her last visitation. She also noted that the superior at Brecon visited the sick in the town when her other duties allowed her to do so. In July of the same year, the music pupils were again successful:

> The success, which the good Lord grants us year after year has earned a good name for the school and its reputation having spread, pupils begin to come from neighbouring localities. The resulting increase in our income enabled us to do something for a few Catholics deserving of help, and we gave their children a place in the school so as to exert a more directly beneficial influence over them.

Father Griffiths, the parish priest, did not hide his joy in having a convent in his poor little mission. It was his hope that one day the mission would have a Catholic elementary school run by the sisters and attended by all the Catholic children, some of whom had to attend the Protestant schools in town. The sisters also hoped that they could realise this dream in the not-too-distant future. However, in November 1912, Father Griffiths was appointed by the bishop to take charge of the parish in Bangor in North Wales. The Annals state:

> He had earned the esteem and the good will of all, so his leaving caused general and genuine regret, especially to the community which had received so much from him. (Annals, pp. 8-9)

Father Finucane replaced him in Brecon. He too greatly appreciated the devoted service given by the sisters, and took a keen interest in everything that concerned the school.

The music lessons became more and more popular, and by 1912 the number of pupils taking music lessons reached forty. Another sister was sent to help Sister Marie Cécilia, the music teacher. By January 1913, the number of pupils in the convent school reached sixty; ten of these were also boarders. In addition, an event happened in the town which was to have a direct influence on the future of the convent school. Another private school, run by the Misses Garlick, closed. As a result of the closure, several new pupils joined the convent school, and the sisters began to have greater hope for the future of their work in Brecon.

The lease of the house in Glamorgan Street was due to expire in March 1913 and the owner made it known that he intended to sell the property. Moreover, the asking price for it was considered exorbitant, a sum which the sisters could not afford. The community went to look at the premises left vacant by the school that had closed, whereupon the rumour quickly spread that the sisters were going to leave Glamorgan Street. On hearing this, the solicitor thought it best to notify the landlord that his tenants were about to escape him. The Annals tell us that the owner took fright and immediately decided to lower the asking price for the house from £1,950 to £1,400 (£88,000 and 64,000 in today's terms). The Annals record this entry:

> We were far from expecting such an outcome and saw in it the hand of God and the protection of St Joseph. The sale was concluded, and St David's is now truly our home. To remind us of this, Sister Amélie des Anges, our superior, had a statue of St Joseph blessed and placed in the hallway.

A few months before this, the sisters were able to give up the laundry work, which they had been doing since 1908 to supplement their meagre income from tuition fees.

In June 1913, when Mother Marie Dominique again made the visitation of the community, she wrote in her report:

> The Sisters are doing good work in the locality, especially through the religious instruction that they give to poor Catholic children who attend protestant schools. The number of pupils in the convent school and of those who come for private lessons has doubled since my last visit [her previous visit had been in April 1910].

The year 1914 saw the outbreak of the First World War in Europe. In Brecon, as in other parts of England and Wales, sewing groups were formed to make warm clothing for the soldiers. The sisters offered their services which were readily accepted and much appreciated. Many large consignments of linen were sent to the convent, from which garments were to be cut and prepared for sewing. The cutout garments were then sent to the volunteers who met regularly at a certain venue. Doing this represented no small enterprise on the part of the sisters, since the number of volunteers who had to be kept supplied with garments for sewing was considerable. Such was the trust that the sisters enjoyed that the manageress of the group would not hear of anyone else doing the cutting out. "At the Convent," it was said, "nothing is wasted, the work is well done and they don't accept money for it!" This fresh instance of devotedness and patriotism earned for the community the esteem of many persons with whom they had had no previous dealings.

During the war years, thanks to the material prosperity of the mining areas that border on Brecon, and thanks to the increased prosperity of local farmers, the number of pupils at the convent school reached the hundred mark. At one time there were as many as twenty boarders, and there were ten sisters in the community. At the same time, the number of pupils taking music and art doubled, resulting in a shortage of space. An army hut was purchased and used for physical education and dancing lessons, and entertainment put on by the pupils.

The gradual implementation of the Fisher Education Act, delayed by the Great War, posed a threat to the schools run by the sisters on account of the requirements with regard to school buildings, to qualified teachers and to the ratio of teachers to pupils. So the superior-general and her council decided to close certain schools in England and Wales in order to be able to strengthen others. St David's Convent School, Brecon, was one of the schools marked for closure, and as the annalist records:

> To the Sisters who had toiled in this foundation since its beginnings, the news came as a great and painful shock. They understood of course the reasons given for the closure, yet one cannot accept without grieving, the abrupt end of a work which has cost so much toil and effort.

When Father Finucane, the parish priest, was told of the decision, he was wholly disconcerted, for the departure of the sisters from Brecon, in his opinion, would spell the end of the mission. He informed the bishop of the diocese who energetically opposed the decision and threatened that, if the sisters left Brecon, he would appeal to Rome. So the superiors of the congregation had to revoke their decision, though they were pleased to discover how much the bishop and the parish priest appreciated the devoted service the sisters gave in Brecon.

The sisters had kept the news of the possibility of the school closing from the parents of the pupils and so school life went on as usual. Even so they were faced with the need of cutting down on the number of sisters needed to teach in these schools. Given that the community's sole source of income came from the fees of the pupils attending the convent school and from private tuition, there remained only one alternative: to close the elementary school which the sisters ran at their own expense. In any case the days of this school were numbered, since it would not be able to qualify for recognition from the Board of Education. Such was the proposal which Father Finucane put to the superiors, who regretfully gave their consent to its closure. The closure of the elementary school in 1921 meant therefore that the Catholic children who had attended it had now to attend the local schools. The sisters undertook to continue the religious education of these children by organising catechism lessons for them, after school hours. These lessons were given in the Catholic church, and were, according to the reports of the diocesan inspector Father Jarvis, well prepared. Even so, it was not easy to remain in touch with these children, who came less and less frequently to Sunday Mass.

Three years later, in June 1922, when the canonical visitation was made by the assistant general of the congregation, the latter in her report wrote:

> Providence continues to bless the work of our house in Brecon. The school numbers 102 pupils, of whom 20 are boarders. Private tuition in art and music is given to 90 pupils. The Sunday school class is attended by 35 young girls, and 49 children come to the catechism lessons. The Sisters still live in the same house where they still have the problem of shortage of space. It is very much to be desired that they should have larger premises.

In fact, a few years later in 1928, Sister Julie who had succeeded Sister Amélie as superior negotiated the purchase of the house next door, called Morganwy **(Plate 14)**, and the community took possession of it in September of that year.

When in 1929, the superior-general made the canonical visitation she was able to record:

> ...our dear house in Brecon has developed since the last visitation. Our Sisters have acquired the property known as Morganwy, which they have adapted to meet the needs of their work. The school continues to prosper and has 117 pupils, 20 of whom are boarders. However, it is much to be desired that there should also be an elementary school for the Catholic children, about 50 of whom attend the catechism lessons given by the Sisters.

From 1930 till 1940, the main topic in the Annals of the community refers to the various changes of superior in the community. Sister Julie was recalled to France in February 1930, and was replaced by Sister Antoine. In November 1937, Sister Antoine received her transfer for Devon. Sister Béatrix ,who spent only fourteen months at Brecon, succeeded her. The main event of her superiorate was to transfer the school from the old house into the new one, "a great improvement" records the annalist, "as the classrooms are now much more spacious and well aired."

In January 1939, after 33 years in Wales, Sister Béatrix returned to France and was replaced by Sister Geneviève, who was to be the last superior of Brecon Convent. She arrived in 1939, the year of the outbreak of the Second World War. The Annals record little or nothing of the effects of the war, except the mention of the hospitality which the community was asked to give to some Ursuline Sisters from Greenwich, whose convent was badly damaged in the blitz, and who had been evacuated to Brecon with some of their pupils.

> We have given them two rooms, our former chapel and our community room; we are doing all we can to make their enforced absence from their monastery less hard to bear. (Annals, p.18)

They stayed until July 1943.

The last decade of the history of St David's Convent, Brecon, was once again plagued by the uncertainty of its future. The opening of a noviciate in Pontypool during the war years for the training of those wishing to join the Congregation of the Daughters of the Holy Spirit, necessitated a juniorate to recruit young girls for the noviciate. As with so many religious congregations, the Daughters of the Holy Spirit turned their thoughts to Ireland as the most fruitful recruiting ground for young people to the religious life. In 1943, the superior of Brecon went to Ireland to look for postulants, and as noted in the Annals:

> Thanks to the prayers offered throughout the colony, several young girls wanting to join the congregation entered the noviciate in Pontypool.

In April 1945, Sister Geneviève accompanied by Sister Mary Ita went for a second time to Ireland to look for postulants. For five weeks, the two travelled through this country, meeting sometimes with success and at other times with failure. Yet a great joy awaited them at the end of their travels: the Bishop of Clogher offered them, for a considerable sum, a fine property and authorised the opening of a juniorate there. (Annals, p.21).

Yet, the future of St David's Convent remained in the balance. Just as the Education Act of 1918 led to the closure of the parish elementary school, so now the new Education Act of 1944 was giving rise to concern for the

1. Jean Leuduger (1649-1722) who inspired the foundation of the Congregation (p.14)

2. The first foundation of the Daughters of the Holy Spirit at Le Légué, 1712 (p.16)

3. Plérin—A wing of the school and first mother house of the congregation (p.17)

4. Mère Saint Georges, the superior-general who sent the sisters to Wales (p.33)

5. The sisters leave Brittany to go into exile (p.34)

7. St Mary's Convent, Monmouth (28 St Mary's Street) (p.39)

8. St Mary's RC Church, Monmouth (p.40)

9. Cartref, St James' Square, Monmouth (Became the convent in 1908) (p.43)

10. St Joseph's Convent, Usk (The first pupils of the private school) (p.49)

11. The Woodlands, Brecon, (first house of the sisters, 1903) p.55

12. The house in Glamorgan Street, Brecon, 1905 (p.58)

13. Pupils of St David's Convent, c.1905 (p.58)

14. Morganwy House, Brecon, St David's Convent in 1928 (p.63)

15. Park House, Pontypool (St Alban's Convent) (p.79)

16. Picton Villa, Carmarthen (St Winefride's Convent) (p.87)

17. Picton Terrace, Carmarthen, (St Winefride's Convent) (p.91)

18. Picton Place, Carmarthen (St Winefride's Convent) (p.91)

20. St Mary's RC School, Carmarthen (p.92)

19. Sister Pierre Lazare "Ma Mère." (p.92)

21. The Old Rectory, Tenby—St Margaret's Convent (p.97)

22. Salisbury House, Aberystwyth (St Padarn's Convent) (p.111)

23. St Michael's Vicarage, Aberystwyth (St Padarn's Convent) (p.118)

24. St Padarn's Convent—A group of pupils, 1946 (p.124)

25. St Anne's Convent, Llanrwst (p.135)

future of the convent school. An entry in the Annals for November 1946 reads:

> The decision of our Superiors is to close Brecon. The blow was all the more terrible, as it was unexpected. We said nothing about it to anyone but stormed heaven asking God to make known his holy will. The same month saw the sad death of Sister Thérèse Albertine. She had been interned at Besançon during the war and there had contracted an incurable disease the ravages of which were so imperceptible that we scarcely noticed she was dying. On Thursday she taught in her class as usual, and on Sunday following she died.

The uncertainty about the future remained until May 1947, when Bishop Petit visited Brecon convent. He was against the closure of the convent. "Never lower the flag," he said. In August of the same year, Sister Geneviève was transferred to Ireland to set up a juniorate. She left Brecon, we are told, on 28 August, and the whole community regretted her departure. An entry in the Annals noted that Sister Marie Apolline also left Brecon to go to Ireland to join Sister Geneviève. At this point, the Annals of the community end rather abruptly. The sadness of the sisters at having to leave Brecon, which they loved so much, meant that they did not wish to air their sorrow in writing.

The final visitation of the community was made in February 1948, the last year that the sisters were in Brecon. There were eleven sisters in the community at this time. It is evident from the report of the visitation that the school was flourishing. The visitor noted:

> The school numbers 114 pupils at present. It is under the direction of a qualified and competent headmistress with a staff of seven teachers, four of them sisters and three lay teachers. The religious instruction of the Catholic children continues to receive priority consideration. As for the Protestant pupils, the sisters avail of the scripture lessons to provide them with clear notions about religion and their religious duties to God. The Sunday catechism is also the responsibility of the sisters, as well as the church music. The Sisters also help in the parish, and do parish visiting.

Rather than allow the school to close, the Bishop of Menevia appealed to other religious teaching orders to take on the school. The Ursulines from Thurles in Ireland accepted to take on the school, and nine sisters of the Ursuline congregation arrived to take over the school and convent. When in the summer of 1948, the Daughters of the Holy Spirit left Brecon, the sisters who were there at that time were transferred to other convents of the congregation. Two sisters went to the community in Abergavenny, one to

Carmarthen and the others to convents in England. It is interesting that, even at the time of writing, over half a century after the Daughters of the Holy Spirit left Brecon, some older inhabitants, who either were taught by or knew the sisters, remember them with great affection and gratitude.

St Alban's Convent, Pontypool 1903-2001

THE FOUNDATION at Pontypool was the sixth foundation made in the year 1903, and was once again the work of the Honourable Mrs Herbert of Llanover. In August 1903, she arranged for a meeting to take place at her home, between Father Degan, the parish priest of St Alban's Parish, Pontypool, and Sister Thérèse du St Esprit (from the nearby Monmouth Convent) who was called upon to be the spokeswoman for the superior-general of the congregation in negotiating this new foundation.

The negotiations went according to plan and, when the decision had been made to open a convent in Pontypool, Sister Thérèse went to view the little house which Father Degan thought would be suitable for the group of three sisters who were appointed to go there. In a letter to the superior-general, dated 4 September 1903, Sister Thérèse wrote a long and detailed account of her visit to Pontypool, which gives a clear picture of the situation.

> I have just arrived back from Pontypool with Sister Marie, my companion. Father Degan met us at the station at Pontypool Road and we travelled by bus to the town itself... He contacted the tenant of the house we are interested in, and asked if we could call there… It is a nice little house though perhaps too small for us. There are three bedrooms into which only one bed would fit, along with a small cupboard, a table and chair. In the room, which is slightly bigger, two beds could be fitted. Downstairs, there are two small rooms, a tiny kitchen and a back kitchen with two taps, four wall cupboards, and a copper tub for washing the linen, and there is also a bathtub. The tenant said that he would be willing to let us have the gas mantles and the blinds on the windows, cheaply. Father Degan has agreed to see to all the arrangements if you agree that we should take the house. Next to it, there is a place for storing coal and wood…there is also a small garden like the one we have at Monmouth, with vegetables. The house is quite new and in very good condition, inside and outside. The rent is nine shillings a week, (about £23.50 in present day currency). The owner pays the rates. Father Degan advises that we rent the house for one year, and if

we get pupils, we could later on move to a larger one. He thinks that the sisters will find that there is a demand for lessons in French, music, art and needlework.

In this first letter, Sister Thérèse also gives a brief description of the Pontypool mission. She writes:

> Pontypool is a town a bit like Monmouth with a population of between 6,000 and 7,000 inhabitants, of whom 700 are Catholics. The mission has four schools, staffed by Catholic teachers. Father Degan oversees these schools and pays the teachers' salaries.

Father Degan took the sisters to visit one of these schools, which had 250 pupils, boys and girls, six teachers and four pupil-teachers. The headmistress welcomed them, and spoke of her wish to see them settled in Pontypool. She expressed her hope that one of the sisters might be able to take one of the infant classes in due course. If she was paid by the parish, it would be a source of income for the community. She hoped that the headmistress would readily allow the sisters to acquaint themselves with these little classes, where the discipline was good. The exact location of the little house they hoped to rent is, unfortunately, not on record, but it was in the Wainfelin area of the town.

Father Degan, the parish priest, was very anxious to have the sisters in Pontypool, as were his two assistant curates. One of the curates said to them during the visit of Sister Thérèse and her companion: "Well, have you decided? Your Sisters are going to come to Pontypool, aren't they? There is good work to be done here." The visit ended with a meal at the presbytery, and then Father Degan took the sisters by bus back to the railway station, where they caught the train to Monmouth, a journey that took less than an hour. Their return tickets cost six shillings.

Sister Thérèse told the superior-general that Father Degan would like a definite answer as soon as possible because the house would be evacuated on 1 October, and the owner was keen to rent it again. The superior-general responded in the affirmative, and the first three sisters for this new foundation in Pontypool were chosen: Sister Marie Geneviève, as superior of the convent, accompanied by Sister Marie Agnès and Sister Ste Sidonie. These three sisters arrived in Pontypool on 13 October 1903. In her first letter to the superior-general dated 1 November, just over two weeks later, Sister Marie Geneviève recounts their arrival. She writes:

> On Tuesday, 13 October, I left the community at Monmouth where I had spent six happy days with the community and would gladly have stayed there longer. With Sister Paul, I arrived at Pontypool Station at

> 10.00 a.m. Father Degan was there to meet us. It was pouring rain, and he helped us on to the bus and came with us to our small home in Wainfelin, Pontypool, which we reached half an hour later, a distance of about two miles from the railway station.

The letter then goes on to describe their arrival at their new home and the settling in:

> The good Father Degan had seen to a hundred and one details in the house and brought in enough provisions to last us a week... My two new companions, Sister Marie Agnès and Sister Ste Sidonie arrived from Ingsdon... We immediately set about unpacking all the boxes, this did not take us long but finding a place for everything did. Our trunks serve us both as storage space and, for the time being, as seating accommodation.

She adds at this point in her letter: "We are glad to want for certain things; the Holy Family, when in exile in Egypt, did not have as much as we have, I am sure."

The sisters lost no time in seeking to find a livelihood in their new foundation, for within three weeks of their arrival there Sister Geneviève noted in her letter: "Already we have seven students for French lessons and five for needlework." The extraordinary speed with which they settled in and began to earn their livelihood is testimony itself to their courage and determination to succeed wherever they settled.

All was not smooth running in those early days in Pontypool. Sister Geneviève notes:

> Last week, we were troubled by boys coming to our door every evening to hurl mud and stones at it, with shouts and whistling. We have reported this to the local policeman and he has promised to keep an eye on our house.

However, worse was to come. On Guy Fawkes' Day, the nature and meaning of which was totally unknown to the sisters in exile in a foreign land, they suddenly found themselves in what seemed to be a state of siege— fireworks blew off at the doors and windows, accompanied by stones and empty boxes, even the letter box gave forth sounds of explosion and terror. No doubt the youth of the neighbourhood had taken it in to their heads to exorcise "Guy Fawkes" who had come down to their town in the guise of "White Ghosts" (the sisters were dressed in white habits). News of this trouble reached the ears of Doctor Haslett, a friend of the sisters, who took it upon himself to go round each school in the district and put the case of the sisters in its true light, to the teachers and pupils. After that, they were never troubled again, either in the streets or at home.

In her next letter to the superior-general, dated 20 December 1903, Sister Marie Geneviève sends her Christmas greetings. There was nothing new to report in this letter, but she recounts the visits she paid to two elderly ladies who were ill, one of them in hospital. Therefore, the work to which the sisters always gave priority, namely visiting the sick and the poor in their homes, was already one of their very early works in Pontypool. Another reaction to the sisters is mentioned in this same letter:

> Yesterday, as we left church, two little girls shyly gave us a penny; the Catholics in Pontypool are, for the most part, very poor.

One of the very first setbacks alluded to at this time came early in the New Year 1904, where we learn from a letter to the superior-general that the number of pupils for French had decreased, as three of the pupils had moved to London, leaving only four for French lessons. Obviously, Sister Marie Geneviève had asked for an extra sister and in a letter dated 16 January 1904, she writes:

> There are already twenty two music teachers in town, so the promised sister will not have many pupils for that subject, but there is only one art teacher, so she may well have a considerable number for drawing and painting.

She also adds that there is new work for the sisters: "Father Degan has asked us if we would look after the church. I replied that we would gladly do so, once the fourth sister had arrived." In this letter, too, she mentions the state of the health of the sisters, which was to plague their early years in Wales. She writes:

> I am concerned about the health of Sister Marie Agnès and Sister Ste Sidonie [her two companions]. Sister Thérèse in Monmouth says she will arrange for them to be seen by a doctor in Monmouth.

In the early days of these foundations in Wales, the communities relied heavily on the mother house in Brittany for some of the necessities of life and the needs of their apostolate. In a letter written on 18 February 1904, Sister Marie Geneviève gratefully acknowledged the various items sent from Brittany. She says: "Sister Marie Agnès was delighted with the sewing machine, Sister Ste Sidonie with the soup ladle," and she thanked Sister St Aristide for the books she had sent. In March 1904, the fourth sister arrived: Sister Marie Béatrix came from Monmouth convent where she had spent a few days after her arrival from Brittany. Sister Marie Geneviève went to Monmouth to meet her, but it was arranged that she should remain there until a piano and materials for her art lessons arrived at Wainfelin,

Pontypool. In a letter to the superior-general dated 20 March, Sister Marie Geneviève wrote:

> We are hoping to be able to move into a larger house…the health of Sister Marie Agnès and Sister Sidonie is a little better. The isolation in which we find ourselves is hard to bear; the number of lessons we give does not fill our days, but we have more than enough needlework to do.

In her next letter, almost a month later, Sister Marie Geneviève reports that Sister Marie Béatrix had arrived and was hoping to give lessons to quite a number of pupils.

In her letter of 20 May, Sister Marie Geneviève reports that the house they had been hoping to have would not be theirs after all, but that Father Degan was looking for another one. She says: "Our daily needs are still met by providence: Mr & Mrs Flood continue to send us three times a week, meat, fish, vegetables and fruit." In this letter, she mentions that they have "four gentlemen and four young ladies for French lessons, another gentleman comes to learn how to play the mandolin, and we have a small class of three for needlework lessons." In this letter too, she mentions the financial state of the community. The accounts for the month of April were as follows: expenditure: 106 francs; receipts: 666 francs.

The first moment of sadness came for the little community following the canonical visitation of one of the superiors from France, who brought a transfer for Sister Marie Agnès. She was transferred to Tenby in West Wales where a new foundation was started in June of the same year that Pontypool was opened. She was replaced by Sister Louis Thérèse. In her letter of 14 June, Sister Marie Geneviève speaks of "the generous spirit in which Sister Marie Agnès accepted her transfer to Tenby." In this letter she mentions that Sister Marie Béatrix was having treatment for her eyes, adding that the sight in one of her eyes was almost gone.

The superior-general always reminded the community of each new foundation of their duty to visit the poor and the sick, as this was part of the reason why the congregation was founded in the first instance. In her letter to the superior-general, dated 30 July, Sister Marie Geneviève wrote:

> In response to your wish that I should visit the poor and the sick, I should like to be able to tell you that I have begun to do so, but up till now, this has been quite impossible. At present, I have to see to all the needlework; the other sisters are kept very busy and what is more, Sister Louis Thérèse needs to do some study in order to be up to the standard expected of her.

The next significant event in the history of the community was the move to a larger house in Pontypool. On 7 April, 1905, Sister Marie Geneviève wrote to the superior-general:

> I am having recourse to you in my present difficult situation: we keep having requests for lessons that we just cannot give. We would need to be six sisters to do all the work, and we are only four…I have also received a request that we start a private school, but now is not the time. We shall certainly get a bigger house but when? I think that they [the church authorities] will decide to build for us, if we cannot get the house not far from here.

On 23 April 1905 when Sister Marie Geneviève wrote to the superior-general, their hope for a larger house was already realised. She wrote:

> Today I can tell you that that we have a big house, one that we least expected to have, and one that seems to be the response to our prayers. It has a yard and a small garden with a green-house. The first boarder will come as soon as we have taken possession of the house.

The new house was situated at 69 Osborne Road, about ten minutes walk from the church. The convent was placed under the patronage of St Alban, the protomartyr of England but not of Wales, presumably because the parish was already under the patronage of St Alban. In her letter to the superior-general in May of that year, the superior writes:

> Here we are in our big house, just ten minutes away from the church. It seems funny to have space in which to move! For the fitting up and arrangements I had a free hand only for the sisters' rooms. Father Degan and the Flood family have seen to all the rest. The little school has not as yet materialised, we have neither desks nor a sister to teach in it, chiefly because, as advised, I tried asking for a higher fee…

Things moved quickly, however, and after the summer holidays. Sister Marie Geneviève wrote to the superior-general, telling her that a teacher from the Catholic school was helping the sisters to set up the private school, and that she came every day for a time to initiate Sister Vincent into the English way of taking a class. By November of that same year, she was able to announce: "Our little class, which began with four pupils, now has seven. They are lovely children, but all of different ability." The parents were delighted with their children's progress and more pupils were beginning to join the four already there. In this letter she asked for more small desks, and for another sister to help with the needlework lessons. She wrote:

> We have as many orders for sewing and needlework as we want, and that is the one way of earning our livelihood. If time allowed it, I could

do nothing but needlework. I have an order for six dozen embroidered napkins, but can give only two hours a day to it...

The first letter to the superior-general for the year 1906 is dated 25 February. In this letter she speaks of her rheumatism. She writes:

> It is something that I have had to live with for a long time now, so I do not worry too much about it except when it becomes so acute that I am unable to do my work.

The news of the school was favourable. There were sixteen pupils in the little school, of different ages and ability. The school fees were very low, as the superior did not dare to ask for higher fees for the 12 to 14 year olds because they were with the infants and, as Sister Vincent had to attend to the others first, she could give only a little time to the older girls. Father Degan had told them that they could have a visit from an inspector at any time, and this was a source of worry to the sisters.

To add to the worries of the community, there was an epidemic of an unnamed disease in Pontypool, and two hundred cases of it were reported in September 1906. The sisters took all the necessary precautions, recommended by the medical authorities. On the educational front, things were looking brighter for the little school. "At the start of the new term we had more pupils than we anticipated." At this time too there is the first mention of boarders. "As for the sewing/dressmaking class," notes Sister Marie Geneviève, "I keep postponing it until we have another Sister, but the girls who have been waiting since July for it to begin, are growing impatient and will go elsewhere, if we do not soon have a Sister to teach them." She also mentions in this letter, dated 23 September 1906, that there was a request from Father Degan that the sisters should give catechism lessons to the children, even though they were so short of sisters. "I told him we would do so; these poor children are given no religious instruction in school."

The epidemic continued to spread during the remaining months of 1906. She noted that hundreds of people were affected by it. In her last letter to the superior-general in 1906 she was still concerned about the epidemic, which was raging in Pontypool. The theatre had been turned into a hospital and nurses were being called in from almost anywhere. "I have promised that, if you will allow me to do so, I shall have a Mass offered in honour of Our Lady of the Seven Dolours, at her shrine not far from here. I shall go there on pilgrimage and leave an ex-voto, if we are protected from this illness." In this letter, she also mentions the progress of their apostolate, stating that they started the new school year with 79 students and pupils: 29 for Art lessons; 11 for French; 11 for lessons in Fancy Needlework and 28 children in the little school. Her only regret was that because of all the work they had to do, there was no time to visit the poor and sick as well. "A lot of children stay for lunch, which means extra work for us. The Sisters have more than enough to do, so an extra Sister would be gratefully received."

While the little convent school continued to grow, the next major concern of the sisters to be gleaned from the correspondence and Annals of the community from 1907 onwards is the move to try to get employment for some sisters in the Catholic primary schools in the locality. This, however, would not be as easy as they might have hoped. In her letter of 12 March 1907, Sister Marie Geneviève wrote:

> For two years now, 'Chapel People' have been proselytising in the area and they have succeeded in excluding Father Degan from the administration of the schools. On the advice of his friends, he is going to present himself again for a place on the Education Committee, in order to be able to defend the interests of the 4 Catholic schools for which he has responsibility.

Some of the teachers resigned from the Catholic schools, because their salaries had decreased so much. One Catholic school at this time was short of three teachers, another of two, and some teachers remained in the schools only in the hope that matters would improve. Father Degan was ready therefore to appoint sisters to these vacancies, where they would find plenty of scope for their zeal.

Events moved more quickly than expected and one week later, the superior wrote again to the superior-general stating:

> Father Degan thinks he can obtain for two Sisters a salary of £40.00, perhaps even £60.00, but to be on the safe side he prefers to say £40.00 to £45.00. If that is at all possible, he would like to have the three Sisters here straight away so that he can appoint them as soon as the teachers whose resignation he is expecting, leave. 'We shall be very happy to share with these Sisters the little we have,' said Father Degan, 'foreseeing all the good that they will do in our dear Pontypool.'

The three sisters who were thus being considered for posts in the Catholic elementary schools of the Pontypool area were at this time completing their teacher training at the Sacred Heart College in Wandsworth. As they were instructed, Sister Pierre Lazare applied for the post of head teacher at Blaenafon, about five miles distance from Pontypool, and Sister Athanasie was appointed as assistant teacher there. Sister Maurice applied for the post of head teacher at Abersychan about three miles from Pontypool. All three were successful in their applications. They were newly qualified teachers who had not served their probationary year, and were obviously unaware (as Father Degan also seems to have been) that before being appointed head teacher in a school with more than fifty pupils, the applicant must have had a minimum of twelve months' teaching experience. In reality, the outcome was very painful for the sisters concerned.

The letters written to the superior-general between December 1907 and July 1908, by Sister Pierre Lazare, Sister Maurice and their superior, Sister Marie Geneviève, afforded glimpses of the trials that they had to suffer in their endeavour to obtain employment within the Catholic sector of education in the eastern valley of Monmouthshire. The letter written by Sister Maurice on 24 December tells, not only of the sisters having to leave the school where they had obtained a post, but also indicates what a beneficial influence they had had on their pupils in the space of the one term they taught there.

> How happy we would be if all our worries about the schools were over, but such is not the case. You know that Sister Pierre Lazare will not be returning to Blaenafon. Last Friday, she bade farewell to her pupils who had already begun to appreciate the benefits of a religious education and become attached to her and to Sister Athanasie... They all wept when they heard that the sisters were leaving; some even went home to get a sixpence, a half-penny or a bit of cake as a parting gift.

Times were difficult on the whole for those sisters who had started teaching in the Catholic elementary schools in Pontypool and the two other centres, namely, Blaenafon and Abersychan, where they were appointed. On 31 December 1907, Sister Pierre Lazare wrote herself to the superior-general informing her that her superior had received a letter from the Minister of Education. It said that Sister Pierre Lazare had been refused the post because of some error in the application form, but the letter also stated that there was no reason why another sister should be refused. Father Degan therefore decided to put in an application for Sister Athanasie for the post in question. She had already taught there with Sister Pierre Lazare, and knew the children and had been initiated into the running of the class.

Sister Athanasie was successful as, in a letter of January 1908, Sister Marie Geneviève wrote to the superior-general saying:

> As Sister Athanasie is the only Sister in Blaenafon, I pay the person who lives opposite the school 1 franc a month to provide a cup of coffee for Sister Athanasie, in the morning, at midday and at 4 o'clock. The school is half an hour's train journey from Pontypool, and there is half an hour's walk from the station to the school…. Each of the three Sisters who go out to school takes with her something to eat during the day.

Sister Pierre noted in a letter to the superior-general on 10 February 1908 that Sister Athanasie had been accepted as head teacher in Blaenafon. There were 80 pupils, boys and girls, in the school at that time, with two teachers instead of the usual three. There was a separate infant school with about 120 pupils. Things did not go well for Sister Athanasie, however, for shortly after she began teaching in Blaenafon the inspector came to the school, and requested that Father Degan should be present as well. The inspector remained all day in her class, asking questions and setting written work for the pupils. He gave a very unfavourable report. He remarked that he had never seen such a class. The inspector said that there should be two other teachers in the class. So in May, Sister Joseph Marie was sent to help Sister Athanasie. The superior in her letter of 7 May wrote: "There is such a lack of order and discipline at Blaenafon. What merit our dear Sisters have in working with these poor, undisciplined children!"

Meantime, the head teacher of the Catholic school in Abersychan gave in her notice at the end of 1907, and Father Degan asked Sister Maurice, the third qualified teacher, to apply for this post. She was successful, and was appointed as head teacher of Abersychan, a school of about 200 pupils with six lay teachers. In July of the same year, both Sister Athanasie and Sister Maurice learned they had not received permanent posts in either school. Sister Maurice wrote forthrightly to the superior-general on 13 July 1908:

> The Education Committee has just renewed the decision that it made last February. So Sister Athanasie and I will be without a school post next September. I am very upset about this and so is my companion. The Committee will not revoke its decision because we have failed to comply with the ruling that, before becoming a head teacher of a school with more than 50 pupils, one must have a minimum of 12 months' teaching experience. Sister Athanasie and I had never taught before, let alone in an English state school… They also gave as a reason for their decision our lack of discipline. In my case this is pure supposition; I still have not had an inspection. The inspector did go to Blaenafon, but one would have to be very credulous to believe that Sister Athanasie was dismissed for lack of discipline. Since 1905, so we hear, no head teacher has stayed at that school for more than 4 months; everyone knows the

lamentable state into which it has lapsed, especially since the previous one was known to have a drink problem.

Thankfully, by 1908 to 1909, things did eventually come right for the three sisters due to the exertions of Father Degan. Sister Athanasie was returned to Blaenafon where she was head teacher until 1920. Sister Maurice Joseph was appointed assistant and later head teacher at St Alban's Elementary School in Pontypool, while Sister Pierre Lazare, after gaining experience at Newport for two terms, was appointed head teacher of St Mary's Parish School in Carmarthen, a post she filled from August 1908 till June 1948. She was most successful as the head teacher of that school.

The sisters were very happy with their house at Osborne Road, but there was insufficient room to accommodate the private school and the increasing number of sisters in the community. The over-crowding of pupils in the private school was causing concern on health grounds. In several of her letters to the superior-general, Sister Marie Geneviève expressed her concern about the sisters' state of health.

> Our house does not afford adequate living space for those who reside in it, so I have begun to look around for a larger one because I am beginning to think that our ill-health is due, in part, to our shortage of living space.

The sisters lost no time in trying to find a larger house. On 6 June 1907, the superior wrote:

> There is a house not far from where we live at present, which would meet our requirements for the next 2 or 3 years, if we converted the stable into a classroom. The rent would be at least £80.00 (£4,000 in today's currency). I shall await your decision before taking the matter any further.

The superior-general obviously agreed the request, for on 28 June we learn

> After many difficulties, the house has been made over to us as from this morning. The repairs and alterations which are due to begin tomorrow will, we hope, be completed by the end of August. We are all grateful to you for allowing us to take this house, so well suited to our needs.

There were, in fact, nine sisters in the community at this time. We learn from an entry in the Annals of the community:

> After the cramped living space of the two previous houses in close proximity to the street with its many inconveniences, the lack of fresh air and of a garden, Glanwern seemed a real paradise. Its lovely garden

and secluded situation afforded the Sisters the quiet and solitude for which their souls pined.

In her first letter to the newly elected superior-general, Sister Marie Alvarez, dated 7 May 1908, the superior of the Pontypool community gave an account of the work of the sisters.

> The new term began last Monday, and God continues to bless our schools. Sister Vincent now has 23 pupils in her class, could you possibly give us another Sister to help her? Sister Henri is initiated into taking a class at Newport. Sister Joseph has 35 pupils for piano lessons; she really would need a second piano. All the Sisters have very full timetables and so cannot give any more time than they do already, to housework. So when you have a spare Sister who is robust and accustomed to doing housework, will you think of us?

At the end of that term, however, Sister Marie Geneviève was recalled to France, having concluded five years as superior of the community. She was replaced by Sister Thomas d'Aquin, who was to spend the next fourteen years in charge of the community.

Sister Thomas d'Aquin addressed no fewer than 85 letters to the superior-general of the time. As reported in the community Annals:

> She began her work at Pontypool with characteristic energy, carried it on with unflagging zeal and a fervent religious spirit, through all sorts of difficulties.

Many of her letters dealt with minor practicalities of everyday life in a community, and the first nine letters she wrote between August and December 1908 were of this nature.

During those early years, the need to have suitably qualified and experienced sisters to teach in the private school was aired in many letters to the superior-general by Sister Marie Geneviève, and by her successor, Sister Thomas d'Aquin. As the sisters also went to the USA as a result of the persecution in France, sisters from England and Wales were sometimes sent to the USA; both Sister Jeanne Odile and Sr St Thomas who had been welcomed to Pontypool were transferred to Leominster in the USA a few months later.

A considerable amount of space in the letters that were written during 1909 is devoted to the long illness and cure at Lourdes of Sister Joseph de St Charles, who was suffering from severe stomach ulcers. This event is also mentioned in the Annals:

> In August, 1909, an event of outstanding interest occurred. Our Lady deigned to bestow a signal favour on one of the members of the

community. For some years, she had heroically borne her sufferings, but that summer, the pain was so intense that permission was obtained for her to go to Lourdes in quest of a cure. Doctor Haslett wondered if she would even reach Saint Brieuc alive. However, full of faith and hope, she set out. She was cured at Lourdes. Great was her joy when she returned to the Mother House in Saint Brieuc. She was in perfect health and all the doctors could do was to witness to the fact, in silent wonder.

Her return to Pontypool was a cause of great rejoicing and gratitude to Our Lady for curing this very sick sister.

In the event, Sister St Thomas herself endured poor health. In her letter to the superior-general in August 1910, she reports that she has been ill, and that the doctor insisted that she should have a change of air. As a result, she went to France where she hoped to visit her former doctor in Lamballe, Brittany. She also mentions in her letter of December of the same year that the sisters were pleased with their Christmas term, that the number of pupils in the school was good, and also those for private tuition. The music results for that year were excellent.

During these years too, the question of accommodation again came into focus. In fact in one of her letters written during 1911, we find mention of an initiative taken by the superior, which would lead eventually to another move for the community. In her letter of 2 December 1911, Sister St Thomas d'Aquin wrote:

> I have just heard that a spacious house with fine outbuildings is going to be put up for sale. The house that we rent at present does not allow for any further development of our works, so may we enter into negotiations with the owner of the house?

However, about three weeks later she was to write again: "It turns out that the owner of the house in which we are interested wants to keep it for two years, so…"

By 1913 Glanwern, their present property, had become far too small. The private school was growing in importance and numbers. Likewise the community had grown in numbers. There were now four sisters teaching in the elementary school in Pontypool and two others who travelled to the school in Blaenafon. so it must have been eagerly, not to say somewhat impatiently, that Sister St Thomas waited for the two years to elapse before the owner of Park House, Mr Hanbury, would sell it. In addition, she wrote in her letter of May 1914:

> The owner of Park House will not be coming to Pontypool until the end of May, so it will be June before anything is settled.

She continued her negotiations, however, for the purchase of Park House. In a letter dated 9 June she wrote that the owner of Park House wanted to keep the stables. He refused to have any repairs done to the house, because he was thinking of having it demolished. His agent was of the opinion that the owner would sell it. On 20 June, she wrote:

> Nothing new to report about Park House except that Mr R. Hanbury is willing to sell it. But English legislation relating to landed estates is so complicated that he does not know whether he is free to dispose of it. So he is going to refer the matter to his solicitor in London.

Some six weeks later, on 31 July 1914, shortly before the outbreak of the First World War, Sr St Thomas was able to report to the superior-general that a decision had been reached; but only after many worries and much anxiety. At the very last moment, the owner refused to sell; so the sisters took out a lease for 14 years, at a rent of £90.00 (£4,000 in today's currency), a year, and the community moved in at the beginning of September 1914. We read in the Annals:

> The house, untenanted for some time, was in a state of great dilapidation, but with immense energy and enthusiasm the young community set to, and cleaned and swept and brushed and polished until it was at least habitable, and gradually, order prevailed over chaos and what seemed interminable scrubbings. Then the community assisted at the first Mass to be celebrated in the most beautiful room in the house, which has remained the chapel ever since.

The new term began in Park House (**Plate 15**), the beautiful manor house set in a park of outstanding beauty. Writing to the superior-general on 22 September, Sr St Thomas told her:

> We have been living in Park House for three weeks now and, even though the process of settling in has not yet been completed, the school re-opened and private lessons began again yesterday. We have a goodly number of pupils but not enough hands for all the work to be done; we'll never manage without help. The house is as big as a mother house.

With the outbreak of the war in August, followed by the German invasion of Belgium and Flanders, refugees began pouring into Britain. Every township got ready to receive them and give them hospitality according to their means. Pontypool was no exception. A committee was formed for this purpose, the superior of the community being a member. To Park House was assigned a number of refugees, thirty in all. One wing was given up to them. They arrived on 26 October. In the Annals we read:

> At first, only utter compassion was felt for these poor, bewildered, homeless people of all ages from five months to fifty years.

Unfortunately, it soon became obvious that only the riff-raff had been sent to the convent. Violent behaviour and drunken brawls, constantly disturbed the convent's peace. And an end had to be made. One evening, the police escorted the delinquents away to HQ in London where they were assigned quarters other than convents.

The committee found more decent folk to be provided with shelter, and St Alban's Convent had its contingent of refugees until the end of the war. In addition to their educational work, the community found many opportunities for practising the works of mercy and for instilling them into the minds of their pupils. They devoted themselves to knitting garments for the soldiers in the trenches, collecting for the parcels sent to prisoners, and giving public concerts to raise funds. All these were undertaken by the sisters and the pupils. The convent had definitely taken its place in the social life of the town.

The second winter of the War was marked by the death of their beloved parish priest. Father Degan had ministered to St Alban's Parish for 23 years. An entry in the Annals for 30 December 1915 states:

> On 30 December, 1915, the Rev Father Degan, the greatest friend the Convent ever had went to his eternal rest, mourned by all who knew him. He had been rector of the parish for 23 years and during that time, had gained a reputation for administrative ability in the official life of the town, as well as for his unswerving efforts on behalf of the needs of his parish and schools.

Father Degan was replaced by Father Lynch who acted as chaplain to the sisters until 1919 when a private chaplain was assigned to them, Rev Father Regnier from the Diocese of Saint Brieuc in Brittany.

St Alban's Convent School progressed rapidly throughout the War and post-War years. From a letter written by Sister St Thomas on 10 October 1917 to the superior-general we learn:

> The school re-opened three weeks ago; we now have 120 pupils, plus 60 for music lessons, 23 boarders and three young girls hoping to join the congregation when they leave school. The sisters in the Catholic elementary school have been notified that, with all the other teachers in the region, they are going to be given a war 'bonus.'

Mention of postulants is made several times in the letters written at this time. In August 1919, Sister St Thomas went again to Ireland to look for postulants, and in a letter written from Glengariff in County Cork to the superior-general she reports "Yesterday we made arrangements for two other postulants to travel with us next Monday."

Throughout the war and post-war years, one consistent theme in the correspondence of the superior was the health of the sisters. In December 1917, she reported that Sister Yves took to her bed, utterly exhausted, with a feverish cold, loss of voice and persistent cough. On the 6 January, she wrote that the doctor ordered a complete rest for the young patient, and six days later, she wrote again saying:

> I am heartbroken, our little Sister Yves has TB. Her left lung is affected. The doctor says that she must leave here as soon as possible.

The war was not yet over, so Sister St Thomas had difficulty in obtaining passports. Once she had succeeded in so doing, Sister Yves was accompanied back to the mother house where she died a few months later, in July 1918.

By 1920, the situation of Park House was as follows. The sisters had a new lease of 21 years, which was all that the owner could grant until his daughter came of age, in five years' time. Then he would be able to dispose of the property, and the sisters would be able to purchase it. The letter which Sister St Thomas wrote to the superior-general at the end of 1920 was a somewhat dispirited one:

> Six sisters and all the helpers in the kitchen are down with the flu, but it is Sister Stanislaus about whom I am most anxious. Our two sisters have been allowed to resign from their posts in Blaenafon without any difficulty…if you allow it, Sister Athanasie could take one of the classes in our convent school. Where can we find the staff we need? And we are short of three sisters for the house. Sometimes the cross becomes too heavy to bear.

In the following year, her letters were also of a rather pessimistic tone. On 26 January 1921, she wrote:

> The news from Pontypool is not good, we are still being affected, I almost said 'overcome' by illness, and as I told you at Christmas, I myself am tired out; the sisters have insisted that I should go to Abergavenny for 10 days or so…

The news from the convent school was more encouraging:

> There are now 200 pupils in the school, 50 of them boarders. May we be enabled to do good to all these people.

Sister St Thomas, tired after her long years spent in the service of the community and of the schools, must have welcomed her transfer from Pontypool when it came. At this time several transfers of local superiors had to be made, to meet the requirements of the new Code of Canon Law. Sister St Thomas was recalled to France, and Sister Thérèse du Saint Esprit, the superior of Abergavenny convent, was sent to replace her.

Sister Thérèse wrote of the wrench it was for her to leave the convent in Abergavenny where she had been superior since its foundation in 1906. It fell to her to continue the transactions for the purchase of Park House from the Hanbury family. In her letter of 16 October, 1922, Sister Thérèse asked the superior-general which sisters' names should appear in the contract to be drawn up… A month later, on 8 November, she informs the superior-general that she has heard from M. Le Brassens, the solicitor, that the asking price for Park House was £3,000, whereas he expected it to be £6,000.

Sister Thérèse goes on to express the hope that Miss Hanbury's Trustees will agree to the first of these two figures, since, as she points out, the property is not in a good state of repair, and the congregation had already had to incur expenses for it. Writing again on 30 November, she reports that M. Le Brassens thinks that the sale will be completed before Christmas — for £3,000 (the modern equivalent of about £75,000) we presume, since she adds: "Lord Treowen tells me that the land alone is almost worth that price."

The purchase completed, the next step was to proceed with the most urgent repairs. In her letter dated 11 January 1923, Sister Thérèse informs the superior-general that the estimate of these repairs, amounts to £1,061 (£27,000 in today's currency). "A considerable sum of money but having examined all that needs to be done, I do not find it excessive."

Nonetheless, she was not free from money worries for long, and she wrote in October of the same year referring to a visit by the Inspectors to the convent school: "We shall soon have to have a laboratory built and improvements made to the school." In fact not long after Sister Therese's arrival in Pontypool, two inspectors had come to look over St Alban's Convent School. One of the two was the Chief Inspector for Wales. It was a private visit, the main purpose of which was to point out what needed to be done before the school could be recognised as efficient, and apparently there was a great deal to be done. The building of the school laboratory was started in late 1923 and completed in January 1924.

As well as ensuring that the necessary building existed for the school, there was also the necessity to have trained teachers. Sister Thérèse mentions the plans for this in her letter of January 1924:

> Sister Arsène, Sister Athanasie and Sister Anne de Lorette are giving time to their studies all the time that can be spared, once they have completed their class preparation.

She also writes:

The higher classes are well provided for as regards teachers, but the four lower ones are taught by teachers who are not up to the mark. We cannot envisage asking for our school to be recognised while this is so.

Sister Thérèse was unfortunately called upon by the superior-general, in the summer of 1926, to change places with Sister Célinia Joseph, superior of the community in Bedford. The implementation of the Code of Canon Law necessitated changes of superiors which must have had an adverse effect on the smooth running of the school and the community. As we learn from the Bedford convent Annals, this was no small sacrifice that these two sisters were called upon to make. We read:

> Called through obedience to take over the direction of Pontypool, Sister Célinia Joseph left the community in Bedford of which she had been the superior for 22 years. Sister Thérèse arrived in Bedford on 16 September. Of her too, obedience required a great sacrifice, that of leaving a work that was dear to her, and Monmouthshire where, since 1902, she had devoted herself...

Of both of these devoted sisters it could be said, as noted in the Annals:

> It is a hard thing for human nature to be uprooted and transplanted, as it were, to new soil when the years are beginning to take a toll on the lifesprings of being.

In fact, Sister Célinia Joseph's arrival in Pontypool was during the Great Depression. We read in the Annals for these years:

> In the 20s and 30s of this century there came to the South Wales Coalfield an era of direful depression. The Great Strike of the ill-paid, ill-housed, ill-fed miners brought in its train hunger and misery and starvation to the valleys of South Wales, and they become known as the Depressed Areas.

This period lasted seven years, during which the convent school, sadly diminished in numbers, still contrived to keep the old flag flying. While the laboratory had been built, the school still lacked a gymnasium. This too was acquired when funds for the equipment were raised by a garden fête opened by Miss Tenison, Squire Hanbury's daughter. Park House also received a new coat of paint inside and outside, and hockey and netball pitches were made in the wood near the river. In this way, Sister Célinia did what she could to give employment to the hungry. Many a family did she relieve from distress in her own quiet way. Queues of gaunt men waited every day at the door of the convent for hot drinks and food, which were never refused; for the 'dole' scarcely kept body and soul together. The sisters who taught in the Catholic elementary school spent their evenings making clothes for the poor children in their own school, distributing garments for the Catholic Needlework Guild, and devising ways and means to clothe the naked and feed the hungry. In these various ways, "the convent became more closely linked by bonds of common love and fellowship with this people so sorely tried."

The sisters lived through the trials and tribulations of the people among whom they lived. When they saw a glimmer of hope in the darkness, they would usually note it in the Annals, as in the case of the following entry:

> At length a propitious day seemed to dawn when King Edward VIII visited the depressed areas of South Wales, showing everywhere deep sympathy and compassion for his people, and a determined will to bring about redress and better things in the near future. His abdication prevented him from carrying out his desires, yet good at length did come of the royal visit, for the eyes of the nation were turned on the hard lot of the miners, and new legislation for its betterment was in the air, when the Second World War called all men to arms.

We can assume that the convent school was successful during the inter-war years, since the main pre-occupation of the superior in the 1930s was the building of a house for the convent chaplain. Sister Célinia wrote about this project to the superior-general on 31 May 1932. She told her that she had contacted the architect, and that as soon as she received the plans and the estimate for the building, she would forward them to the superior-general. In her letter two months later in July she wrote that the contract for the chaplain's house was signed, and work on it had begun. The estimated cost was £685 (£27,000 today). By 1935, Sister Célinia was able to report to the superior-general that the building of this house which was called 'The Hollies' had been duly completed. The first occupant was Father L'Helgouach SM, the third of the French priests to have served as chaplain to St. Alban's, since 1919. He was succeeded by Dom L. Baron, a Benedictine monk from Kergonan Abbey, in Brittany. He remained in Pontypool till the end of the Second World War when he was replaced by Father F. Jordan, a secular priest from the Archdiocese of Cardiff. When he left, the clergy of Pontypool parish began once again to take it in turns to serve the community, as they had done in the early days. Sister Célinia had in fact served four mandates as superior of the community and finally in 1938, with her health failing, she was replaced by Sister Marie Albertine. Sister Célinia remained in Pontypool until her death in 1947. Sister Marie Albertine had been in Pontypool since 1919. She taught science in the convent school at the time of her appointment as superior. The shadows of World War II were already looming on the horizon.

After the invasion of France by the German forces in May 1940, communication with the mother house in Saint Brieuc became increasingly difficult and before long, virtually impossible. This made it necessary for all the communities of the Daughters of the Holy Spirit in England and Wales to be governed, at least for the duration of the war, by a provincial superior resident in Britain. Sister Albertine was chosen by the sisters in England and Wales, but she pointed out that given the present war-time situation, it would be better to appoint a sister who was a naturalised British citizen. Her opinion was endorsed by Monsignor Godfrey, the Apostolic Delegate, when the matter was submitted to him. Six months later in response to the communication she had been able to send to Saint Brieuc, by diplomatic channels, a reply was received appointing Sister Jeanne du Calvaire as Provincial, with Sister Marie Albertine as her Assistant. It was at this time too that the need for a noviciate within the province became clear. Pontypool was chosen as the setting, and it was to Sister Marie Albertine that the task fell of setting one up for the English-speaking candidates who wished to join the Daughters of the Holy Spirit.

Thus it was, in a spirit of faith and trust in God, accepting everything as his will for them, that the sisters lived their ministry in Pontypool. St Alban's Convent School flourished during the post-war years. All the convent schools run by the sisters had to be recognised as efficient by the Ministry of Education, and the sisters worked hard to achieve this. We shall return to the subsequent history of the foundation at Pontypool in a later chapter.

CHAPTER SIX

1903: Foundations in West Wales

St Winefride's Convent, Carmarthen 1903-1970

AN INTRODUCTION TO A BRIEF ANONYMOUS HISTORY OF THE CONVENT in Carmarthen (1903-1950) recounts how, in Catholic times, the place had been a centre of fervent Catholic life, with a special devotion to Mary, the Mother of God. After the Reformation, Carmarthen was one of the first towns in Wales to struggle back to the faith. So when the Daughters of the Holy Spirit arrived, they found a warm Catholic atmosphere emanating from a parish already possessed of a church, a school and a monastery; a spiritual luxury that few places could boast of at the time. The site for the church had been donated by the Herbert family of Clytha, of whom it was said:

> They stuck to their original Creed through good and evil, through state persecution and social obloquy from the time of Henry VIII onwards.

St Mary's Church was built between 1851 and 1852, at the expense of Miss Catherine Richardson. The Congregation of the Passionists, founded by St Paul of the Cross in Italy in the eighteenth century, arrived in Carmarthen in 1889, and, led by Father Dominic the first superior, they settled in the presbytery. They also opened Mass centres at Cardigan, Llandovery, Llangaddock, Llandrindod Wells, Ammanford, Burry Port, Kidwelly, and Llandeilo. This was still an era when Catholics were not kindly received in non-conformist Wales, and there were occasional attacks on them in the press, where the church was accused of being full of "pagan and medieval accretions" and of being the "worst and subtliest of enemies." When, for example, the Catholic church was being built in 1852, each evening the building was knocked down by those who did not approve of having Catholics in the town. This went on till a guard was set up outside the church to protect it.

The names of the benefactresses associated with the foundation of the Daughters of the Holy Spirit in Carmarthen, in March 1903, are those of the Honourable Mrs Herbert of Llanover, of Miss Abadam and of Dr Johnson of Carmarthen. These ladies were eager to have Breton sisters come to Wales and work for the Welsh people. The first two of these were converts to Catholicism, while the third was a Protestant. The principal sources for the history of the foundation at Carmarthen are kept in the Archives of the Maison Mère, Saint Brieuc, File 12G5, and File 8T5.

Sister Marie Théodose was the sister sent by the superior-general to negotiate the foundation with Miss Abadam, a member of one of the most notable families in the County of Carmarthenshire. She was: "a woman of remarkable intelligence and burning zeal for the conversion of Wales, she wanted other Catholic missions to be able to benefit from the presence of a Daughters of the Holy Spirit community". It was she, too, who steered Sister Marie Théodose towards the future foundations at Brecon and Aberystwyth. A name that remains linked with hers is that of Dr Alice Johnson, who exercised her profession at the hospital for the mentally ill at Carmarthen, and who hoped that, one day, the sisters might be able to work with the mentally ill. It is mentioned in the Annals of the community that these were "two noble souls whom providence had placed there to guide the sisters with their lights and encouragement through the difficulties inseparable from a work such as that with which they were entrusted".

Miss Abadam wrote to the superior-general in February 1903 telling her that she had found a house for the sisters, which they could rent for five years. It was called Picton Villa (**Plate 16**), and she wanted a reply before the 1 March. She also added that she was certain that the sisters would be able to earn a livelihood in Carmarthen with little difficulty. Dr Johnson wrote to Sister Marie Théodose on 8 February inviting her to come before 1 March. She said that she had already found six pupils for their school and three more would come for the summer term. She also invited the sisters to take on the visiting of the sick. Another letter from Miss Abadam to Sister Marie Théodose a few days later told of repairs to the house. As the decision to open a foundation in Carmarthen was quickly arrived at, she also said that she was glad that Sister Marie Théodose was coming to open the foundation. In this letter she also tells her to contact the Honourable Mrs Herbert to keep her informed of developments. In her eagerness, Miss Abadam had even announced French lessons for the 26 March, although the sisters had not as yet set up their Carmarthen foundation. She also asked that the names of the sisters needed to draw up the Act of Foundation should be sent to her.

Monsignor Morelle, the ecclesiastical superior of the congregation, had written to Bishop Mostyn of Menevia for permission to open a convent in Carmarthen, and the latter replied that he would be pleased to welcome the sisters into his diocese, if they could find a house in Carmarthen suitable for their community and mission. The house at Picton Place, which they were advised to rent, had a large garden and eleven rooms for the new community. However the repairs, which needed to be carried out before the sisters took possession, were very slow. This new foundation was given the name St Winefride's Convent. St Winefride was a popular saint in the area, and her well in North Wales was a great centre of pilgrimage, where so many miracles were reputed to have taken place that it was called 'The Lourdes of Wales.' Sister Marie Théodose stayed on for some time with the five sisters who were sent to form the community. Sister Ste Barbe Le Jeune, superior, Sister Marie Isodore Le Mayer, Sister Louis Marie Loaec and Sister Anna du Sacré Coeur, arrived in Carmarthen of 25 March 1903, the Feast of Our Lady. They expressed their feelings as follows:

> As did our heavenly Mother, we voice our apprehension, feeling so young, so powerless, so unworthy. 'The Holy Spirit will cover you with his shadow.' Nothing is impossible to God... Strengthened by this assurance,we uttered our 'Fiat'.

Miss Abadam helped them in every way, and both she and Dr Johnson tried to find pupils for their proposed school. It was even noted that Dr Johnson supplied them with food.

The foundation at Carmarthen, unlike some of the other foundations opened in Wales at that time, had a fairly secure beginning, and flourished, despite many difficulties and setbacks, for a total of sixty-seven years. At the beginning of April, a week after the arrival of the first sisters, Bishop Mostyn wrote them a letter to welcome the sisters to his diocese and promising to visit them when he next visited South Wales. He wrote:

> I welcome you to the Diocese of Menevia. Do not contemplate coming all the way to Wrexham to see me. I will come to see you when next I am in South Wales.

It was not long before the sisters became known in the parish and neighbourhood. The first requirement, as always, was to earn their livelihood, and soon after their arrival

> several Protestants came to ask for lessons in French and needlework. Gwen and Freda Llewellyn Jones and Elsie John were our very first pupils, and thus our daily bread was assured. This income was of course, inadequate for meeting all our expenses, but poverty and suffering serve, do they not, to set the seal on works cherished by God.

An Irish family entrusted two of its daughters to the sisters, to form a small class. These were Josephine Gilsenan, aged thirteen years, and her sister Marguerite, aged eleven. These two, together with Mary Bland, formed the nucleus of a little class; the future St Winefride's Convent School.

> Such were our small beginnings, but we trust that this modest sowing will bear fruit under the beneficent rays of the Divine Son...

The sisters were also asked by the parish priest to look after the sacristy and church linen, and to visit the poor and sick members of the parish. In a letter of 19 August, Sister Marie Théodose mentions a visit to the workhouse:

> Yesterday, Sunday, we went to the workhouse to visit a poor young girl who after having lapsed from the Catholic faith, has returned to it. A wasting disease is slowly taking her to the grave, but she does not seem to realize this and insists she feels less ill. While we were there, a woman about eighty years of age came to see us and said: 'We noticed your white habit as you walked through the room and we ask you to come and speak to us' This was only our second visit to the workhouse but already we were looked upon as friends.... Ah! If only you could see these wrinkled faces light up with joy whenever they see us coming! One of them said: 'I would never have thought that nuns could be so good and kind.' What an idea they must have of us? Once they come to a true appreciation of the selfless devotion of our sisters, our cause, which is one with that of the Divine Master, will be won. The more I see of these poor people, the more firmly I am convinced of this. (*La Colombe*, 1903).

One of their greatest difficulties in this new foundation, as in all the other foundations in Wales, was their inadequate knowledge of English. On 9 April 1903, in a letter to Monsignor Morelle, Sister St Barbe wrote

> I shall have to ask for the gift of speaking English, if I am going to be able to manage. It is so painful to be unable to communicate with families. To be obliged to keep silence when one is longing to express sympathy or gratitude! I am beginning to speak, just a little, and can understand more or less what is being said in a conversation.

Writing to the superior-general on 19 August 1903, she says,

> We have a small number of children on whom we can count to start a
> small elementary class. I am hoping their number will increase once we
> become better known. There are many young children in the surrounding
> areas, and all of them live about a mile from the other schools. I was told
> by a kind Protestant lady the other day, that what is really needed is a
> school for six to ten years olds.

The problem was how would the opening of a private school by the
sisters affect the parish elementary school? Father Madden, the parish priest,
was obviously concerned and may well have expressed his concern in a
letter to Bishop Mostyn. In an extant letter, the bishop wrote to Father
Madden, saying:

> It was never my intention that they (the sisters) should start an
> elementary school in opposition to the existing school, and what is more,
> the sisters have no certificates for teaching so as to satisfy the Board of
> Education. But encourage the children to attend their school when they
> leave you, to still further themselves.

In a subsequent letter to Father Madden, the bishop told him that he had
told the sisters that they could take who they liked at their school, as long as
they did not take any Catholic children attending the parish school. In the
autumn of 1903, however, when the superior-general and Monsignor
Morelle, the ecclesiastical superior of the congregation, visited the
community on 3 October, there was no mention of the school plans. The
only mention of the visit in the community Annals was the following:

> How to describe the joy that filled our hearts? What a precious grace
> it was for our souls! Our good Mother General spoke to us in words
> of comfort, encouragment and advice. Strengthened by this two-fold
> blessing, we continue our mission with greater courage.

In order to prepare for the opening of a school, which was obviously
destined to take pupils up to the Matriculation Examination for the older
pupils, Sister Ste Barbe went to Aberystwyth on 3 November. She wrote:

> Given my responsibility with regard to an examination as important as
> the London Matriculation, I felt obliged to get in touch with a few of the
> professors at University College, Aberystwyth, in the hope of being
> able to arrange for a correspondence course. Providence so ordered
> things that I was in for quite a pleasant surprise. On the very day I
> arrived, the sisters in Aberystwyth [the foundation at Aberystwyth had
> opened in the summer of that year] received an invitation to visit the
> university buildings. As it was the day when the students had a free
> afternoon, Sister St Lazare decided that I should go at 2 o'clock. It was

> with keen interest that we traversed the vast rooms, which serve as lecture halls, laboratories, and other rooms...I asked to see the lady principal who was in charge of the women students. What a gracious welcome we received from her! How unaffected and charming she was! I spoke of the possibility of having a teacher from the university. She promised she would look out for a young girl who might accept to come to us as an 'au-pair' teacher.

We learn in a letter dated 26 June of that year that they had secured the services of an English teacher and that she was satisfactory. But still the number of pupils remained very small.

Although they had the bishop's blessing, the sisters' hopes for their school were not to be fully realised. They still needed someone to teach the examination class, and they asked to have a sister from Olney, another foundation in England. By 1906, however, they found an English teacher and although she fitted in well, the number of pupils was very small, probably because elementary education for Roman Catholics was already provided in the parish school. The idea of the sisters was to have a private school for pupils of secondary school age in order not to overlap with the existing parish school. Very few Catholic parents could afford to pay for secondary education and there was an excellent high school in the town.

The school received little or no support or encouragement. By 1906, there were no more that nine pupils in the school after three years of its existence and, in order to attract more pupils, the sisters bought a large property called Wauniago outside the town; they moved there on 19 September 1906. Sad to relate, the number of pupils did not increase; rather they decreased, because of the distance of the new property from the town. Still they struggled on in that building for seven years, till 1913, and on 13 February they left and moved to 29 Picton Terrace (**Plate 17**), until another property better suited to their needs could be acquired. By the end of the year they had twenty-four pupils. Two years later they moved again to Picton House (**Plate 18**), which was to be the permanent abode of the sisters while they were in Carmarthen. The two sisters, whose names remain linked with the convent school were Sister Yves du Saint Sacrement le Menager and Sister Angélique du Sacré Coeur Nedelec. With occasional help from other sisters who were placed in Carmarthen for a longer or shorter time, they each had responsibility for one of the two classes that the school comprised. Sister Yves taught the older pupils, Sister Angélique the younger ones. The age range of the pupils in these classes was considerable, and their level of attainment varied widely. Sister Yves, for example, had in her class "the equivalent of four separate standards".

Nevertheless, she proved to be a good teacher. Her untimely death in 1918 contributed, no doubt, to the factors which led to the closure of the school.

They continued with the private school, despite the setbacks, but it was to be in St Mary's parish school, which had been in existence for forty years before the sisters came to Carmarthen, that their future in education lay. This school was constructed on the site of four or five old houses in Dame Street (later known as Mill Street). It was built to accommodate a hundred pupils and it was financed by the sale of the field adjacent to the cemetery. In 1907, the head of the parish school gave notice of retirement. Father Wilfred, the parish priest, asked for a suitably qualified sister to present to the Borough Education Committee with a view to her becoming the head of the parish school. Sister Ste Barbe, the superior of the community, wrote to the superior-general and put the case by asking for one of the five sisters who had just completed their teacher training at St Charles Training College in London. Her request was granted and, in January 1908, Sister Pierre Lazare (**Plate 19**) was appointed as the new headmistress of the parish school, a post which she held till 1952, that is, for nearly half a century. Sister Pierre was a capable teacher and organiser with a good sense of humour. Nothing ever got her down, not even the dilapidated state of the school buildings. The school grew rapidly, and by 1913, there was urgent need for further accommodation which was satisfied by converting two cottages in Mill Street into an infants classroom.

Over the years the fabric of the school deteriorated to such an extent that zinc baths and buckets had to be used to catch the rain that frequently poured in. For many past pupils, the mention of their early school days would conjure up the picture of rain dropping into buckets and bathtubs while a harassed sister struggled to teach her pupils under the shelter of a large umbrella. This was the experience of Sister Pierre for the first fifteen years of her time as headmistress of St Mary's School, Carmarthen (**Plate 20**). Then in 1923, a new school building costing £2,550 (£66,000 today), was built on a new site near the church. It was blessed and officially opened by Bishop Mostyn on Tuesday of Easter week, 1923. The pupils responded to their new and cheerful surroundings by producing work which won consistently high praise from the School Inspectors. At the same time their spiritual growth was assured. Since their school was situated so close to the church, they 'lived and moved and had their being' in a Catholic atmosphere.

For the next twenty years there was quite a succession of superiors and sisters in the Carmarthen community. Sister St Barbe, who was the first superior, was recalled to France in 1910. She was succeeded by Sr Paul who, at the end of a three-year mandate, was replaced by Sister St Urbain, who was replaced seventeen months later by Sister Albertine. The lattter remained as superior for seven years to be replaced by Sister Marie Thomasine. It fell to Sister Albertine to arrange for Picton House to be made habitable for the community and the convent school, which was situated, in very cramped conditions at 29 Picton Place. She had the house surveyed by an expert, and an estimate for repairs drawn up. By now, it was wartime; and materials and manpower were in short supply. At the same time, she was anxious to do something for the Belgian refugees in Carmarthen and the surrounding area. She explored with the architect (who happened to be one of the chief members of the local committee for refugees) the possibility of providing work for those refugees who had experience of building and repair work. So work on the more urgent repairs was begun on 29 June and two months later, on 30 August, 1915, the sisters moved to Picton House. The repairs included making two well-aired and pleasant rooms into classrooms, with a play-room underneath. The remainder of the repairs would have to wait till they could afford them.

When the new school year began in 1915, there were thirty-six pupils. By 1919, there were eighty-four pupils in the parish school and forty-four in the private school. The number for the private school sounded encouraging, but it was decided nevertheless that there was no future for the private school because of the demands made by the Fisher Education Act of 1918, the requirements of which could not be met by the meagre resources of the sisters. Consequently, St Winefride's Convent School closed at the end of the summer term in 1919.

The year 1930 represents a kind of watershed in the life and history of the community as it was marked by the beginning of Sister Pierre's long and fruitful superiorate. In January 1930, Sister Pierre was called upon to animate and govern the community in addition to carrying out her responsibility as head teacher of the parish school. She was also the community annalist, and kept the Annals till her death. The year 1935 saw the official opening, attended by many clergy and notables, of St Mary's Hall. It had been paid for by the parish, but recognised by the education authorities as an extension of the school premises. The hall was to prove of great advantage, not only in the promotion of a more serious and vigorous social life among the parishioners, but also in providing additional educational facilities for the children of the school. The next landmark in the life of the community was the Depression of the 1930s, the decade of the great slump and large-scale unemployment. In January 1938, Sister Pierre wrote:

> The number of pupils in our school has diminished considerably; this is due to unemployment which drives people to seek work elsewhere.

On the other hand, the evacuees who came to Carmarthen during the war helped them.

In September 1939, war was declared. The Annals of the community give an account of the effect on the community. At the outbreak of the war the following entry in the Annals states

> War is declared. It is with heavy hearts that we listen to the news coming from our beloved country and sense the danger in which our loved ones are going to be.

Again on 1 May 1940:

> A great sorrow for us all in the English colony: our beloved France is vanquished, demoralised and occupied by the Germans. From now on, we have no contact with the mother house.

The entry in the Annals for 24 December 1943 mentions the presence of American troops in Carmarthen: Midnight Mass was celebrated for the troops stationed there. She adds:

> All too soon they will perhaps be in France, sacrificing their young lives to free it from the oppressor.

The year 1943 proved to be a year of waiting and resignation. Through the Red Cross, the sisters were able to receive brief news from their families, at rare intervals. It was also noted during that year that the classrooms were no longer quite so full. The evacuees were gradually returning to the towns they had left on account of the air-raids.

Finally in 1944 the entry reads:

> A memorable year. The year, which saw the liberation of our beloved country. We have been following the events every day since the landing of the allied troops. When in the news, we hear the names and places so dear to our hearts we experience a thrill of joy. One evening, we heard the wonderful news: 'Saint Brieuc has been liberated by American troops.' The sisters will be able to travel to France again.

The post-war years did enable the sisters to visit the mother house and their own families once again, often to find that they had lost loved ones in the war.

St Mary's parish school continued to flourish under the capable management of Sister Pierre who, together with the community of five sisters, devoted the succeeding years to the education of the children of the parish, and continued to assist in parish work and visit the poor and the sick in the town. Successive inspectors' reports commended the school, and life in the post-war years was uneventful. The school grew from strength to strength. Bishop Petit, the newly appointed bishop of the diocese, paid his first visit to the community on 14 September 1947. He told the sisters how pleased he was with their work, and the influence they had in the parish.

In June 1948, Sister Pierre Lazare retired after forty-one years teaching in the school as head teacher. Almost the entire Catholic population of Carmarthen and beyond had passed through her hands. Although she was glad to enter upon a period of comparative rest (she remained as superior of the community), it was not without regret that she felt she had to hand on the torch to someone else. On 29 June, in the presence of Father Rector of the monastery, and his curate, the members of the education authority as well as of many parents and pupils, Sister Pierre Lazare was presented with various tokens of gratitude and appreciation.

At the time of the celebration of the golden jubilee of the presence of the sisters in Wales, Sister Pierre was due to attend the celebrations but unfortunately fell sick and was unable to attend. In the same year, it was the centenary of St Mary's church in Carmarthen, both of which were marked by a fitting celebration. For the parish as well as the community, it marked the end of an era. Sister Pierre, "Ma Mére" as she was known to all, was loved and respected by Catholics and Protestants alike. Her influence was felt far beyond Carmarthen. A considerable number of people showed the affection and esteem thay had for her by coming to pray beside her mortal remains and .by being present at her funeral. She now rests in a little cemetery near the church and the school she loved so much. The parishioners put in a stained glass window of Our Lady, in St Mary's parish church, in memory of a great teacher and friend.

A succinct and fitting conclusion to this chapter on the first fifty years of the Daughters of the Holy Spirit in Carmarthen is to be found in the *Souvenir of the Centenary of St Mary's Church, Carmarthen, 1852-1952*, where we read:

> The sisters have been a heaven-sent blessing to the parish, laying the foundation of the faith in successive generations of children and assisting in the work of the church in every possible way.

Sister Mary Enda Loughnane replaced Sister Pierre Lazare as head teacher of St Mary's parish school in June 1948, and we shall return to the subsequent fortunes of the school in a later chapter.

St Margaret's Convent, Tenby 1903-1917

THE FOUNDATION at Tenby was the third of the six foundations made in Wales in the year 1903. Unlike the foundation at Carmarthen where the Annals of the community, normally a rich source of information, were scrupulously kept, there are no extant Annals for St Margaret's Convent, Tenby, and there is no reference in the source documents to indicate whether they were ever written. So the source for documenting the history of this foundation comes from letters exchanged with the superior-general by Sister Benôit Marie, the superior of the community. (File 12 G7).

Preparations for the opening of a foundation at Tenby began only a few weeks after the opening of the convent in Carmarthen. Sister Marie Théodose, who had responsibility for the initial arrangements, wrote to the superior-general in a letter dated 12 April 1903, to give a report on her visit to Tenby. It was a certain Miss James who helped to establish the founadation at Tenby, although Miss Abadam was in some way involved too, since there is a reference to her in one of the early letters. Miss James was described as a woman with plenty of common sense, very practical and a person who spoke her mind clearly. It was she who conceived the extraordinary idea that since Tenby was a seaside resort, the most likely work for the sisters to do there would be to set up a laundry, and take in washing. She could promise only a few French lessons, which would not provide enough remuneration for the sisters to live on. Miss James also approached the bishop to get his permission for the establishment of the foundation. Bishop Mostyn agreed to the foundation, and Miss James asked for a quick decision from the superior-general. Father Moore, the parish priest, was also glad at the prospect of having the sisters at Tenby. He promised to give them charge of the church linen, and catechism lessons for twenty children.

Miss James then proceeded to negotiate the renting of a property in Tenby, known as the Old Rectory (**Plate 21**). In a letter dated Easter 1903, she informed Sister Marie Théodose that she had received a first letter from Miss Fothergill, owner of the property in question. A few days later, a meeting took place between Miss James and Miss Fothergill and it was arranged to rent the Old Rectory for £60 a year. Writing again to Sister Marie Théodose, she indicates the type of work the sisters would undertake:

I have no doubt you will do very well here with a laundry service, some French lessons and, if you wish, visits to the sick. The Fothergills will supply you with vegetables; they are keen for you to rent their property.

A few weeks later, Sister Marie Théodose went to see the bishop and, on 3 May 1903, she wrote to the superior-general:

The decision has been made with regard to Tenby, and all is in order. Bishop Mostyn would like Wales to become another Brittany [presumably referring to religion]. I told him we had about one hundred sisters we could send here.

This statement seems to be in strange contrast to what follows, when the sisters seem to be in short supply to operate the laundry. Towards the end of June, negotiations were completed and Sister Marie Théodose and Sister Benoît Marie, the superior-elect of the new foundation, received two nights' hospitality from Miss James who was not pleased that the lease had been signed without her seeing it, as she could have obtained easier terms. In her next letter to the superior-general on 1 June, Sister Marie Théodose, on the recommendations of Miss James, had to write the following statement to the superior-general:

The bathing season will soon commence in Tenby, some five hundred visitors are expected since all the boarding houses are fully booked. So it is vitally important that the laundry should be in operation within the next fortnight, since to start with, the installation will be minimal given the small space in which it is to be set up. We can hope to have it ready in time to begin accepting customers, if you can ensure that we have the personnel to do the work, and for the reputation of the house it is important that it should be so.

Miss James set about organising the laundry, and asked for six to eight sisters to do the washing, drying, folding and ironing. This was to be the first foundation in Wales where the sisters were destined to earn their livelihood from engaging in domestic labour, although in an earlier foundation established in Devon, they were obliged to take in washing too in order to survive. The superior felt that they would risk having no requests for French and music lessons, when it became known that the sisters who were not lay sisters did laundry work. In fact, as a religious congregation, the Daughters of the Holy Spirit seem to be rather unique in that they never had lay sisters in the congregation. All the sisters were of equal rank from the foundation of the congregation.

The house was blessed on 24 June by the parish priest, Father Moore, and the sisters moved in immediately afterwards. The bishop indicated that he would like the Blessed Sacrament reserved in the house, and Mass to be said in the convent occasionally. The next event was the arrival of the furniture from France for the new foundation. We can assume that it came from the convents which were compulsorily closed. It was noted that a lot of crockery got broken. Sister Benoît Marie requested that the mother house should not send any more cast-iron cooking pots, which were heavy and unsuitable for English stoves. They set about arranging the furniture and had to make a few essential purchases. The superior informed the superior-general that she would send for Sister Hilaire and Sister Olive Marie who were at Carmarthen, and she adds:

> May St Margaret who seems to be the ideal patron for our new convent help us in these our beginnings. I have to organise the French lessons next week, then rush over to Brecon Convent and if Sister Benoît Marie needs me, come back to Tenby next week, and then rush before going to Aberystwyth.

There is no indication in the correspondence as to why St Margaret was chosen as their patron. The parish was called Holyrood and St Teilo, and had been founded in 1888.

In her letter to the superior-general dated 25 June, Sister Marie Théodose wrote:

> There is an advert in the local newspaper announcing that our laundry service will start in a fortnight and not one of us is able to run it. We need to have a sister in the house who can speak English.

By July 1903, we learn that ten sisters now formed the community: one for needlework, two for laundry, three for ironing and one for catechism. Two new sisters arrived on 11 July. The laundry work proved very heavy. Sister Marie Théodose wrote:

> A fortnight ago, we had 1,270 items to launder, so it is impossible to give a break to those who do the ironing. Out of the twelve sisters only two understand English. There is only one able to translate for us and give catechism lessons.

On 30 June, 1903, she wrote again to the superior-general saying she was still waiting for two persons with experience of laundry work. She regrets her ignorance and that of Sister Marie Théodore about setting up a laundry. She also said that a lady in Carmarthen had undertaken to find a profitable outlet for their daisy table runners. She even proposed sending some of the sisters' daisy work to be sold in London. Once Sister Marie Théodose had left Tenby to see to the needs of Brecon and negotiate for an

Aberystwyth foundation, it is from the letters of Sister Benoît Marie that we glean information about the early community and its works.

In one letter Sister Benoît Marie mentions a Miss Agnes Chew who helped them with errands and receipts. But she adds sadly: "The people of Tenby do not understand the first thing about religious life." The refrain of many of the early letters to the superior-general was the continuing need for more sisters to help with the laundry work. In September of that year the sisters received a visit from Mère St Georges, the superior-general. Mgr Morelle, the ecclesiastical superior, arrived the following day. *La Colombe*, 1904, decribes the joy of the sisters at this visit:

> The prospect of this visit was a source of great rejoicing among the sisters. The visitors arrived, accompanied by Mrs Gregory, a friend of the sisters, who had met them in her carriage. On the very afternoon of her arrival, the superior-general went to Pembroke Dock to meet Father Kelly who wanted a community in his parish. During their visit to Tenby, they also visited the benefactors of the sisters. They were received with great courtesy by the Hancocks, a truly devoted and Christian family. Miss James and Mr Gregory, who were away at the time, regretted being unable to share in our gladness. Father Moore, the parish priest, although he was unwell at the time, gave the visitors a warm welcome.

In a letter to the superior-general, dated 4 November 1903, Sister Benoît Marie writes

> We now have the Blessed Sacrament reserved in our chapel, thanks to the kindness of Father Moore who has lent us a ciborium.

The community at La Roche Derrien in Brittany sent the sisters a number of items for the chapel. Other news of a more domestic kind referred to the blankets they were expecting:

> The blankets we are waiting for have not arrived yet; perhaps they have gone astray. What should I do about a request we have received for French lessons to be given in a hamlet about 8 kilometres from here?

Two weeks later, however, her fears were allayed. She wrote again to the superior-general, to say that the blankets had arrived and were put straightaway on the beds. She said they were also delighted with the other (unnamed) items that were contained in the cases.

The letters from Tenby to the superior-general frequently referred to the health of the sisters, and one wonders whether the work in the laundry was too strenuous for most of them. In a letter of 23 December, Sister Benoît Marie mentions a flu outbreak in the town and in the community.

One of the sisters is suffering from rheumatism. On 12 January, she writes: "Sister Théodorine Marie is ill and will need to be replaced." On 29 February, she writes "Worrying illness of Sister Théodorine Marie, who is waiting to hear when she should leave for Brittany." She mentions that they have a lot of work with the laundry, "but we thank God for it since it is the means of earning our daily bread." Sister Benoît Marie accompanied Sister Théodorine to France, and brought back two other sisters with her: one for the Aberystwyth community and one for the community in Monmouth.

In May, she writes again to the superior-general with a request for two more sisters who would not be afraid of hard work. She writes:

> The health of the sisters at Tenby is not very good; out of the eleven, only four or five are strong enough for the work to be done.

In July, two more sisters arrived. In her letter of July, Sister Benoît Marie says:

> The needlework items that were displayed in London have all been sold. The handkerchief sachet was bought by the Princess of Wales.

In her letter of September 1904 she writes:

> Surprise visit from an American lady who bought some of our articles and paid for them very handsomely.

While some sisters joined the community, others moved elsewhere. In December 1904, Sister François de Borgia was transferred to the community at High Wycombe, to be superior there. The increase in the amount of laundry work to be done was a constant cause of concern for Sister Benoît Marie; during the winter months, they were finding it very difficult to get the linen to dry.

Having established themselves at Tenby despite their many problems, the year 1905 was a year of celebration for the sisters. The feasts of St Joseph and St Benedict were occasions of particular joy that year. On 19 March, the Mass for the Feast of St Joseph was celebrated by the former Benedictine Abbot of Caer Maria in Brittany. In the afternoon, vespers were sung in the convent chapel and the altar servers and a number of curious adults were waiting to get into the chapel. There are many incidents in the correspondence illustrating their complete trust in the help of St Joseph. Finally, they were still short of one pound.

> There was a ring at the door, and one of us ran to open it. The caller had already disappeared, though not without slipping through the letterbox an envelope containing 'the pound we needed', and the words 'From a friend'. Imagine our surprise and gratitude. Ste Thérèse of

Lisieux was right when she said 'Whoever prays to St Joseph with confidence never fails to be heard.'

The Abbot prolonged his visit to Tenby after the celebration of the feast of St Joseph in order to celebrate the feast of St Benedict two days later, since it was also the feast of Sister Benoît Marie, the superior. He received hospitality from the Hancocks, a devoutly Catholic family. But as noted in *La Colombe:*

> The good Lord saw fit to permit that a bereavement should cast a shadow over our little celebration. Sister Benoît Marie received word of the death of her aged mother. But she would not hear of declining our feast-day wishes. She gave of herself with a serenity which edified us, as well as attenuating the awkwardness with which she carried out our little programme. ...How ironic the fate which mingles happiness with sadness and brings a smile amid the tears! But such is our condition, the corrective to all earthly celebration, lest we take the shadow for the reality and lest we forget heaven when tasting the charms to be found, even in exile...

Four months later, the correspondence turns again to the need for more sisters for the work involved with the laundry. In her letter of 29 June 1905, Sister Benoît Marie requests that Sister Abel Marie be replaced before the summer bathing season began, and in July she wrote: "This is the height of the season and we have work in abundance." She mentions that Sister Elie is still plagued with rheumatism. The strain and the worry of the work and the financial situation caused distress to the superior herself. So in August of the same year, one of the community, Sister Athanase de Jésus, took it upon herself to write to the superior-general giving news of Sister Benoît Marie's health, saying:

> She has succumbed to fatigue and to all the internal troubles during the past months.

In her letter of 3 September, things had improved, for Sister Athanase writes:

> The fever has abated but has left her (the superior) extremely weak. Mrs Wetter and Mrs Gregory have taken a keen interest in our invalid's progress and shown many kindnesses.

By October 1905, however, Sister Benoît Marie herself writes again to the superior-general thanking her for her prayers for her recovery. She also airs her financial worries, and mentions that the income from the laundry during the season was enough to pay their rent. She also adds: "We have a lot of needlework to be done in time for Christmas." During the season, the washing took three days, the ironing three days and the rest of the week was given to sewing and embroidery. The French lessons were on the increase, to the delight of Sister Athanase.

As was the case with nearly every foundation in Wales, the premises soon became too small for the needs of the sisters, especially as they always had in mind to start a school wherever they set up a foundation. Tenby was no exception to this practice. The lease on the premises that they had rented was up and they had to look elsewhere. In her letter of 3 December 1905, Sister Benoît Marie writes:

> Saddened by your letter of 16 November asking me to look for another house. I have done so and found none with a rent below £40 (approximately £2,000 today). I have asked Mgr Vaughan if he would rent the Priory to the sisters; I am awaiting his reply.

Mgr Vaughan replied on 1 December 1905, as follows:

> Sorry to hear that you are going to give up the laundry work which provides you with an income during your time of exile…you cannot hope to make a living from school work because I just cannot see where the pupils would come from. I would have been happy to rent the Priory to you, were it not for the fact that it is already occupied.

On the day of the receipt of this letter, Sister Benoît Marie forwarded it to the superior-general, and added that for the two other places for rent that she had looked at, the owners were asking £40 and £50 a year respectively. She adds:

> If Miss Fothergill insists that we leave the premises as they were when we became tenants, we shall have to incur considerable expense.

Happily, the decision to leave the Old Rectory was reversed. Sister Benoît Marie's post-Christmas letter speaks of the lovely Christmas the sisters enjoyed with Midnight Mass in the convent chapel. She also says that Mrs Fothergill was anxious that the sisters should remain at the Old Rectory and reduced the rent by £10. By this time, she was able to confirm that the people of Tenby were increasingly well disposed towards the sisters, and very generous with their gifts.

Although there is no mention of the exact date on which they started a little school, in her letter of 29 December, Sister Benoît Marie mentions the fact that the children acted a little play *Le Réveil de Jesus* (Jesus Awakes), and that the parents were delighted. There are references to this little school in subsequent letters although there are no extant letters for the year 1907. The first letter for 1908 is dated 20 April, and in this letter, she merely refers to the feast of Easter and that the church was beautifully decorated for the paschal feast, and drew many visitors. Again she says: "In the community we have had flu for several weeks," and she makes an allusion to a brief canonical visit made by the assistant superior-general to the community. In a letter of October 1908, there is also mention of the little school. She writes

> A lady has made enquiries as to what it would cost to send her three children to our little school; if they come, that would give Sister Athanase ten pupils.

The correspondence between the Tenby community and the mother house became increasingly rare during the last few years of the foundation's history. In the one extant letter for 1909, Sister Benoît Marie simply sends her good wishes to Mère Marie Alvarez who was elected as superior-general in 1908. She writes: "All the sisters at Tenby are trying to work for the spread of God's kingdom and for the conversion of souls." In this letter, too, she speaks of an accident and the miraculous escape of a workman who fell 15 to 16 feet while doing repair work on the dome of the house. The only other item of interest is that she promises to send the community accounts for the year by the end of January.

Mother Marie Dominique, the provincial of the communities in England and Wales, paid a visit to the community in May 1910, and in a letter dated 22 May, Sister Benoît Marie thanks her for her visit and for the letter received following the visit. She says that she feels drained, on account of the uncertainty of the house. In response to the letter received from Mother Marie Dominique, Sister Benoît Marie writes:

> Thank you for having pleaded our cause. There is a great need to have more sisters here; this foundation would be one of the most flourishing, if only we had enough people.

On 30 May 1911, Sister Benoît Marie wrote to the superior-general congratulating her on her re-election. That year too, there was a canonical visitation of the community made by Mgr Vaughan. In this letter there is no mention of the school or the laundry. She merely gives news of the sisters, and mentions that a French student had taken three of the sisters for a day's outing to Carmarthen, to visit the community there. In her next letter of 14 August, once again she is concerned about the health of the sisters. Sister Elie who is suffering from blindness had spent a few days at Miss James's, and she remarks: "The pain is less acute, but according to the oculist it will be two months before she is cured." In this letter she mentions that a rich widow, Mrs Pritchard, recently converted to the Catholic faith, would like to open a house in Cardigan, in West Wales, but there is no further reference to this request so we can assume it was not pursued by the superior-general and her council.

Increasingly, the problem of the health of the sisters preoccupied much of the time of the superior. Sister Benoît Marie wrote again, in December, to Mother Marie Dominique, the provincial, to give her news of the health of Sister Elie, and of her own deteriorating health. She said that she had made a pilgrimage to the shrine of St Winefride in North Wales, to pray for a cure for Sister Elie, but as we learn subsequently, the hoped-for miracle did not happen. Through the intervention of a charitable lady, whose name is not recorded, Sister Elie was admitted to the French Hospital in London and underwent an operation. This is the last reference to Sister Elie in the correspondence, but we learn later that she was transferred to the convent in Bedford when she left the hospital.

In April 1913, we have one of the last letters from Tenby to the superior-general for three years, as there are no extant letters for the years 1914 and 1915. In her letter dated 20 April 1913, Sister Benoît Marie mentions that the Anglican monks on Caldey Island had recently been received into the Roman Catholic Church. The sisters from Tenby were invited by the Abbot of Caldey to take part in the procession of the Blessed Sacrament on the island on the Feast of Corpus Christi. An account of the event was published in *La Colombe*, 1914. In this account, we have reference to the pupils of the school, about which there was so little reference in the correspondence relating to the foundation. The account of the trip to Caldey Island for the procession reads as follows:

> On Thursday we went to the Procession of the Blessed Sacrament. Let me tell you how I, who am lame and scarcely able to walk, was able to undertake this journey. First of all, Sister Angélique pushed me in my bath chair as far as the steamer. As it was high tide, there was no difficulty in getting me on board. After a crossing that lasted one and a half hours (about twenty minutes today), we reached the island. The monks had kindly arranged for two men with a little carriage to be waiting to take me to the monastery. We arrived just in time for High Mass, which was sung by Bishop Mostyn. I had not heard the singing of this beautiful Mass since 1902 (the year she left Brittany for Wales), so I kept thanking God for it.

In the afternoon, there was tea for everyone: for the sisters, at Miss Myers' (a benefactress of the monastery); for the children, at the procurator's; for the people, in the meadow. The monks did the serving. Soon the bishop and several Benedictine monks joined them. The bishop served the tea, reminding them of the gospel scene in which Jesus multiplied the loaves in a place "where there was grass." The memories of that day on the Island of Caldey would remain with them for a long time.

This type of happiness was not to last. Soon the sisters were to receive sad news from the superior-general. On 31 March 1916, Sister Marie Alvarez, writing on behalf of the superior-general, announced the closure of the Tenby community. The sisters were to inform the owner as soon as possible and see if they could get the lease terminated that very month. The letter concludes:

> Let us know promptly of the outcome of your dealings with the owner, also let us know your thoughts about closing the laundry.

On 12 April 1916, Sister Benoît wrote to the superior-general:

> Your decision pains us deeply. Our landlord being away with his regiment, I have addressed my letter to him at his property in the North of England.

She also gives details of the little school, which was doing well. She concludes:

> We can manage here until 1917, provided you see fit to leave six of us at St Margaret's.

The news of the proposed closure of the convent was clearly unexpected. Normally, the superior would have been kept in touch with all the proposed decisions regarding her community. One might ask on this occasion, whether Mother Marie Dominique, who was consulted about developments in previous years, had carried out the negotiations with the superior-general since she was *au fait* with the situation in Tenby. In fact, in her letter of 27 April, Sister Benoît Marie asked the superior-general if Mother Marie Dominique could come and see what could be done. A few days later, she wrote again to the superior-general:

> Colonel Fothergill's military duties do not permit of his dealing with our request, so we shall have to approach his solicitor.

The laundry was to be closed down as requested. Her next letter was dated 27 April and it read:

> A reply has been received from our landlord, refusing to terminate the lease before it is due to end; the laundry will be closed down on 29 April.

Again she asks that six sisters should be allowed to stay. She herself expresses a willingness to go wherever she may be sent, ready to accept all "so as to obtain your recovery" (the superior-general was in poor health herself at this time).

One month later, she wrote to the assistant superior-general:

The announcement of the departure of four of our sisters came as a painful shock. It is very difficult to make arrangements for travel during wartime.

At this time there were 24 pupils in the school. On the 1 June she mentions, "We have five small pupils who are boarders." Judging by the small number of pupils in the school after thirteen years in Tenby, it seemed obvious that there was no future in education for the sisters there.

The year 1917 was to be their last at Tenby. Sister Benoît wrote:

> I am sending an inventory of the furniture. The parents have been notified that this will be the last term. Given our undertaking to restore the stables and adjoining room to their original state, we are going to have to have a certain amount of work done. May I remind you that Sister St Hilaire wishes to return to Brittany for good. I am enclosing a banknote to help with providing warmth for our sick Sisters.

This little gesture of generosity in the midst of their own privations, and at the time that the community was faced with closure, illustrates the strong bonds of unity and fraternity among the members of the congregation.

By this time, therefore, the sisters were ready for the inevitable, and did not wish to prolong their departure from Tenby. Sister Benoît Marie wrote on 25 March:

> I am grateful that you have seen fit to shorten this agonising time which would have been hard to endure until the end of June. The school will close on Wednesday of Holy Week; then we shall prepare for our departure. What is to become of our little maid, Marie Le Roux?

The last letter written from St Margaret's Convent, Tenby, was dated 5 April 1917, and in it we learn that the sisters had already received their transfers to the various other communities in Wales and England. She writes:

> Sister St Hilaire is disappointed to be transferred to Bedford, may I ask you again to allow her to return to her own country? I think we shall be ready to go to Carmarthen on Thursday, 12th. I am trying to find a workman to dismantle all the stoves and pipes, it is not easy to find one because here as elsewhere, almost all the men are in the army.

When the sisters finally left Tenby, Sister Benoît Marie was sent to the convent at Buckfast in Devon, and remained there until 1924 when as a semi-invalid she retired to the Ingsdon Convent, Newton Abbot. Sister St Hilaire was finally allowed to return to France. The other sisters were sent to the other communities of the congregation already established in Wales and England. Sister Félicien was sent to Pontypool; Sister Athanase and Sister Jean du Christ to Brecon. Sister Elie went to Bedford, and Sister

Véronique de Juliani had left the previous January for the foundation at Pwllheli in North Wales. A total of twenty-seven sisters passed through St Margaret's Convent, Tenby, during the fourteen years of its existence.

St Padarn's Convent, Aberystwyth 1903-2004

SISTER MARIE Théodose, the envoy from Saint Brieuc, was responsible for the foundation at Aberystwyth as she was for the other early foundations in Wales.

As already mentioned, she was spurred on in her negotiations by Miss Abadam, an ardent Catholic from Carmarthen who seemed to want nothing more than to see numerous communities of the Daughters of the Holy Spirit established among the Welsh people. As she rightly urged, Aberystwyth, a university town in mid Wales, would be a key place in which to open a community, with prospects for the future. Miss Abadam was all the more insistent that Sister Marie Théodose should act quickly and do all that was possible to secure a place in Aberystwyth for the Daughters of the Holy Spirit, as there were other religious, exiles like themselves, looking at Aberystwyth as a place in which to settle. In effect, the letters exchanged between Sister Marie Théodose and Mère St Georges and Mgr Morelle, the ecclesiastical superior of the congregation, during the months of June, July and August 1903, afford an insight into all the effort Sister Marie Théodose had to put into negotiating this promising foundation. Whereas the foundation at Tenby was centred on laundry work, the one at Aberystwyth was destined to become the house of studies for the sisters in their pursuit of academic excellence for themselves and their proposed school.

In a letter dated 18 June, written from Carmarthen, Sister Marie Théodose gives the superior-general the following report:

> For Aberystwyth, I wrote to Mgr Mostyn and received his reply on 13 June, saying: 'I will give you permission to establish a house at Aberystwyth like the ones you have established at Carmarthen, Brecon and Tenby, but I cannot promise that the sisters will be able to follow the courses at the university, until I have consulted the other bishops about this.'

The report continues:

> I wrote to the parish priest, Father Baggaly, who gave me an appointment for next Wednesday morning (17 June). I went with Sister St Barbe to see him. (Father Baggaly speaks French which was a great

help in the negotiations). He was most welcoming, although he is very poor. We looked at several houses for sale, and rather liked one that was called 'Rosario'. He would prefer to have us to help him rather than the other religious we saw there, who were also looking for a place to settle. There are only 50 Catholics in Aberystwyth, most of whom are poor. He said that he thought we would be able to earn our daily bread, and mentioned possible kinds of work. On the train journey, we engaged in conversation with two young Welsh students who supplied us with a good deal of information about the university. They said they would come to us for French lessons. This would be a source of income for us, provided the sisters sent to begin the new foundation were up to the mark. We would also need a good musician.

The superior-general agreed to the foundation at Aberystwyth. She wished the sisters to rent rather than buy a house, and hoped that the parish priest would be able to advise them on this. Sister Marie Théodose wrote to the superior-general on 10 July, this time from Brecon convent. She said:

> It really is good of Father Baggaly to spend so much time trying to find a house for us. He had suggested one that he thinks will do and asks for a reply by 10 August. He suggests that, when the time comes, I should go with the sisters who are to form the first community. What reply shall I give him?

Miss Abadam also continued to follow the negotiations for the opening of the new foundation in Aberystwyth. In July, she wrote to Sister Marie Théodose:

> You must take this house and you must secure the lease for it without any further delay. Don't be afraid of the responsibility laid on you by the mother house; your fear is just one of the obstacles by means of which the devil is trying to prevent this foundation destined to be more successful than all the others. ...I sense that the reason you are delaying to secure the lease is to save a little money on it, but you must be prudent in small matters and imprudent in greater ones.

In her letter addressed to the general bursar at the mother house, dated 20 July, 1903, Sister Marie Théodose wrote:

> I am sending Miss Abadam's letter to be translated into French by Sister Emmanuel de La Croix. When she has done so, please give the translation to the general council. As you'll see, it is a strong, well-argued case for Aberystwyth. It is difficult to be diplomatic with her, she is so perspicacious, so tenacious. I could perhaps go with one of the sisters to found Aberystwyth on 1 August.

By the end of July, the superior-general wrote to say that she was sending Sr Paul Aurélien and Sister Berthe Joseph for the new community in

Aberystwyth. She also asked what furniture they would like for the house, and she said that the general bursar would send money with the sisters travelling from Brittany. She also told Sister Marie Théodose that she would have to stay in Wales a little longer, since she says: "You cannot leave until Aberystwyth has its superior, and we have not found one yet." So Sister Marie Théodose and the two sisters destined for the new community at Aberystwyth took possession of Number 2 Penglais Terrace, Aberystwyth; rented premises. The foundation was placed under the local patron saint of the area, and thus was born St Padarn's Convent, Aberystwyth.

The arrival is recorded in *La Colombe*, 1904:

> It was on 7 August 1903 that Sister Marie Théodose, accompanied by Sister Paul Aurélien and Sister Berthe Joseph arrived at the rented accommodation that had been found for them at Penglais Terrace, Aberystwyth. The very next day, Sister Marie Théodore had to leave them on their own in this unfamiliar, barely furnished house, but Father Baggaly had promised to come and fetch them at dinner-time. He duly arrived at 11 o'clock and took them to the house of Mrs Owen who made them very welcome. Unfortunately, the good lady did not speak French and only one of the sisters knew a few words of English. So they found themselves in one of those situations, which are just not funny for those involved. At dinnertime, fresh embarrassment, what was the English etiquette to be observed? There were frequent long silent pauses, and then the sister who knew no English managed to find a word. "Water," she said, as Mrs Owen was taking a stopper off a decanter of wine. Tears came to the eyes of the latter and her face showed that she understood the embarrassment of the poor sisters. In the afternoon, she accompanied them to the railway station, and stayed with them there until Sister Marie Théodose arrived. Such misunderstandings and occasions of embarrassment because of the sisters' poor knowledge of the language were a frequent occurrence. Many of them were amusing, and these experiences alone could fill volumes.

On the very day they arrived in Aberystwyth, Sister Marie Théodose, with some alacrity, wrote to the ecclesiastical superior of the congregation about the early beginnings. She wrote:

> The priest at Aberystwyth, poor himself, understands our poverty and will do all in his power to help us. The words he spoke when presenting the sisters in the parish go to prove that...

To the superior-general on 16 August she wrote:

> The sisters are happy in their poverty. We have the sympathy of some Protestants too, who are trying to find work for us to do. One of them

came to clean the house for us, giving her service free of charge. She will come again from time to time without accepting money. A large store in town has promised to sell the needlework that we do.

The pioneers obviously lost no time in starting to earn their livelihood, and with all the fervour of this new beginning, they courageously struggled to cope with their initial poverty and need.

Less than three weeks after their arrival, the sisters had the joy of a visit from the superior-general and the ecclesiastical superior, who were making a visitation of all the foundations in Wales. They arrived at 4 o'clock in the afternoon on Saturday, 26 September and stayed until 11 o'clock the following Monday. From Aberystwyth, the two visitors went to Borth, about five miles away from Aberystwyth, to look at a property which Miss Abadam thought the congregation would do well to purchase, in case the sisters were exiled from the mother house. (This large property, a hotel, was purchased, but sold later, after a rather acrimonious dispute, since the congregation was not turned out of the mother house in Brittany). With regard to the visit, it is recorded in the Annals of the community:

> The next morning alas! They had to leave us to go to Carmarthen. Despite the sadness of this separation, we felt strengthened by their words of advice and by their blessing. If the bitterness of exile seemed all the greater, the desire to work for the glory of God and for the growth of our dear congregation on foreign soil made easier the sacrifices we were generously making.

On 30 August, Sister Marie Théodose wrote again to the superior-general saying:

> There is a mysterious benefactor, about whom I have already written to Mgr Morelle, who wants to acquire a house for us that is as good as two 'Rosario'(the house they wished to buy when they first arrived in Aberystwyth).We could set up a laundry there, have a large henhouse, take in students during the term and families during the holiday season. It is about 8 to 10 minutes walk away from the church. The gentleman is prepared to pay half the rent. Seeing that I was hesitant about it, he promised to pay the last term's rent for the house where we are now. What shall I do? The matter is urgent.

Two days later, she wrote again to the ecclesiastical superior saying:

> The gentleman is anxious that we should settle for Salisbury House, rented or bought. Others are interested in acquiring it: the university as extra accommodation for students, and speculators who know that in the grounds there is a well containing water that is much in demand for making soda water. Unless I hear a 'no' from the mother house, I shall

settle for it. If the answer is 'no', then the gentleman will purchase the house for another work. The present owner is going to see to a few necessary repairs and the tenant-occupier, a Belgian lady, is going to give us certain useful items. The gentleman is anxious to interest the whole of Brittany in our work; this by means of conferences and a Review that he intends to edit himself. He assures me that *La Colombe* would prove of great help to him and he requests that the next number of it should be sent to his address in Paris.

The reply to this letter was swift, for on 5 September, 1903, the superior-general wrote to Sister Marie Théodose:

Our good Father Superior passed on to me your letter of Friday, and the one which followed it. The hand of providence is evident in all these events. I wholly approve of your moving to another location, and am anxious for you to be able to settle in there soon. The superior and the sisters must have arrived by now.

Sister St Lazare, the superior and five other sisters duly arrived, three for studies and one for the kitchen. Soon after the visit of the superior-general, the first request for lessons was received, which was a great relief to the sisters since the prospect of almost total inactivity had been hard to bear. It was the university that first asked for lessons. Miss Brebner, Professor of French, came to ask the sisters to give her and her students a course of lessons in French Literature. An entry in the community Annals at this time shows that the sisters were being accepted at Aberystwyth:

Little by little we won the sympathy and esteem of the population, and visits to St Padarn's Convent became more frequent. People called to see us, to talk with us and to enquire about our situation and our works.

The house that they had rented in Penglais Terrace was much too small, and totally inadequate for their future works. So in the month of November they moved to Salisbury House in Llanbadarn Road. **(Plate 22)** Several Breton compatriots, who were spending five months in the area to sell their onions, generously helped them with the move. The community now had eight members for, at the end of October, Sister Louis du Sacré Coeur who had her Brevet Superieur (equivalent of the G CE examinations in Britain) was sent to help the three young sisters (as yet novices) who were to study for their matriculation, and she was also to give private tuition in French to the persons who requested it.

The aim in each foundation was to set up a school, and St Padarn's was no exception to this. The school began with a class for young children, and there was an advertisement in the local newspaper that the class would open on 10 January 1904, when the other schools in town began their new term. Mr Owen sent his little daughter to this class, but she was the only pupil for the whole of that term. On 16 April, a second pupil arrived, but progress was very slow as regards the admission of pupils. The sisters were longing for the day when they could bring together all the children who attended the Saturday catechism class and give them a really Catholic education. Their hope was that when they gained Welsh degrees, this dream might be fulfilled.

The main goal of the early years in this foundation was to get the sisters qualified to teach in the schools in Wales, and much of the correspondence deals with this topic. Before gaining admission to the university, however, they had to study for the matriculation. The sisters worked hard at their studies. The syllabuses they had to follow demanded, in their opinion, a great deal of memorising. For the English people, it seemed to the sisters, learning was more a matter of erudition than of reasoning. The Lord seemed to bless their progress, however, and in due course they qualified for admission to University College, Aberystwyth. Mr Owen took a special interest in their studies and, despite his heavy workload, insisted on coming once a week to talk to them about English Literature and poetry. He assured them that sisters having a university degree and being able to speak Welsh could not fail to win the confidence of parents who would give them the preference in their choice of education for their children.

Their life at the university was strange to them, at first, and no doubt was a source of curiosity to their lay student colleagues. Extracts from letters to Mgr Morelle describing their first days at university were printed in *La Colombe* (1905, No. 2)

> On the first day of term, the students had to go to the principal to obtain his approval for the course of studies they wished to follow. We were very apprehensive about doing this, but great was our surprise at the politeness and kindness with which he received us… On the next day, a more testing duty awaited us: we had to present ourselves to an assembly of all the professors, but here again, the Lord was with us, and the professors, whose courses we are going to follow, put us at our ease. As we mingled with a crowd of 500 students who eyed us with a certain astonishment we felt less assured. However, we were not entirely on our own, some of the students had made our acquaintance during the last year and they gathered round us offering to render various kinds of services.

The sisters were placed in the front row of the lecture hall, so that they could understand the professor more easily. At the end of the lecture, some of the professors would enquire whether or not they had found it difficult to follow. The entry in the Annals for 3 March 1905 states:

> We are beginning to feel less out of our element than we did when we started our course, and it has to be said that we meet with nothing but respect and kindness from professors and students, so we are hoping that with God's help we shall be successful. The subjects which we have to study hardest are Latin (which we began to study only a year ago) and English Literature in which we can scarcely hope to compete with the English.

The sisters' plans for a private school in the town progressd very slowly indeed. An entry in the Annals in the autumn term returns to the little school, St Padarn's Convent School, with only three pupils. The entry for 12 September 1905 states:

> The little school reopened on 12 September. Two more children, Ada Pears and Alice Bath came to join our first pupil, Dorothy Dixon, all three are soldiers' daughters. A tiny fragile nucleus, but we saw it, as the grain of mustard seed, which we hoped would grow. During this first term of the school year, things progressed though always slowly. Nevertheless, the music lessons and the French lessons were sufficiently numerous to provide a source of income for the house.

In November of the same term, there was a canonical visitation of the community by the bursar general of the congregation. In her brief report she writes:

> The studies are well directed. The teaching of the catechism and the visiting of the sick are for the present the only 'works' possible, and the sisters attend to these as best they can.

As in many of the other foundations of the congregation in Wales, illness was a frequent preoccupation for the sisters. At the end of December 1904, Sister Marie Olive was sent from Brecon convent to join the community and to teach Mr Owens's two little daughters; Mr Owen was one of their benefactors. She was no stranger to the sisters in Aberystwyth and she was welcomed in the community. Her arrival brought the number of sisters to fourteen, and the house was full. But an entry in the Annals says:

> Alas! We had no idea that within the space of a few months our numbers would be reduced to 9, nor that the year 1905 would be marked by such trials.

In March of the following year, Sister Marie Olive was taken ill. The doctor thought she was suffering from influenza, but despite the prescribed treatment she did not really recover and on the night of Easter Sunday, she deteriorated and her impaired sight indicated something much more serious. Finally, she was diagnosed with a brain tumour, likely to lead to total blindness. She was taken to the community at Ingsdon in Devon, and the doctor there confirmed the diagnosis of the two Aberystwyth doctors. She returned to France to the mother house. The Annals note:

> Devoted care and fervent prayer notwithstanding, our dear invalid's sight continued to fail and the pain in her head to cause her intolerable suffering. She died on 29 November, aged 24. In the same year, illness struck again. Sister Louis d'Assise felt very tired at the end of her year of studies. During the first days of August, she became extremely weak, and the doctor did not hold out much hope for her. When the sisters realised that there was no hope, they helped her to prepare for death. At 4 pm on 12 September she died peacefully, surrounded by the community. When the news of her death spread to people of the town, messages of sympathy poured into the convent, from rich and poor alike, from Catholics and Protestants. The funeral took place on 15 September. Fathers Méréour and Tanter and the superior from the Convent in Pwllheli (where by now a foundation had been established) insisted on coming to the funeral. All our catholics, Mr Owen, the principal and some of the professors of the college joined in the funeral procession to the cemetery where Sister Louis was laid to rest alongside the graves of other catholic students. During her illness she had said: "When I am in Heaven, I shall pray for this house." The effects of her intercession were soon experienced; four new pupils Catherine Rowland, Elsie Davies, Muriel Pears and Victor Young came to join the six pupils we already had.

As regards St Padarn's Convent School which began with one pupil, it is interesting to note that two years later there were still only six pupils. In January 1906, however, things began to change. The sisters were asked to take two little Catholic boarders from Birmingham, Billy and Conrad Powell. It is recorded in the Annals:

> For the next two years, they were the pride and joy of the house, which they delighted by their mischievousness and unaffected piety.

In June of that year, a visit was received from one of the general councillors of the congregation, who noted

> There is now a small class of fee-paying pupils but it leaves something to be desired as regards the discipline which makes for the keeping up to date and care of books etc. And the teachers themselves need formation in some of the areas of the subjects taught.

The first reference to the teaching of Welsh is significant, for a majority of the population in Aberystwyth spoke Welsh. The entry in the Annals read: "Welsh pupils should be given lessons in Welsh."

The new school year of 1906 to 1907 began with the admission of several new pupils: Lucy and Elsie Price, Gladys and Dilys Wood, Maggie Jones, Mona Treharne, and in the course of the year, the nucleus of the kindergarten was formed by the arrival of Kathleen Paul, and Frank and Herbert Murray. Then at Easter, the nephew and niece of the superior of the community, Yvon and Yvonne Menut, from Brest, came as boarders, bringing a French element, something that was appreciated by the parents of the other pupils. This was the year that saw the school truly established on a more solid basis. To the initial aim of the foundation, that of obtaining university qualifications that would entitle sisters to teach and take posts of responsibility in English schools was now added the running of a day and boarding school, which soon became the most important work of the convent, together with numerous private lessons in French and Music.

The purchase, in November 1906, of Salisbury House and its outbuildings secured the future of this educational establishment. The end of the school year brought success for the student sisters. Sister Marie Henri passed her second year examinations with success in all subjects, while Sister Jeanne Du Calvaire was awarded her BA degree and received the traditional insignia at the degree ceremony on 21 September 1907. In February 1908, the community had the joy of welcoming the assistant superior-general from France who made a canonical visitation of the community. In her written report, she noted

> The school, which at present has 14 pupils shows an improvement with regard to discipline and with regard to written work, and creates an overall favourable impression. The piano lessons are well given and will be perfect once the teacher has acquired better fingering and a looser wrist movement.

In June 1908, Sister Marie Henri took her final examinations and was awarded her BA and when the new school year at St Padarn's began, it was Sister Marie Henri who was made its first headmistress. The school continued to grow and develop, the number of pupils rose from 22 to 34, and the course of studies preparatory to the various examinations was well organised and taught. In July of that year, the first of the student sisters to be unsuccessful in her studies left, without having obtained her matriculation and no other sister was sent to take her place. "This" in the words of the

Annalist: "marks the end of an era for St Padarn's" because it was some time before sisters registered for a degree course at the university.

In April 1910, Mother Marie Dominique came to make the canonical visitation of the community. In her report, she drew attention to the fact that whereas the convent school continued to be governed well, little or nothing had been done by the sisters to help the poor children of the mission, and the superior is asking whether it is not time to start a class for these children. Father Baggaly had requested it and the bishop wanted it. The convent school at the time of the visitation had 36 pupils and was progressing well. In the year 1910 also, Sister Lazare de Béthanie, who had been the superior of the foundation since it opened, was transferred to another community and Sister Marie Amélie, who was to be a member of the community for the next 37 years, was appointed as superior of St Padarn's Convent.

The next development in the work of the sisters in Aberystwyth was the setting up of a mission school. It is recorded in the Annals of the community that in October, 1910, "the school," or more exactly the class for the Catholic children of the Mission, had begun. When its doors opened on 2 October, twelve small children came to attend the lessons given by Sister Berthe Joseph. For the next nine years, it served both the educational and pastoral needs since, as the Annals record, the contact with the children facilitated reaching out to parents, in particular to those who were not well instructed in the faith and those who had lapsed. Three years later, in 1913, the mission school had 18 pupils. This small school suffered the same fate as the other small mission schools that the sisters tried to run in addition to their private school. The requirements of the Fisher Education Act of 1918 brought about its closure. The Annalist writes:

> One of the victims of the new Education Act was our little Mission School, started by Sister Berthe whose devotedness and competence had kept it going.

It was an *école de charité* (Charity School) *par excellence*. The funding for the room that housed it and for all the basic educational requisites, came entirely from the community's funds. Yet, since it did not have the required number of pupils (to obtain recognition in terms of the Act) it was, to the deep regret of the sisters, compelled to close its doors and send the pupils back to the state schools.

Meanwhile, the problem of lack of space, as in many other foundations was also present in Aberystwyth. As the years went by, it became increasingly clear that Salisbury House, the second location of the sisters in Aberystwyth, did not provide adequate space for the community and the school with its fourteen boarders. For a long time the sisters dreamed of having more room in which to live and work. It was decided therefore to build a new school, and this new building was completed in September 1913. This resulted in a surge in the number of pupils seeking admission to St Padarn's Convent School.

Then the First World War began. Just a few entries regarding the war are made in the Annals for these years. We read:

> The outbreak of the Great War which filled our hearts with anguish and foreboding, also made us experience, in a way that was new, the rigours of exile. Our share in the material privations, which it brought, was minimal, but the trust which the superior had to place in providence to help her provide the wherewithal to satisfy the healthy appetites of the young, was heroic. One consolation that we had at this time was to be able to come to the assistance of those less fortunate than ourselves: we were asked to take in some 20 Belgian refugees. We were able to provide them with food and shelter, also with schooling appropriate to their need... We are pleased to record the lasting gratitude of these families, for the blessing of the poor draws down the blessing of God. We were able to help not only the refugees but also the wounded. At the invitation of the Red Cross, the superior spent long hours at the bedside of the wounded in hospital.

Once the war was over, and the Fisher Education Act began to be implemented, thought had to be given to the re-organisation of the convent school, which was now attended by about 100 pupils, 36 of them boarders; a far cry from the single pupil when the school opened. It was also necessary to ensure that the headmistress and other members of staff had the necessary qualifications for the school to obtain official recognition. In the first instance, Sister Marie Henri the headmistress was sent to Cavendish Square, London, to obtain her postgraduate Diploma In Education, while other sisters began a course of studies at home. Two new classes were formed at this time and another two planned, but the allocation of more rooms to the school meant that the community had its living space reduced. During the canonical visitation of the superior-general in July 1919, she wrote that it was consoling to see how the school had prospered and grown. But she added that it was a matter for regret that the new building (1913) was not more spacious.

The problem of the shortage of space was resolved, for a time at least, by the purchase of the former vicarage of St Michael's Anglican Church **(Plate 23)** In 1921, it was owned by two elderly ladies who, finding that its upkeep was now too much for them, decided to sell it. But Sister Lazare, the superior since the foundation at Aberystwyth, did not have the satisfaction of seeing this new development in the history of St Padarn's brought to completion. The implementing of the 1918 Code of Canon Law with its new regulations regarding the duration of the mandate of the local superiors meant a change of community for her. In September 1921, after nineteen long and fruitful years in Aberystwyth, Sister St Lazare was transferred to Caernarfon, where another foundation had been established.

Sister Marie Thomasine who, with the authorization of the superior-general and her council, and with the help of Mr Nee, their solicitor, had negotiated the purchase of the Old Vicarage, replaced her. The contract was signed on November 1921, and the move was effected during the Christmas holidays. Sad to say, Sister Marie Thomasine was in hospital when it took place. For a long time, her health had been less than good, and the doctor decreed that she should undergo surgery without delay. She spent two weeks in the hospital in Aberystwyth before returning to the community for a long period of convalescence. At Easter she was sent to Caernarfon for a change of air and in the summer the doctor advised that she be sent back to France to rest.

In the year 1922, when the assistant superior-general came on a canonical visitation of the community, she wrote

> The newly acquired property of the Old Vicarage now houses the chapel, the community and the boarders, an arrangement which will facilitate the development of our works in Aberystwyth and make possible a greater contribution to the spread of God's Kingdom. The trial at present is the illness of Sister Marie Thomasine whose recovery from the serious operation she had is very slow.

During her absence, Sister St Elodie had been entrusted by the superior-general with the care and direction of the community, which numbered nineteen sisters. As Sister Marie Thomasine did not return to Aberystwyth, Sister Ste Elodie was appointed superior of the community.

At the start of the academic year 1922-23, after an interval of fourteen years another sister, Marie Albertine, began to study for her Bachelor of Science degree at the university college. The number of pupils in the school in September 1922 was very encouraging, and more children began to come in from the outlying rural areas, so they had to form a special class for the

Welsh-speaking pupils "in order to make it easier for them to learn, and for the sisters to win their trust." Many of the pupils were boarders and despite the purchase of another property, they had difficulty in housing all of them. Sister Ste Elodie had to find a way of remedying this, and with the permission of the superior-general she arranged for the garages behind the Old Vicarage to be converted into a building, which comprised a playroom, two dormitories, two bathrooms and toilets. Finally, at Easter 1924, this building was ready, and the pupils were delighted to move in when they came back after the Easter holidays. The sisters too were delighted because they were now able to spread out a little into the rooms vacated by the boarders.

A greater problem still was to face the sisters in the year 1924. It was the fiftieth anniversary of the foundation of the Catholic church in Aberystwyth, and a vicious campaign was mounted against the sisters by a rabidly anti-Catholic group (the Kensitites). For fifteen days they spread all sorts of calumny about them, distributed vile pamphlets and tried to dissuade parents, whom they stopped in the streets or called on at home, from sending their children to the convent school. It is noted in the Annals as:

> an embittered struggle which filled our hearts with anguish: were we going to have to capitulate and leave the town? The unconquerable faith and unshakeable confidence of Father Hook, who had succeeded Father Baggaly as parish priest, allayed our fears. "God," he said, "protects his own; remain calm, suffer patiently and pray." Our trust was restored by these words, and we calmly waited until the storm had spent itself. We continued to give lessons and our pupils took their exams, but when the term came to an end we could not help wondering whether or not these dear children were leaving us for good.

This was the year, too, when the first two pupils of St Padarn's Convent School who had been successful in their matriculation examination gained a place at the university. They were the first two pupils to have passed right through the school and qualify for the university and their names are recorded: Beryl Hughes and Kathleen Miller, and this in a year when it was noted: "the powers of Hell sought to destroy us." The following year, another pupil, Roma Evans, passed her matriculation with flying colours:

> The good Lord thus blessed the efforts of his valiant teachers, giving the little school the success that would ensure its future.

The year of 1926 saw two more sisters join the community to study at the university, after some initial preparation before beginning in October. This year, too, saw many changes of personnel in the community.

> This year was one which affected us very much since it was going to mean the loss of a dearly loved and deeply respected sister who with utter selflessness had devoted the whole of her religious life to the community and to the school of which, it could be said she was the foundress.

Sister Marie Henri had to leave the community where she had spent all her religious life, the pupils she had seen growing up, and the university town where she had pursued her own studies. Sister St Elizabeth, who was an Oxford graduate, was also called upon to make a sacrifice since she was leaving Bedford Convent School, where she had spent many years, to replace Sister Marie Henri, as headmistress. In 1927, there was a new priest appointed to the parish. He was Father Michael McGrath, a future Archbishop of Cardiff.

The entry in the Annals for 1931 speaks of the exceptionally high number of pupils, twenty-four in all, who had left at the end of the summer term. The year 1931 also saw the first General Chapter of the congregation, held at Saint Brieuc in the mother house. It also brought elections for a new superior-general, and Sister St Charles Borromée was elected. The following year, she made a canonical visitation of the community, arriving on 27 April 1932. She was accompanied by Sister Louis du Sacré Coeur, who was delighted to see again the place where she had spent two happy years (1903-1905). The superior-general, anxious to help the sisters in every way she could, and finding that the distance between the convent and the school gave rise to all sorts of difficulty and inconvenience, decided there and then that a school should be built on the same site as the convent, and she instructed the superior to start making arrangements for this to be done. On the advice of Father McGrath, the parish priest, the diocesan architect was invited to draw up plans and submit an estimate, and on 3 August 1932, the workmen arrived and work began on the new school.

After five months the new school was ready for occupancy. An entry in the Annals for January 1933 says:

> Deo Gratias! We began the new term in our lovely new school...five months steady work has resulted in the construction of a building with which we are truly delighted. And how pleased we are that we no longer have to leave the convent twice a day, and in all weathers, to walk to the school.

In February it was noted:

> Providence continues to watch over us, and we give thanks that without too much delay, a purchaser has been found for our old school. The negotiations between our devoted Mr W.P. Owen and the *Urdd Gobaith Cymry* were satisfactorily concluded and so on 7th of this month, Salisbury House passed into other hands.

The year 1934 passed without incident as regards the school, but on 2 November, a letter arrived from Saint Brieuc with a message that saddened the sisters. It announced the transfer of the superior, Sister Amélie des Anges, who was named as superior of Ste Anne de Brest, in Brittany. The entry in the Annals states:

> As often happens in the working out of God's plan, while he takes away with one hand, with the other He gives and so it was for us, since the sister appointed for us to succeed Sister Amélie was Sister Marie Amélie...

who had already spent 25 years in the community.

The following year saw another canonical visit carried out by the assistant superior-general, Sister St Amélie, who was accompanied by Sister Marie Théodose, who had been responsible for the opening of the foundation in Aberystwyth, thirty two years earlier. How pleased she must have been to see Sister Berthe Joseph who was one of the first sisters to accompany her on her mission to open the foundation at Aberystwyth in 1903. In her report the assistant general, Sister Ste Amélie, mentioned the school as follows: "There were 98 pupils, 26 of them boarders; they all loved their school and wished to be a credit to it..." In that year too, Father McGrath, the former parish priest of Aberystwyth, was consecrated as Bishop of Menevia. The superior of the community and Sister Berthe Joseph went to Wrexham for this event so that the congregation would be represented at the consecration of someone who had shown great concern for the interests of the sisters. In December, the bishop paid a first visit to the community. It is noted in the Annals:

> He shared with us his plans for extending the reign of God in his vast but poor diocese. One thing that was of particular concern to us was the announcement that the Carmelite Fathers would take responsibility for our little parish, from the following September 1936.

In 1936, the Congregation of the Daughters of the Holy Spirit decided to send a sister to a mission in Manchuria in China. One of the sisters from St Padarn's Convent, Aberystwyth, had volunteered for this mission, and on 12 February she received a letter from the superior-general telling her that her wish to be one of the missionaries leaving for Manchuria was to be realized. The sisters shared in the joy of Sister Mary Alice, though they were sorry to see her go. Some three weeks later she left Aberystwyth to go to the mother house to say goodbye to her beloved parents, before setting sail for America where she was to join her future superior, Sister Marie Céline.

Another painful letter was received in Easter week in the following year, 1937, recalling Sister Berthe Joseph to France. We read in the Annals:

> Every change made in the community is painful, but this one was particularly so...With her departure the last link with the very beginnings of our house will be severed, for Sister Berthe Joseph had been here since the very beginnings, that is, a total of 34 years...We shall remember her for her unfailing devotedness and for the solid virtues of which she was always an example.

The school year 1938 to 1939 was a year when no outstanding event marked the school year, but the school could record the success of all their pupils who took examinations, in particular the success of those who took the Higher Certificate, and as always they thanked God for the success. September 1939 however, saw the declaration of war, with all the uncertainty that brought for the sisters living away from their own country. An entry in the Annals states:

> Our poor little Sister Adèle Emilienne, who had left us a few days previously to return to her family in America, had a miraculous escape from the first disaster of the war, the sinking of the *Athenia* on which she was to have sailed had various unforeseen delays not prevented her from so doing.

In community she was replaced by Sister Agnès Marcelle who, being of Polish origin, was very much affected by the sufferings of Poland, partly on whose account Britain was at war with Germany.

On the school front, 1939 was a good year. At the beginning of the school year in September, the number of pupils was the highest ever, about 130, with a maximum of 35 boarders. This was because the fearful anticipation of brutal warfare prompted many parents to send their children to safety amid the Welsh hills, where the enemy planes would not penetrate. For the same reason the University of London was evacuated to Aberystwyth. The community readily gave hospitality to Ursuline sisters from Brentwood, but unfortunately they had nowhere to offer to the three Marist Sisters who had to find lodgings in town. Aberystwyth also welcomed as evacuees the Daughters of Charity from Birmingham, and the girls in their care. These became known as the Plynlimon girls after the name of the hotel in which they were housed for the duration of the war.

Further reference to the war appears in the Annals for the year 1940:

> Each passing day we follow the dreadful events of this terrible year: the invasion of Norway, Belgium, Holland, the capitulation by the king of the Belgians, the evacuation of Dunkerque and finally the armistice between France and Germany announced on the radio one morning in May. Since then there had been no communication with France. What was happening to the their superiors and sisters and their families?

Letters that had been written to them before the armistice were returned without having reached their destination.

> Oh the anguish of those terrible days! One needs to have lived through them, if one is to have any idea of what they were like…

London and other major cities were the targets of heavy bombardment from the air. During the last weeks, large groups of evacuees from Liverpool arrived in Aberystwyth. The superior encouraged all the sisters to start knitting garments for them.

In 1942, the impossibility of communication with France necessitated the appointment of a provincial superior of the congregation, with responsibility for the communities in England and Wales. Sister Jeanne du Calvaire, the first sister to graduate from University College, Aberystwyth, was chosen. During the year a few messages sent via the Red Cross brought the sisters news from the mother house and from the sisters' relatives.

> We scarcely feel the material privation experienced in the occupied countries, and so we pray ceaslesssly for those who suffer the outrages of this war.

The year 1944 was a year they would never forget. After a four-year silence, they received a letter from the superior-general informing them that Brittany had been liberated. Such was their joy at the good news, that they immediately sent off cards to their families. The entry in the Annals for 1945 reads as follows:

> The war is over! We begin to entertain the hope that our superior-general will soon be able to visit us. In fact, on 24 September, a phone call from our devoted Miss Henn informs us the superior-general, accompanied by Sister Anne Elizabeth, had arrived in Bedford Convent. We pray that the Holy Spirit will guide her and enlighten her during this first visit to the province after the long years during which all communication with the mother house was impossible.

One of the aims of the foundation in Aberystwyth, as stated earlier, was to enable the sisters to study for degrees at the university. Despite the difficulties of the war years, this continued. In 1942, two sisters graduated with a BSc and a BA respectively. One of them went to St David's

Convent, Brecon, and the other to the community at Bedford. Another sister began her degree course the year the war ended, and yet another graduated with a BA Degree in 1947. The 1944 Education Act made further demands on the schools and as mentioned in the Annals for that year:

> In our convent schools the need for fully qualified teachers required by the Education Act is great.

The demands of successive education acts indicated to the sisters how precarious a future their school would be faced with in order to comply with educational legislation. No longer would St Padarn's School be regarded as an entity in itself, however successful, but its future would be linked to that of all the other convent schools run by the sisters, in Wales and England.

In the post-war years, it became increasingly evident that St Padarn's Convent School was one of the convent schools which did not have a very secure future. In September 1945, there were 115 pupils on register, just 22 of them boarders **(Plate 24)**. In November of that year, the provincial superior, her assistant, the former headmistress of the school and Sister Geneviève from Brecon (where the convent school was also threatened with closure), met to discern, under the guidance of the Holy Spirit and the protection of Our Lady, as also St David, the patron of Wales, the future of St Padarn's School. Later in the week they were joined by two Carmelite priests, one from the parish, the other from Sittingbourne, who had come to plead the cause of the school. Like the disciples of Emmaus they went away sad, for it seemed that all was over. In the evening of Sunday, 10 November, the provincial re-convened everybody, and the final decision was made. She made this announcement: "Aberystwyth will continue, but as a junior school as from September 1947," that is, two years later. So as to be able to continue their secondary education, fifteen day-pupils took the scholarship examination for the county school in Aberystwyth, and twelve of them were successful; four of these obtained their matriculation.

In April 1948, there was again a strange turn of events. The provincial made the canonical visitation of the community, at the end of which she wrote a report which affords a comprehensive description of the community and school. The report stated:

> The school, which years ago was on the brink of closure, has had a new lease of life and the number of pupils shows a marked increase, from 90 last September to 105, 28 of whom are boarders. The teachers are competent and determined to do their utmost to inculcate in their pupils the love of God, and a sense of duty. The children are

remarkable in their good behaviour, and the respect that they have for their teachers.

The sisters also did parish work, and gave catechism lessons to the children who were unable to attend a Catholic school. They did all in their power to assist the local clergy, and the Carmelite Fathers were very appreciative of their services. They still hoped to have a school for the Catholic children in the parish. During the following years leading up to the golden jubilee of the province, the sisters turned all their attention to preparing the convent school to be recognised as efficient by the Ministry of Education, and we shall return to the subsequent history of St Padarn's Convent in a later chapter.

Chapter Seven
Expansion: Foundations in 1904

St Anne's Convent, Llanrwst 1904-1909

THE FOUNDATIONS OF THE DAUGHTERS OF THE HOLY SPIRIT THAT were made in North Wales have this in common, that they were made in areas where the Breton Oblates of Mary Immaculate (OMIs) had already established a mission, which they called the *Mission Cambro-Bretonne*. We find the first mention of it in the letter which Père Goulven Trébaol OMI addressed to the superior-general of the Daughters of the Holy Spirit on 18 December 1903. He wrote:

> The evangelisation of our Welsh separated brethren has been entrusted to the OMIs by Bishop Mostyn with the approval of His Holiness Leo XIII.

A small parish bulletin headed 'The Breton Mission, Llanrwst, St Tudwal's Church,' and giving the times of the Sunday and weekday services, is dated 1 December 1901. This seems to have been the year when Father Trébaol came to the tiny parish as priest in charge. As a Breton himself, it was only to be expected that before very long he would call upon the Daughters of the Holy Spirit to come and work with him.

Negotiations with the congregation began in 1903, and when he wrote to the Vicar General Mgr Morelle, on 8 December 1903, Father Trébaol began with an announcement:

> I am pleased to be able to tell you that the house for the good sisters of Llanrwst will be ready to receive them on 1 January 1904. It is my wish shared with Father Crosier and our little flock that the sisters should come as soon as possible. New Year's day would be a good date, and you with their mother general could come and install them. I am promising to send you the Welsh version of 'Gourc'Hemenou doue,'

which the Bretons know so well, as an exercise for those readers of *La Colombe* who are learning Welsh.

Ten days later, in reply to the letter from the superior-general informing him that the sisters would come soon, Father Trébaol wrote:

> Great was my joy, shared by all who knew of it, on learning of the imminent arrival of our dear sisters. May Mary Immaculate obtain for them a safe journey, and bless their ministry in this dear country. I shall be at the station to meet these good religious, and there are devoted persons here who are ready to give them a hand and to ease as much as they can the sisters' first days in exile. No need to say that Father Crosier and myself will be just as eager to do likewise. It is not for me to tell you what name to give your community, but if I may, I'll suggest a few: St Tudwal's Convent, The Breton Convent, Convent of the Holy Ghost, St Winefride's, St David's, St Anne's. May I also take the liberty of asking you to send a good musician and excellent singers? These are the two gifts that are much needed here. I hope that you will have about ten children to begin with (I have six who come regularly to the catechism lessons three times a week), some French lessons and one music lesson for the harmonium. No doubt, visiting the sick will prove essential for reaching out to the people and earning their good will. And above all, there is prayer.

The sister chosen to be the superior of this new foundation was Sister Louis de St Yves who had previously spent six months learning English with the Franciscan sisters in Taunton, Somerset. The other sisters who were to form the community were: Sister Renée de St Anne Kergoat and Sister Marie Cécilia Elien. Sister Louis and Sister Renée arrived at Llanrwst on 4 January 1904, and took up their abode at Number 5, Carrington Terrace, a property rented from a Mrs Parry, which thereafter became known as St Anne's Convent, after the patron saint of Brittany.

Three days after their arrival at Llanrwst, Sister Louis, the superior, addressed her first letter to the superior-general. She wrote:

> I have decided not to wait until the octave of our arrival before writing to give you my first impressions. Our house is very nice, very convenient and shelters us from all unwelcome prying. I cannot convey to you the joy with which Father Trébaol and his companion welcomed us, when we arrived here on Monday at 7 o'clock in the evening. I enclose the word of welcome which the good bishop had sent Father Trébaol for us, a few days ago. Our house was blessed yesterday: four OMIs, three of them Breton, two Breton sisters and three benefactresses were present at this simple moving ceremony.

The mission of the sisters of St Anne's Convent, Llanrwst, began with-out delay, and four days after her first letter, Sister Louis wrote again to the superior-general to give her information of the work they had undertaken:

> The other day, I began teaching the catechism to two little girls who came to the mission. I shall visit the sick and, if possible shall call at homes in Scotland Street where the poor live. Our sisters are going to give lessons; three have already been asked for, in Music and French. Sister Renée de Ste Anne who has a lovely voice is going to sing solo at Mass on Sunday, while Sister Marie Cécelia will provide the musical accompaniment for the singing. The children will be around us. We are going to have to learn Welsh; this will not take too long, I hope, thanks to the lessons that Father Trébaol gives us and thanks to Mrs Parry who is especially kind to us.

In a letter dated 20 January, Sister Louis reports:

> We have not yet started to give lessons—everybody seems to be waiting for our musician, Sister Marie Cécelia, to arrive before they start coming for lessons. Father Trébaol keeps on asking us when she will come. Our small purse gets emptier by the day: 15 shillings to the carpenter, 25 shillings for rates to be paid in advance. Even so, Providence takes care of us: over and above the provisions, which were in the house when we arrived, we have received 25 francs, sent by the superior of the convent at Taunton. Whenever I think of the burden you have to bear, I pray for you; especially when I am in the little church where, every morning, we are almost the only ones present. The two Fathers recite the prayer of the breviary aloud, while we say our Rosary, before assisting at the two Masses which follow.

The sisters had high hopes for their mission in Llanrwst, and good will was not lacking. Nevertheless, the first year was to prove a difficult one, especially for Sister Louis. The letter she wrote to the superior-general on 2 February almost a year after their arrival was printed in *La Colombe*, and by now she was aware of the great difficulties which they would have to endure. As happened in other places, the arrival of the sisters among the people who had not seen nuns before dressed in their unfamiliar white garb, provided various kinds of reaction, not all of it friendly. For example, the grammar school boys played pranks on the sisters: coming to ring the door bell and then running away, putting stones and earth in the doorway. Not knowing quite how to deal with this, Sister Louis asked a workman who had come to do some repairs to report it to the police. A kindly policeman came that evening and asked if he could wait indoors until the boys came to play their pranks. Once they had started, he crept out the back door and caught them, and he took their names. Sister Louis did not want them taken into custody for the night, but she requested that they be reported to their parents. By next morning, everyone in the neighbourhood had heard of this, and affirmed that the boys would not come again.

This letter also contained information about the work of the sisters. It said

> We need all the patience, prudence and courage that we can muster, if we are going to 'throw helve after hatchet.' For the most part, our Catholics are Irish immigrants who are Christian only in name, and most of them are poor. If we have too much to do with them, the Protestants are going to look down on us, and that will damage our hopes for the future (the hoped-for private lessons and a school), and yet we have the duty to instruct these poor Catholics, the women and girls at least, to bring them back to the practice of their faith, through our visits to the sick, our catechism lessons and the advice we can give. It is now that I feel all my weakness, and I call upon the merciful heart of Jesus to help us to do His work and to guide us in our difficulties.

Although the letter does not mention the total number of Catholics in the little parish, there was obviously only a handful, for she does mention in her letter that there were only eight baptisms in the parish in two years. The letter also gives a description of the poverty of the little Catholic Church in Llanrwst. In this letter, too, we have the first mention of a new mission being opened in Pwllheli, where the congregation would later open another foundation. The parish priest spoke Welsh fluently and the people appreciated his sermons in Welsh.

Sister Louis's letters point to the difficulties that constantly plagued their mission in Llanrwst. Her next letter of 28 February 1904, tells of her tribulations but also of her courage:

> With the help of your prayer and the grace of my life as a missionary, I shall accomplish small things in the Master's Vineyard, and I will accept trials with patience, trials that are inevitable, since we find ourselves in a stronghold of Protestantism, and with very few Catholics, who are often less that edifying. Despite this, our good Father Trébaol remains undaunted. He is pleased to know that his sister (who was coming from Brittany to work for the sisters) is on her way and he sends you his warmest thanks for all your kindness to her. All four of us are busy helping with the preparations for the visit of our good bishop.

There was a longer interval between this letter and the next one dated 9 April. It was a significant letter, containing important information about the beginning of St Anne's Convent School, Llanrwst, a school that was never to materialise! It begins with a word of explanation for the long silence: "I ought to tell you about the Bishop's visit and thank you for the harmonium" (she had been too busy to write).

> Father Trébaol has announced the opening of the school for next Monday, 11 April. The first class will be in the dining room, and it is very sparely furnished. The names of twelve children have been registered as pupils. We have asked Sister Célinia Joseph for some help on how to teach; a few books and sundries have been ordered from London until such time as you can send us some more. And I would be grateful to receive some more money; we still owe money for the rates and for three months' rent. What a nightmare money can be, and what a cross to have to think about it everyday! Our five Music and French lessons bring in a little money, but not enough to meet daily needs and to pay the rent. Boarders will provide a source of rent, but for that we would have to have another house.

The superior-general would not have remained insensitive to these calls for help, and it would appear that she asked Sister Louis to come to the mother house at Saint Brieuc to talk things over. In her letter of 25 June, she says "I shall probably arrive at Saint Brieuc on the 29 or 30 July with my little postulant, Miss Devon", who was joining the congregation. From a letter which Sister Louis wrote on her return from Saint Brieuc to Llanrwst, it was evident that while she was in Saint Brieuc a decision had been reached not to continue with the school. In her letter she writes:

> On the advice you gave me, on the recommendation of Sister Marie Angélina, and after asking the opinion of Father Trébaol, we had decided not to re-open the school/class for the children of the poor Catholic families. But now, Father Trébaol has changed his mind and came to ask that we should re-open the school, saying that somehow, from somewhere, he will find what is needed to be done to keep it going. Sister Renée is very tired so I can see only one thing to be done, namely, to ask you to send another sister, one who knows English and is able to teach. All my time is taken up with the running of our little household, and the care of the church and my visits to the sick.

Another sister arrived at Llanrwst, as requested. Sister Olivier Hammon came from the convent in Olney, Buckinghamshire. Sister Marie Angélina, the general bursar, promised to send some furniture for Sister Olivier Joseph's class, which was very poorly equipped for her four pupils. The latter was also preparing for her matriculation examinations. Father Trébaol had undertaken to give her Welsh lessons. A crisis occurred in the community at this time, the exact nature of which is not on record. It led to Sister Louis' unexpected departure from Llanrwst, an event which is not recorded in any of the later correspondence. From the subsequent letters written by Father

Trébaol himself, however, the crisis seemed to centre round Sister Louis herself, and probably had arisen because of her unsuitability for the job of superior of the community.

The parish priest, Father Trébaol, addressed the remaining letters for this period to the superior-general. He wrote in December 1904 apologising for the fact that there were so few pupils attending the school. He said that this was not his fault or the fault of Sister Louis; he felt that the problem arose from the prejudice of the local Protestant population. The lack of a livelihood for the community, and his inability to pay the sisters for their work in the parish, had led him to propose that the convent should be closed. Father Trébaol continues in the same vein in his next letter to the superior-general:

> I know that the work here has not succeeded as well as I hoped, but was it reasonable to hope for more? Above all, I would ask, is Sister Louis as much to blame for this as some have been quick to say? Be that as it may, I beg you for the sake of my own peace of mind, for that of the community, especially of Sister Louis herself, to make a decision with regard to the future.

Soon afterwards, Sister Louis left Llanrwst and was sent for a time to Ingsdon in Devon, before joining the community at Abergavenny.

During her time as superior of Llanrwst, Sister Ste Thérèse, the successor of Sister Louis as superior of the community, wrote thirty five long letters, five to the superior-general and thirty to the general bursar. These describe the sorry state in which she found the small community, the difficulties that had still to be faced; and the brave attempts to establish a work that would not only ensure a livelihood for the sisters, but also enable them to contribute to the evangelisation of the poor in Llanrwst.

It was from Belgium, where she had been superior of the community at Ramecroix since 1902, that Sister Ste Thérèse was called to Llanrwst. In the long letter which she wrote to the general bursar, Sister Marie Angélina, on 12 January 1905, she recounts her long journey:

> Southampton, Carmarthen, Pwllheli and now the painful bit, Llanrwst. The only good I can find is the great kindness of Father Trébaol, the parish priest. As for myself, what good can I hope to achieve, since one needs to be able to speak their language, if one is to win over the Welsh. I simply do not know where I can find the time to learn it. As for the school, there are 9 children between the two classes: Sister Renée has six pupils (Catholics), what was supposed to be the future of the parish school. Sister Olivier has three little Protestants, who are grandchildren of Mrs Parry, the community's sole benefactress, who died a month

ago. The Parry family faces ruin because of the elder son's misconduct; its lands and houses, including the one we occupy are to be sold in June. As I am not acquainted with the locality, I have asked Father Trébaol to find us another house we could rent.

Mrs Parry (Junior) came to visit the sisters after the death of her mother. She encouraged them to start a private school for girls in Llanrwst, but they would have to go about it in the right way. For one thing, they would need to separate the fee-paying pupils from the others. She stressed that the people of a certain social class would not support a school where the poor children were under the same roof as the fee-paying pupils. Another important condition would be to have, at least to start with, a teacher who was English; lastly the sisters could advertise in the local press. Father Trébaol was of the same opinion as Mrs Parry. Such a project would necessitate the renting of another property, which would mean that they would have two rents to pay, and already the house they were renting was going to be sold.

The next move as regards their work, as she mentions in her letter of 13 February to the superior-general, was the removal of the class for the poor Catholic children from the convent to the presbytery. At this time they had ten pupils for the mission school, and Father Trébaol vacated his room to give them a classroom. But they were still very confined with regard to space. They had no playground, and the front door opened directly onto the street, so the pupils had to stay in the one room all day.

> Sister Renée goes over to the presbytery for the school hours and comes back as soon as they are over. This keeps her very busy…we have two lady boarders, they are the daughters of the late Mrs Parry, and needed to be in Llanrwst for a time.

She also gives news of the private school. Father Trébaol found a qualified English teacher who had given up full-time teaching and was willing to come for two days to teach whatever subjects she might be given. She mentions in her next letter that this teacher was a Protestant, and that Father Trébaol had asked the bishop whether she could teach in the convent school. The bishop agreed, and if the superior-general were in agreement they would be able to employ this teacher. She concludes her letter as follows: "Only through the schools shall we be able to do any good and earn our living."

Most of the correspondence for the next year dealt with the problem of acquiring a house in which to live, and with news of the private school. On 27 February, Sister Ste Thérèse wrote again to the general bursar, indicating that she had not received an answer from the superior-general to her last letter. "I am very surprised", she wrote,

> that I have not received a reply to the letter I wrote a fortnight ago. The main things that I need to know are: 1.) If I may put an advert about the school in the newspaper; 2.) If I may accept the teacher about whom I wrote to the superior-general; 3.) The big question of the house about which I have already told you and which I went to view last week. I am really worried about it; we cannot remain where we are, and we need the sort of house that will allow of our future works. The house in which we are living is going to be sold on 19 May. I am able to trust in providence; what kills me is the lack of works. I do not get a chance to visit the sick because here whenever anyone falls ill, the doctor is sent for and if there is any need for someone to provide care, he can send the nurse.

In her letter of 28 March 1905, even though the negotiations for buying a house are in progress, she still feels unsure of the future.

> Once again, it is the question of the house that brings me to you. We have taken the first steps towards purchasing it; in other words, Father Trébaol has asked the solicitor to ascertain what would be a just price for it. If you knew the moral agony this causes me! The future, as I see it, is so dark; if it turns out that we are unable to have any works, what shall we do with this big house, which may then prove a burden for the congregation. I'll tell you quite frankly the more I study persons and things here, the less trust I have for the future. It is the merchant class which is dominant in Llanrwst, most are Calvinistic Methodists and quite hostile to Catholics. They will not be in any hurry to send their children; so where will the pupils for our school come from? We cannot expect to receive anything from anyone here in Wales; quite the reverse, we have to give of what we have and that is what we are doing. We pay for absolutely everything in the poor school for the Catholic children, including pencils and paper; we also launder the church linen. In his pastoral letter the bishop made an urgent appeal to the generosity of Catholics in places where the mission cannot be maintained for very much longer. It is to be feared that the Mission here, which is so poor, will not last.

She says that the opening of the private school was fixed for after Easter of that year, but she adds:

> We have received no requests yet for a place from prospective pupils. It is to you that I prefer to tell all this, because you are better acquainted with our situation and I am certain that you will settle with the superior-general what is best for us.

Two days later she wrote:

> The solicitor has just informed Father Trébaol of the sale price of the
> house, it is very steep, £1,400 (£70,000 today)

Sister Ste Thérèse, like her predecessor, also paid a visit to the mother
house, for her next letter to the superior-general, dated 15 April, begins
with an expression of gratitude for the visit.

> How good it was to see my sisters, Sister Mary Eliza, and Sister Marie
> Madéleine (who were her blood sisters)…Here at Llanrwst, I am
> feeling my exile more than I did in Belgium, and the distance from the
> mother house is so much greater, not to mention the difficulty of not
> knowing the language. I have never been accustomed to such a solitary
> life as I live now. As a result, I have found the last three months the
> longest in my religious life. I expect that the general bursar has
> acquainted you with what I wrote to her about the purchase of the
> house… I am waiting for her reply. Father Trébaol, after speaking to the
> solicitor, is in a hurry to know your decision. How worried I am about
> this house! What I really want at this moment in time is that a sister from
> the general council would come to Llanrwst; I do so need to be
> enlightened and guided.

News about the house figured in her next letter to the general bursar:
she told her she was waiting to hear from the owner of the house, before she
wrote again. When he did contact her, the owner maintained his original
price of £1,400. Having looked round for another house to buy, she said
that they found one that she went to view with Father Trébaol and Sister
Renée. Her description of this house is as follows:

> It is not easy to describe but I would say that its outbuildings are
> pleasing and much better than those of the other house. In appearance,
> it resembles a country presbytery. Its surface area is 40 acres. It is priced
> at £1,350 but the lady owner who is anxious to move from the locality,
> and is prepared to sell for a mutually agreed price, seems willing to make
> concessions.

The next few letters to the general bursar dealt with the purchase of this
house for the community. On 2 May 1905 she wrote:

> This morning, Father Trébaol received a letter from the agent of the
> lady who is willing to let us have her house. This gentleman asks that
> we give a definitive answer as soon as possible since, if we do not have
> the house by a private agreement, it will have to be put on the market.
> We know that the present owner paid £1,000 for it and it is now worth
> £1,300; the lady having added to it a playroom for her children.

Writing a fortnight later, on 17 May, Sister Ste Thérèse sounds an almost jubilant note:

Deo Gratias! I have given my signature and received that of Mrs Lewis' agent. It was only after a long-drawn out discussion that we were able to agree on a price. I told him that I was prepared to pay just £1,100 (£56,000 in today's currency), solicitor's fees included, and that I was not ready to negotiate any further. Before leaving, he told Father Trebaol that he was sorry to see the property go for such a low price, but added that the owner was happy to see it go to nuns. We shall pay by instalments. Mrs Lewis will vacate her house by 1 July, on which date we shall move in. Once all the paper work has been completed, we shall have it examined and approved by a Catholic lawyer in Caernarvon (a Mr Nee). The agent said it would be good to do this. I am happy at having thus made acquaintance with a number of Protestant families who encourage us by saying that a private school for girls is needed in Llanrwst. The Fathers are even happier than we are at this purchase.

One wonders at their daring in trying to buy a house with so little resources, and also the fact that they still had no pupils. So the superior undertook fund-raising activities. She had written about ten begging letters to various persons. She also asked the superior-general if Sister Renée who was going to the mother house to make her annual retreat, would be allowed to make appeals on behalf of their poor, yet well-loved Mission. Five days later, she wrote again, this time to say:

I have been to see the cottage; there I met a photographer taking different views of the property: Mrs Lewis wants to have these as a souvenir of the home where she brought up her 7 children. She promised me one of these photographs, which I will send to you as soon as I receive it. From there, I went to the bank to draw out the 2,750 francs from Saint Brieuc. This transaction has cheered me up considerably. The date for paying the last instalment will be 1 July after which we may take possession of the cottage. I promise that I shall repay you as and when our circumstances allow. Now our only problem is that of finding pupils. Father Trébaol wants me to invite you to come to Llanrwst when we take possession of our new house.

Nearly a month later she sends the photographs of the cottage that she promised.

This will give you some idea of what the cottage is like (Plate 26). The sale of Mrs Lewis' furniture is due to take place on the 29 June. We have already begun to pack our bits and pieces so as to be ready to move on 1 July. Since the lease on our present house will not have quite expired, we intend to lease it to a family from Paris who will be coming to Llanrwst for two months. Mr Nee, our Catholic lawyer from Caernarfon, has studied the title deeds and finds them in order. It embarrasses me to have to tell you that the contents of my purse have increased by only 80 francs, and yet I have written some thirty letters asking for assistance. It will soon be 1 July when payment for the cottage will have to be completed. The thought of having to ask you for such a considerable sum daunts me and yet I cannot do otherwise.

The next event was the move to the Cottage. On 14 July 1905, she wrote about her financial worries once again. The solicitor's fees were very steep, but she did not regret having his expert services, since she was assured that the title deeds were in order. Mr Nee, the solicitor, had altered the name of the Cottage to St Anne's School, since there was a law in England which was in abeyance which allowed the government to seize property belonging to religious, with the exception of houses that were used as schools. At the sale of Mrs Lewis' goods, Sister Ste Thérèse bought some gardening implements, and a few other indispensable objects, all for £12. The house and the garden would need a lot of tidying up.

In her letter to the general bursar dated 8 September, she mentions the lady boarders.

> The two ladies from Paris are still with us; they are very good and devout. Madame Andrade has had a grotto made for us, under the tree opposite the front door. The statue is very beautiful. It was blessed on 1 September. These two ladies pay 35 shillings a week for their rooms; they pay for the coal and gas also, which benefits us. It is Madame Andrade who is our organist for the duration of her stay, and when she leaves, Father will regret this very much… I do so long for you to come to Llanrwst to bring us enlightenment and advice. I could not sleep last night for worrying lest Sister Olivier Joseph should be taken from us, since whatever works we may eventually have, I need a sister who can compensate for my inability to speak English.

Sister Olivier was transferred to Caernarfon just a few weeks after this letter was written.

The next problem recorded in the correspondence for these years refers to the future of the OMI priests who were running the mission. Bishop Mostyn disapproved of having two priests residing in Llanrwst, whereas he had only asked for one. The rule of the OMIs stated that there should be at least two members in each community. "And what of ourselves?" she writes:

> We have the house, it is true but we are still going to have to find money for the rates and taxes, which in Mrs Lewis' time amounted to 325 francs, not to mention maintenance. I am sorry that when I write to

you, I am always worried and sad. After the failed attempt to start a fee-paying school, I simply do not know what other work to try and organise. Needlework done to order brings in so little. I have thought of a day nursery for which a fee would be charged, but I do not know whether this would be possible in Llanrwst.

Sister Ste Thérèse's next letter to the superior-general dated 20 September 1905 says:

I am rather late in thanking you for sending us a young sister to give music lessons. Sister Olivier Joseph has taken over the Mission school where she has two new pupils who are Protestants. Since they come from poor families it is to their advantage to have free schooling. The little school affords us consolation and hope, because we count on these children for the future success of the Mission. We long for you to come and see our new residence.

Her next letter to the general bursar was pessimistic about the convent school. She writes:

I am more than heartbroken that not a single pupil has come to us. All the visits we made have yielded no results. I can only conclude that these people are insincere and that it is a spirit of hostility to Catholicism that keeps them away from us. I have tried to start a day nursery. Sister Renée was devoted enough to walk all the streets of the town, looking for small children. If I could have agreed to take them for nothing, several would come. So what can we do to earn our daily bread? You mention sewing; I very much doubt that the shops in town would accept to sell our work, given their prejudice against us. The two nice ladies from Paris left last week…As for the Fathers' situation nothing has been decided yet. The Bishop, so we hear, cannot find the extra £80, which the OMI General Administration is asking for, so probably one of them will have to go.

The problem centring round the two priests in the mission featured in many subsequent letters. In her next letter to the general bursar, she wrote:

Father Trébaol is back from his travels, and is very happy to have seen the loveliest sanctuaries in France. Madame Andrade, one of the ladies who stayed at St Anne's Convent, entrusted him with her son, a young man of 20 who is doing his year's study in rhetoric. This will represent an added source of income for the presbytery since he is going to pay £8 a month plus 25 shilling for beer.

The Provincial of the OMIs was awaiting Father Trébaol's return before calling a meeting of the four priests who were serving on the Welsh Mission. The meeting was held at Holyhead. The impression with which they came away was a very unfavourable one. There was talk of closing down the Missions at Llanrwst and Pwllheli on account of lack of resources.

Sister Ste Thérèse's last letter to the superior-general for the year 1905 was dated 21 December.

> We thank you for having taken part in our Christmas draw. We managed to sell 80 tickets, which is very good, given the attitude of people here. We are preparing a Christmas tree for our little pupils; it will be a joyous celebration for the children as well as for all the adults who may come.

The first two letters to the superior-general for the year 1906 continued in the same vein of frustration and waiting. In her letter of 12 February, she wrote:

> The mountains here are covered with snow; it is very beautiful to see but it prevents our children from coming to school. Their numbers continue to fall; they are poor, often without shoes and other necessities of life. Our works show no development, and as you will see from our accounts, our earnings are minimal. The two Fathers are still here, and no decision has been made about their remaining. We are all tired of waiting to see what will happen.

The decision came for Father Trébaol, for in her letter of 17 April she writes: "Father Trébaol has just told us of the letter he received from the vicar general saying that he is not to remain at Llanrwst."

The canonical visitation of the community took place at the end of May of that year. Sister Marie Angélina, the general bursar, came to Llanrwst and wrote in her report:

> At Llanrwst, I found a delightful community that is very united and well maintained; this includes the class of 12 pupils who are well mannered and attached to the sisters. This is a class for the poor; a work for which the sisters are wholly dependent on Providence, which it must be acknowledged, has not failed yet. There is a vast amount of good waiting to be done here. It would be more easily done if the sisters were in a position to give alms to the poor, thereby drawing souls to themselves and through them to the good Lord. But for the present they have no income that would allow them to do this. Sister Ste Thérèse, now that she is beginning to make herself understood in Welsh and in English, has promised to start visiting the Catholics with a view to doing them some good, morally at least. Together we went to see the dark street where most of them live. Ah! What misery there must be hidden there? Sister Renée de Ste Anne, well loved by her children, also achieved a great deal: all of them can recite the catechism answers perfectly; some can spell without making a single mistake, and one little boy confidently

worked out on the blackboard an addition in pounds, shillings and pence. And the children sang, all of which gives hope for the future, even though Llanrwst is the 'boulevard du fanaticisme.'

Since the sisters had so little success with the school, they turned once again to the idea of laundry work, or at least a certain Mrs Rownsley conceived the idea. This lady did not think that the sisters would ever have enough pupils to run a school. So she advised the sisters to open a laundry. She would rent three bedrooms and another room upstairs in the convent. She would also rent the garden, which she would cultivate. Mrs Rownsley offered to initiate this laundry work, and meet all the expenses of installing a laundry in the cottage, where there was enough space for it. When Sister Ste Thérèse wrote to the general bursar on 11 June, she told her that she had been to visit Mrs Rownsley again.

> She received us most graciously and is going to be *Une petite Providence* for the Mission. Not only is she going to pay the board of the little Selter girl, she is also going to pay that of a girl from the mountains. So next Thursday 14 June, we shall welcome our first boarders. By then the Cottage will have been blessed since it is going to be our privilege to have the Corpus Christi procession of the Blessed Sacrament in the convent grounds. Please let me know whether the Superior-General would allow me to take them. Mrs Rownsley seems devoted to the Mission and to us. She will await your reply before notifying the owner of the house, which she has rented until May 1907, when she would come to us, if you find it good that she should do so.

The laundry project took pride of place in subsequent letters to the superior-general, as it was seen as a means of earning a livelihood for the sisters. Mrs Rownsley was prepared to employ a woman to do the washing, but she was very keen that it should be a sister who took responsibility for the ironing, at least to begin with. She asked for a sister from Tenby or from Ingsdon who would be accustomed to smoothing and starching linen. Mrs Rownsley was also doing all she could to find outlets for the sisters' needle-work. The sister experienced in dressmaking and embroidery which the superior had asked for did not come, but the sisters of High Wycombe had been so kind as to send some items as models.

An interesting letter dated 14 November 1906, contains information of the work of the sisters at Llanrwst. Sister Ste Thérèse writes:

> At last, I am responding to your request for information about our works.

She gives a list starting with the Mission school with its ten pupils. She also mentions visiting the poor Catholic families in the Mission, looking after church linen; making clothes for poor children, and music and singing for parish worship.

> They also held a Sunday meeting for the school children and young Catholic girls...All these works are wholly benevolent, and bring us nothing by way of income. We should like to be able to do more but it has not pleased the good Lord to render our zeal any more fruitful yet.

Her subsequent letters to the superior-general also deal with the laundry project. She writes:

> I beg you once again to send us a sister as soon as possible, because the laundry work is due to begin very soon. We have heard that we can count on the custom of two main families in Llanrwst. Mrs Rownsley is actively searching for a woman to do the washing but, like myself, she is counting on having a Sister to do the ironing. She wants me to write to Mr Chauveau and ask him to send the three main items we need: a washing machine, tumbler and a large tub. She is hoping that he will agree to the payment being deferred which makes me think that she intends to contribute to the cost. My visit to Amiens was a wasted one. The good Father Superior who took a kind interest in the Mission at Llanrwst gave me 50 francs. Sister Emérienne showed me round the laundry there.

A short time later Sister Ste Thérèse wrote:

> We are still waiting for another sister to come. We have begun receiving linen to be laundered and we have no one to iron it. Imagine the embarrassment it causes me. Mrs Rownsley has arranged for a young woman from Liverpool to come and do the washing, work for which she will be paid 25 shillings (£63 now) a week. A young girl from Llanrwst will come and help; she too will be paid by Mrs Rownsley, who for the present is meeting all the expense. I had intended to send you my accounts for the year but am unable to do so now because on returning from Amiens, I had to take to my bed.

There is an account of the running of the laundry in one of Sister Ste Thérèse's letters to the superior-general. This letter to the superior-general is dated 23 February 1907. It reads:

> All the washing was done on Mondays, by the maid, the girl from the Mission and Miss Trébaol, who insisted her services should be accepted. The sisters gave a helping hand on Monday afternoons, by washing the woollens—following Sister Elie's method.

They would do this only until the girls were able to do it. On Tuesday mornings, the sisters helped with the blue rinse and the starching, and in the afternoons they were free. The remainder of the week was given to sewing. The laundry work brought in thirty shillings a week, but they had to deduct from that the cost of the starch and the soap. Still the laundry work brought in enough money to provide the basic needs of the community. It appeared that Mrs Rownsley soon used up all her money, and she left the sisters to manage the laundry by themselves.

As soon as one problem seemed to be solved, another one usually replaced it. The next one centred on the departure of Sister Ste Thérèse from Llanrwst for the USA. She was obviously very reluctant to move, for in her next letter to the superior-generaal, she writes:

> I have been filled with remorse for my lack of generosity in not responding affirmatively to your wish. Today, the Feast of St Joseph, I experience the need to tell you that I am available to be sent to America. If it is not too late, and if you need me for this, I will gladly go to the new world, there to work for the glory of God and the good of souls. My first sacrifice will consist in moving away from the mother house, the second in leaving the Mission of Llanrwst where I am ready to continue working if such is your wish.

In her last letter from Llanrwst, she asks to visit the mother house before leaving for the USA.

Sister Ste Thérèse was succeeded as superior of the community in Llanrwst by Sister Marie Alix who stayed for only a few months, during which time she wrote two letters to the superior-general, both of which are rather negative and dispirited in tone. On 17 November 1907, she wrote:

> I have waited for a long time before writing to you because I was hoping to be able to send you good news from Llanrwst. But alas! I can see that the time has not yet come for the conversion of Wales. It is heartbreaking; hardly anyone at the Sunday Mass. With regard to the laundry, I keenly regret that money was spent on it. It will not do any better than the other works. No custom to be had from the town, and if any one of the few customers that we do have let us down, we would be without bread during the winter. And the sisters' health is so poor. What a hospital this is! They envy the lot of maids in France who have less fatigue and more comforts (which is a reminder of the thoughts of the prodigal son in the gospel). A letter received from Sister Ste Thérèse informs me that our maid, whom she had brought from her home parish in Brittany will not be staying here, once her year of service is ended. So I am faced with the necessity of asking you to send a sister who is strong, to help Sister Michel Marie Le Bars, otherwise we shall have to give up the laundry work which is our sole source of income.

In a more critical frame of mind, she adds:."I am sorry that Sister Ste Thérèse and the general bursar, at whose initiative the laundry was set up, are not here to run it."

Her second letter of 19 December is in a similar vein.

> I am surprised to learn that you have not received my letter which I
> wrote the very next day after receiving your cheque. Thank you for
> your kind generosity to us. I am pleased to tell you that peace, union
> and charity reign in our little community. The wish that we all share is to
> be able to do some good around us. But alas! The ground is arid and the
> seed scarcely grows. School attendance is down; yesterday only five
> pupils came out of the twenty or so on the register. Their fathers are
> miners; here one day and somewhere else the next. In November we
> accepted two children as boarders, then made enquiries about their
> parents' circumstances, only to learn that they are insolvent. So as you
> might expect we hastily returned these children their parents. As for the
> laundry, it is with great difficulty that we manage to obtain even the
> small amounts that we are owed. I shall send you our accounts at the
> beginning of January.

Sister Marie Alix in fact only stayed in Llanrwst as superior for nine
months and then returned to France. Sister St François Borgia, who had
been superior of the community at High Wycombe, replaced her. Sister St
François was aware of the difficulties that her new community had been
experiencing and she realized that, as at High Wycombe, its income would
have to come to a large extent from orders for needlework and embroidery.
So in her first letter to the general bursar dated 27 May 1908, she requests
that Sister Barthélémy Marie whose gift for sewing she had appreciated
when they were together in community, be returned to her, and she
continues:

> Really we cannot manage without having 2 more sisters. Yesterday, our
> fourth boarder arrived, a charming 6 year old, but boarders add to our
> already considerable workload. Our school children, they now number
> 22, pray the 'Hail Mary' every day for your intentions. You cannot
> imagine how I love these children already, and I am experiencing a joy
> that I have not known for a long time.

Sister Barthélémy Marie was not sent to Llanrwst as requested, but
instead Sister Louise Hélène Le Moan was sent from France. On 3 October
1908, Sister St François wrote to the bursar general:

> Thank you for sending us Sister Louise, she seems content to be in
> England. She does not know how to embroider lingerie but she does
> know how to make Irish lace, so that will be perfect. I think it is going to
> be difficult for Sister Dominique to settle in Wales; everyday she sighs
> for Brittany.

Sister Dominique du Rosaire Hallequin was one of the two sisters sent during the summer to join the community. The second was Sister Rudolph Marie Cariou, sent to help Sister Renée in the schoolroom.

The following letter, dated 7 November 1908, tells of difficulties connected with the school. Father Trébaol, it would seem, left a letter for Sister St François saying that he was going to close the Mission school. Whereupon she went, with Sister Renée, to see him:

> I said: "if on Sunday you announce the closure of the school, on Monday I shall re-open it." To this he replied "I'll forbid the children to come, I don't want there to be a Catholic school any longer," and he continued to speak like a man who was out of his mind. What will there be left for us to do in Llanrwst if the school is taken from us? The mines are closing down and the parents of our boarders are moving away to seek their fortune elsewhere, four of the children have gone already. The father of two other children has written to me saying: "I think I am going to take my children away." What will be the outcome of all this?

Father Trébaol was now the sole priest in charge of the parish, his confrère having had to leave because the parish was too poor to support two priests.

The first three letters for the year 1909, written by Sister St François, tell of hardship. In her letter of 16 May she wrote:

> To your question: 'How are you managing with regard to money?' I have to answer that the winter proved difficult—3 long months without any work. My dear companions did the impossible (sewing) and we just managed to subsist, but we were not able to pay our little maid, and I am wondering where I am going to find the 200 francs that she is owed. Would you allow us to try to do without a maid? We could all lend a hand with the cooking and washing etc. I have said this to the sisters and they are willing to try, if I show them... After this, we shall have tried everything possible, and I just cannot see what there remains for us to do. The Catholics are moving away from Llanrwst; we still have few children and for the good of their souls, we are glad to devote ourselves for as long as the Lord Jesus wishes. I am not asking that you should reduce our number because we would not then suffice for the work on which we depend for our livelihood. To meet our current expense, for food, garden, maid, rates etc. we need to earn six shillings and sixpence a day, and to earn that we have to ply the needle unceasingly, since we haven't a single lesson, and are never likely to have any. Do not envisage sending another sister to replace me. I cannot bear the thought of how painful it would be for her: if she had no liking for needlework, and if she were slow in doing it, then she

would soon grow discouraged, and feel unable to provide for the community's daily bread.

Her letter dated 14 June 1909, begins with some account of how the community are managing without a maid. She also gives news of the Mission.

> Yesterday, three of our children made their First Holy Communion. How sad it was! They had no preliminary retreat/instruction, just confession at half past eight in the evening before. And yet, Father is Breton, and how differently things are done there. Father is losing heart, and keeps on talking about leaving. His parishioners, it is true, afford him no satisfaction; he cannot get them to come to Mass, and he never has any one for Holy Communion, except at the convent. What a sorry mission it is! We pray that we may not lose heart. My health has improved, thank you; though I still suffer from headaches sometimes. This is probably due to worrying about the Mission.

A few weeks later, Sister St François received word of the decision to withdraw the sisters from Llanrwst. Her last letter from there dated 3 August, 1909, records their grief at having to leave:

> Our house now stands empty, but I do not want to leave it without writing to you from here for the last time. In keeping with your wish, as conveyed by Sister Dominique, we shall go this evening to Caernarfon for the night, and the following evening to Pontypool, from there we shall set out for Plymouth, and hope to be in Saint Brieuc by Saturday evening. How I am longing to see you! My heart is so full of anguish, and the grief of the sisters adds to my own. When they see my tears, their own begin to flow. Again, may the Lord accept our suffering in reparation for the faults we have committed here, for the good of our beloved congregation, and for the salvation of these poor blind souls?

Eighteen sisters were placed at St Anne's Convent, Llanrwst, during the brief existence of this foundation. Of those remaining when the foundation closed in August 1908, three of them returned to France and one was transferred to the USA.

The history of the foundation at Llanrwst is a sad one, and presents a picture of struggle for existence, and efforts, in so many areas, which failed. The inability of the sisters to earn their livelihood by setting up a school, and resorting to laundry work and needlework, must indeed, as Sister St François admitted, be a cause for tears. It was a foundation which began, as we saw, with great hopes for the future. The sisters had been asked to go there by Father Trébaol, one of their own compatriots, but the five years and nine months that they spent in Llanrwst must register as one of the least successful ministries of the sisters in Wales.

St Mary's Convent, Pembroke Dock 1904-1908

THE FOUNDATION at Pembroke Dock was the second of the four that were made in Wales in 1904. The negotiations for it began on 1 October 1903 when the superior-general, in the course of her brief visit to the already established communities, responded to a request from Father Kelly, the priest in charge at Pembroke Dock, that they should meet to discuss the possibility of having a community of sisters there. The idea of a foundation at Pembroke Dock was initiated by Miss James of Tenby and, as a preliminary step in the process, Sister Marie Théodose visited Father Kelly. There was a population of fourteen thousand in Pembroke Dock at that time, of whom four hundred were Catholics; there had been a Catholic mission there from 1843, and a church since 1865.

After her return to France, the negotiations continued with the superior from the Tenby foundation, Sister Benoît Marie. In a letter dated 17 October 1903 we read:

> Father Kelly paid us a surprise visit yesterday afternoon. He would like the sisters to earn their living by private tuition and needlework classes. He finds the laundry work that we do in Tenby too tiring, and does not really like to see us engage in it. He wants the sisters who come to Pembroke Dock to be able to visit the people living around them, and he would like them to instruct the Catholic children, numbering seventy-four. For this reason, Father Kelly requests that you send at least one sister who knows English. He is unable, as yet, to start a Catholic school. He would like to hear from you as soon as possible lest, as might easily happen, other sisters move in before we do.

The main obstacle to the foundation, as in many other cases, proved to be the finding of a suitable house for the sisters to rent in Pembroke Dock. In the end, Father Kelly vacated his small presbytery near the church in Meyrick Street, for the sisters to live in, and he moved to some other accommodation. This decision was to prove a great source of disagreement later on between the sisters and Father Kelly, not long after the foundation was established. No Annals of this foundation have survived, if ever there were any, so the source for tracing the brief history of St Mary's Convent, Pembroke Dock, is the correspondence between its only superior, Sister St Thomas d'Aquin, and the superior-general (Archives, Maison Mère, Saint Brieuc, File 12G 12).

Once she had been appointed as superior of the new foundation, Sister St Thomas d'Aquin came from France to the convent in Monmouth where, in the community of Sister Thérèse du Saint Esprit, she tried to learn a little English. In a letter to the superior-general, dated 3 December 1903, she writes:

> Though I try very hard, the progress is slow. I am able, however, to pray the rosary in English but it will be a long time before I am able to express myself with the same facility as our sisters in Monmouth [where the foundation was made two years earlier]. Sister Benoît Marie has just written to me saying that the foundation at Pembroke Dock should be made by Christmas, or at least such is the wish of the good Father Kelly who would like the sisters to start giving lessons at the beginning of January. If his plans come to fruition, then I have only a fortnight left here… I shall be leaving Monmouth with a very small amount of English, fortunately the companions you are going to give me will know more. I go into the kitchen here several times a day to watch Sister Paul at work. Though I am not a 'cordon bleu', I think I shall be able to manage to do the cooking at Pembroke Dock. I am glad to be in Wales and I shall assure you that I shall put all my good will into doing what you expect of me. Sister Benoît has offered to send two sisters to help to put up the beds, as soon as she receives word that our furniture has arrived.

By the time Sister St Thomas wrote her next letter, dated 12 January 1904, she was already installed in Pembroke Dock. The foundation was known as St Mary's Convent. It was placed under the patronage of Our Lady, since the mission was called St Mary's, and many of the foundations of the Daughters of the Holy Spirit in Wales, as we have seen, took the patron saint of the existing mission. Sister St Thomas wrote to the superior-general to tell her that certain problems prevented them from arriving at Pembroke Dock as proposed on 4 January. The furniture which was sent from France for their house had not arrived, because it was addressed to Pembroke, rather than to Pembroke Dock. So the sisters only arrived there on 8 January. They first of all prayed on arrival at their future convent, and then went to meet Father Kelly. He invited them to stay for an evening meal, but they declined as they felt that six of them were too many to impose on Father Kelly's generosity, so they returned home. He sent them a tin of salmon, bread and butter and some oranges, he also sent them cutlery and serviettes, and they had a lovely meal together.

The sisters who formed the new community at Pembroke Dock were the following: Sister St Thomas, superior, Sisters Anais Le Flock, Jeanne de Ste Angèle Le Cousin and François des Anges Le Fur. Sister St Thomas gives a brief description of the house in her first letter of 12 January:

> Our house, as you know, is very small; you saw the single ground-floor room, one end of which Father Kelly used as his sitting room, the other as his dining room. It would be a great help if we could have a partition erected. There is no attic, so our trunks have to remain in our bedrooms; the cellar comprises 2 small rooms, one of which serves as our kitchen cum-dining-room, the other as the laundry. There is a fine garden where we can hang out the washing to dry.

Father Kelly formally announced the arrival of the sisters to his parishioners, and encouraged them to make contact with the sisters. He was of the opinion that the sisters would be asked to give lessons once they became known. Their first work was to be responsibility for locking the church door after Mass. Father Kelly, who was very zealous for the good of souls, tried to recruit children to come for an hour's instruction in the evenings, and not only for religious instruction but also for French, drawing and needlework, so that they would not be put off by too much religion. Soon he recruited twenty-one boys and girls, who were to come for the first time on 25 January 1904, within two weeks of the sisters' arrival in Pembroke Dock. This meeting depended on whether the sacristy could be made ready by then, because it needed cleaning. They would be asked to pay three pence for each hour's instruction.

Father Kelly also announced at the following Sunday Mass that the sisters were willing to give private tuition, at their house, in French, art and music to all who would be interested in this, Catholics and non-Catholics alike. The sisters would need textbooks for these lessons, so immediately they requested that books be sent with the sister who was coming to Pembroke Dock the following week from Brittany. The initial accommodation problem was resolved in this way. Father Kelly agreed that they needed two rooms in which to give private lessons. Soon a lady came with her six-year-old daughter to ask for lessons in French, English and painting. When she saw the one long room where the lessons were to take place, she offered to improve it. She told her husband, Mr Swann, about it; he contacted a joiner, and workmen were sent to put up a partition, and to clean and polish the floor. The demand for private lessons was more speedily forthcoming than at Llanrwst, for soon after their arrival in Pembroke Dock, two ladies came to ask for lessons in French conversation, and they said that they had been in touch with two others who wished to share in this lesson. The sisters found it difficult to decide what fee they should charge, but fortunately they knew that at Monmouth the sisters asked for one shilling per lesson, and they thought this would be the price they should charge.

In her next letter to the superior-general, dated 5 February, 1904, Sister St Thomas reported that the religious instruction classes that Father Kelly had asked for had begun on 25 January; that fifty two children had turned up on the first evening and that, since then, the number had grown to sixty, which was as many as the sacristy could hold.

> As I think I have already told you would be the case, the R.I. lessons comprising the catechism, bible history, church history and the gospel, are followed by a short French lesson. This, I think, is what draws the children, but given that their age range is from six to sixteen, it makes for difficulties. Sister Ste Anais and Sister Ste Angèle are present for the R.I. lesson so as to hear English spoken; after that, they help Sister François des Anges with the French lesson. All these children are thrilled to be learning our language and think it is very clever to be able to say "Bonjour! Bonsoir!"

In the early days, the inability of the sisters to understand or speak English fluently was a great handicap, and yet they soon had requests for two needlework classes, one for young girls and one for ladies, for which the fee was one shilling an hour. Sister St Thomas expresses this when she says: "None of them knows French, so I have to have recourse to my needle when trying to show them a row stitch." The sisters were also fortunate in having several families in Pembroke Dock who befriended them. Among them, mention is made of the Swann family, the Misses Walsh and Flanagan, all of whom helped them in various ways.

From the two letters which Sister St Thomas wrote to the superior-general during March 1904, we learn that their work was progressing satisfactorily. The sisters by then gave ten lessons a week in French and four in needlework, all of which were well remunerated. Unfortunately, there was not much demand for music lessons because music teachers were already very numerous in Pembroke Dock. It was soon felt that some of the sisters would need further study to prepare them to give painting lessons, and Sister St Thomas asked if she could send one of them to Carmarthen to learn from Sister Marie Isidore. Their benefactors continued to be generous to the sisters:

> one of them has provided us with linoleum for the stairs. Our little house looks quite good now but it is too small. Of the two small rooms on the ground floor, one is used for the little class, and the other for the

private lessons; so at times we have nowhere to receive visitors, except the hallway. Yesterday, a gentleman, the headmaster of one of the schools here, came to ask for a course in French Literature, but we haven't a single text we could study with him. I should be most grateful if you would arrange for the works of some French authors to be sent to us. We are now giving thirteen private lessons in french each week. The people continue to be well disposed towards us; the great difficulty is the language.

In this letter, there is mention of "the little class." This was obviously the beginning of what the sisters hoped would eventually be a convent school.

In the only letter that she wrote during April 1904, Sister St Thomas began by offering Mère St Georges, the superior-general, feast day wishes, for the feast of St George, her patron. She also gives news of the activity of the sisters.

After Easter two young ladies came to ask to be shown how to make bobbin lace; this was something that I had first to learn how to do myself. However, they seemed satisfied with what I showed them and did not suspect that I, too, was only a beginner. We ourselves are not finding enough time to learn English, so would you allow us to work at it until half past nine in the evening? It is only in the evening that Sister François can give time to helping us.

From their studies to the surroundings in which they lived:

Here at Pembroke Dock we are surrounded by the sea on all sides but one, and need go only 100 yards to find ourselves out in the open country, which is where we go for our walks. The land is quite high above sea level and the winds often strong; when the winds get in our cloaks we really look a sight! A few times we have ventured out without our cloaks. May we continue to do so?

The main topics of interest in the letters which Sister St Thomas wrote during May 1904 were the expected new addition to the Swann family, the financial situation of the community, various benefactions, and the possibility of putting up a school building for the Catholic children.

The Swann family are expecting a new baby soon. I cannot tell you how kind and generous this family is to us, nor how it grieves me to be unable to find words adequate to convey our thanks. I should dearly like to give them something for the baby as a token of our gratitude. May I do so? Our financial situation, thanks to kindly providence, is quite good. I think that we are going to be able to make ends meet; I very much hope so since you have so many other expenses. For two months now we have had enough fresh eggs to make a meal of them every day and on Fridays, our fish is supplied gratis. Yesterday, I went to pay the doctor's fee for Sister Marie Desirée's treatment; he told me in French: 'Je ne charge pas les personnes comme vous; vous me trouverez toujours quand vous aurez besoin.' (I don't charge people like you, you will always find me when you need me). We meet such kind and generous people in this foreign land that, were it not for the language, we wouldn't feel that we are in exile. Our English is getting a little better. Thank you for allowing us to have a lesson in the evenings.

In response to the announcement that a new baby was expected in the Swann family the superior-general wrote to Sister St Thomas saying that she would send a matinée coat and two little bibs. Almost three weeks later, Sister St Thomas was still waiting for them so, when she wrote on 24 May, she began by expressing her concern at the delay.

We have not yet received the gifts for the Swann baby that you announced in your letter of 9 May. I tell you this so that if the parcel has gone astray, enquiries can be made about it. The other day, I asked Father Kelly whether or not he was thinking of having a school built for the Catholic children. He replied that funds are lacking for this so it is just not possible. There are about 80 Catholic children of school age and some families are very reluctant to send their children to the Protestant school.

A longer interval elapsed between the foregoing letter and the next one, dated 23 July 1904, perhaps on account of some of the difficulties it reports: in particular the difficulty, in the absence of Sister François, of communication with outsiders. There were increasing difficulties resulting from shortage of space.

When I told Father Kelly that we would have to look for a larger house, he replied "Alright, you look for one if you can afford to pay for it". We have looked for one but in vain. We made a novena to St Anthony; I spoke to Father Kelly again, asking if he could not have a schoolroom built. He reflected and this time answered that it would not be altogether impossible. This gives us a glimmer of hope.

In eager, if not well founded anticipation, Sister St Thomas continues: "With your permission, the sisters would like to make a small contribution to this building, out of gratitude to their friends and acquaintances."

The next big event in the life of the sisters, which was the beginning of difficulties for them, was the move to 49 Guyther Street. Sister St Thomas wrote excitedly to the superior-general:

On Friday evening, we were told that there is a house to rent just five minutes walk away from the church. We immediately went to view it, and found that it has several advantages. We have spoken to the owner who is asking £23.00 (£1,200 in present day currency) rent a year for it. It is in need of a few repairs but she is going to have these done and will keep her offer open till September. She is willing to rent it for a period of three years or more. I asked Sister Benoît Marie to come and see it; she finds that we ought not to hesitate to rent it. Father Kelly agrees that it would be better for us than his house in which we are at present, and says that it would be a mistake not to take it. So, will you let us know what arrangements we should make with the owner of this house? It will enable us to increase the number of children in Sister François' class, but the evening R.I. lessons would still have to be given in the sacristy, since there is not a room in the house big enough to take 30 to 40 children. I have given Father Kelly to understand that he ought to start making arrangements for the building of the parish schoolroom, but how can we get him to make a start?

This was a time of great hope for the sisters, but, as so often happens, things did not go quite according to plan, and in her letter of the 21 August, Sister St Thomas tells the superior-general that on account of the absence of the English sister (Sister François) the repairs had not yet been completed. "This is creating a problem because we have to vacate our present house before September." Another cause of disappointment: the sister sent to replace Sister François (who had been sent to study in Aberystwyth) did not seem nearly as fluent in English. By September 1904, her letter to the superior-general brought the news that

> We have moved house and are now living at 49 Guyther Street; here at least we have room to turn round. Why ever did we not come here at the start?

There are no letters extant for the months of October to December 1904. This is unusual in the history of the foundation, since the superior of each convent wrote very frequently to the superior-general. However, as we learn from a later letter, Sister St Thomas' health was giving cause for concern. Problems began to surface in what they hoped would be a time of growth for the community. The first letter for 1905, dated 1 January 1905, seems to indicate that Sister St Thomas had begged, though in vain, for a sister who would be capable of replacing Sister François in the little convent school.

> I am very upset that you are unable to give us another *Soeur Anglaise* to teach in our little class; it began so well and now will fall below standard.

Together with this letter, Sister St Thomas sends the accounts for the community's first year: Expenses: £102. 4.10 (£5,300 in present currency).

Receipts: £122.18.6 (£6,400). After some three months silence, she wrote again on 17 April 1905, explaining that she had been ill for over five weeks;

> My sisters cared for me devotedly and, had my recovery depended solely on them, I would have been better long before this. In their name, and in my own, I ask you to accept our warmest and most respectful wishes for your feast day (the feast of St George) next week.

In May of that year, Mère St Georges was re-elected as superior-general for a third triennium and on May 15 Sister St Thomas wrote to offer her the "Humbles hommages de filiale submission et de profond respect" of the community at Pembroke Dock, and she continues:

> My health is much improved so, while I thank you for your kind authorisation to take things easy, I shall not now need to do so. At present we have 15 pupils in our little class but it remains a nightmare to me, the cause: the ability of the young sister in charge of it is below standard.

To judge from the following letter, dated 19 June, it would appear that Sister St Thomas was about to go to France for treatment .She writes:

> I thank you for the permission to do this. I hope that French medical science will find a cure for the ills from which I suffer. I can come via Paris without making too great an inroad into our funds.

During her time in France, over the summer, Sister St Thomas must have discussed her problems with the superior-general, and perhaps it was then that she was told that she could look for more accommodation. In the letter she wrote on 1 December, we read

> As you advised, we have just rented another house at one minute's walk away from ours. We are going to transfer the little class there and use it for art lessons also. But how are we to find the money to pay two rents and to furnish the place? It is rumoured that the dock is going to be closed; this will spell ruin for Pembroke Dock.

The letter which Sister St Thomas wrote on Christmas Eve was a more cheerful and positive one:

> Thank you for your generous donation with which I shall be able to furnish the second house and pay for the repairs that are needed, after having 20 children in it... The Christmas party was a great success; children and parents alike were delighted with it. Sister Jeanne has gone to Carmarthen again for more help with her art lessons. Sister Mary Patrick and Sister Marie Augusta have gone to Tenby for the Midnight Mass. Next week, a young woman of 22 that Sister Marie Augusta has been instructing is going to be baptised and make her first Holy Communion. You will be pleased to know that when he examined the

108 children that we have had for catechism lessons, Father Kelly seemed quite satisfied. I must say that the sisters put all their heart and soul into the lessons, so as to make up for their deficiency in English.

The year 1906 marked the beginning of the increasingly strained relationship between Sister St Thomas and Father Kelly, which would eventually result in the withdrawal of the sisters from Pembroke Dock. Very likely, her inadequate grasp of the English language contributed to the misunderstandings which led to recriminations on both sides. The first mention of this comes in a letter Sister St Thomas wrote to the superior-general on 8 May, in which she complains that Father Kelly wanted the sisters to move into his house (was this the one he moved into when he vacated the one in Meyrick Street to make room for the sisters?) and was showing his displeasure at her refusal to consider this. She ended this letter with a plea for the general bursar to come as soon as possible as "we do need to see her." At the time that the sisters were involved in their move, Father Kelly was probably progressing with plans for his new parish school.

The news of these strained relationships obviously came to the ears of the bishop, for when she wrote again on 27 May, Sister St Thomas reports on the appointment she had just had with the bishop, Mgr Mostyn:

> His lordship listened with kindness to what I had to say. I told him about Father Kelly's attitude towards us and of his intention to invite other religious to take charge of his school and to live in his house. In reply, the bishop said that Father Kelly had written to him explaining why he found it necessary to call upon other religious. I can see that the bishop is reluctant to intervene for fear of making things worse. He says he will come to Pembroke in the autumn and meet with Father Kelly at our convent.

Things were not going very smoothly for Father Kelly either; from what Sister St Thomas wrote to the superior-general on 21 July, it would appear that he was finding it difficult to obtain teachers for his proposed school and that the likelihood of obtaining government funding for it was remote.

> So he has proposed that in the meanwhile the building be used for the evening catechism lessons and for our private class, provided we take his house. I replied that I would have to ask your authorisation to do this…

Three days later:

> Father has not mentioned the other religious again since the visit of the Assistant General from France. He met with the bishop recently and must have settled the matter of his school… Our parish covers a vast

area and some families live so far away from the church that the children never come to it. To remedy this state of affairs we have begun giving catechism lessons in the town itself. While Sister Anais is away in France, I go there every Sunday, accompanied by our little maid, an hour's walk along difficult roads. It is a difficult apostolate. Please pray that when school re-opens [the sisters' private school], we shall have some new pupils; we have only 13 at present.

Sister Ste Anais, who had been the senior member of the community since the beginning, did not return to it after her holiday in France. She had been given a transfer to Olney in Buckinghamshire. Sister St Thomas wrote to the superior-general:

> The departure of Sister Ste Anais pains me deeply. And I should be grateful if you yourself would break the news of it to Father Kelly. Yesterday he told me that the Catholic school would be blessed on 19 August and be opened on 1 September. So please send us, as soon as possible, a sister who speaks English, to take this class. We are still having problems with Father Kelly.

These problems become more evident in her subsequent letters. Her next letter of 15 August read:

> I had been writing to you when, in church this evening, Father Kelly handed me a paper to sign: This agreement he told me has been drawn up on the instructions of the bishop. I am sending you a copy of it, herewith, and beg you to let me know by telegram whether or not I should sign it. Father is going away on Monday for three months and he wants the matter settled before he leaves. The conditions are not ideal. But we are prepared to accept them because there is so much good to be done here.

This document that she was meant to sign was undoubtedly a written undertaking to rent the house that Father Kelly had vacated on his return to the presbytery when the sisters vacated it and moved to Guyther Street.

In the interval between the previous letter and the next one, two new sisters had been sent to join the community: Sister Anne de Gonzague Fauchet and Sister Renée du Sacré Coeur Marc, and on the 5 September, Sister St Thomas wrote thanking the superior-general for these two companions she was good enough to send to Pembroke Dock. In this letter, she gives news of the private school. At that time, there were twenty three pupils in the school, and there were sixteen students. She spoke again of the possibility of the dock closing, and what it would mean for the town. She adds:

Although we have very little paid work, our field of apostolate is vast: 3 of us teach the catechism every evening to 50 children of all ages, and then there is the Sunday school in town for which I have responsibility; add to that our visits to the poor and the care of the church, and you have our time-table. Father Kelly has gone away for three months, so no Mass, except on Sundays.

There was no cheerful or encouraging note in Sister St Thomas' next letter in which she sounds really woe-begone. In her letter dated 22 November 1906, she writes:

> Everywhere the sisters are preparing in fervent prayer for our feast on 8 December. Here we have been without a priest since 25 August. He did come back for a three-week period but has gone away again. I recommend myself and my companions to your prayer; never before have we experienced the feeling of being exiles...It will not surprise you to learn that our funds have run out, and so, with a heavy heart, I am obliged to have recourse to your charity in order to be able to pay the rent at the end of the year.

The superior-general passed on this request to the general bursar, and on 17 December Sister St Thomas acknowledges receipt of the money by registered post. She writes:

> It grieves and humiliates me to be obliged to have recourse to your generosity. As I told you in my last letter, we have been without a pastor for months; unable to put up with this situation any longer, our Catholic people demanded a priest, and since the 1 December, a Benedictine priest has served us, (probably one of the exiled monks from Kerbénéat). We continue with our catechetical work and visits to the poor; these latter are especially appreciated. The sisters' health is good; peace and charity reign among us.

The first letter written in 1907 is dated 18 February. Its main point of interest concerns the parish school. She was able to report that Father Kelly was in the process of obtaining approval for his school which was due to open in September of that year, with Sister Anne de Gonzague as an assistant teacher. The head teacher had not as yet been appointed. Before she wrote again, there was a canonical visitation of the community, and her next letter refers to this. When Sister St Thomas wrote to the superior-general on 4 March, she told her that the difficulties had not been resolved, even with the canonical visit. She then asked if they could take the house Father wanted them to have, in order to make life easier for them. She ended her letter:

Given our present situation, I was not really able to enjoy the stay of our dear visitors (the general councillor and general bursar), however, the appreciation of our little community which they expressed was very comforting. They said that they were satisfied with everything, a precious testimony which did us a great deal of good.

In her next letter, which was written only a week later, Sister St Thomas writes with a gleam of hope for the future. She says:

In reply to your letter, I would be inclined to say that Father Kelly is reasonably hopeful about his school. At present it is the local authority, which is proving the greatest obstacle to the realisation of his plans. But I would hesitate to affirm that the school would be operational by next September.

Then she goes on to describe her own daily routine:

My life is a vagabond one, always out and about; the sisters have as much as they can do, so are never able to save me from having to go out on an errand or a visit. You will be pleased to know that Father Kelly seems to be a bit better disposed towards us. He came to wish us a happy feast day and sent us a superb cake.

The communities in Wales always followed with interest the happening in France and the difficulties the sisters there were experiencing as a result of the enforcement of the anti-clerical educational legislation. Sister St Thomas' next letter, dated 26 December 1907, refers to this concern. She begins:

The sisters at St Mary's offer you their good wishes for the New Year. We have read in the *Semaine Religieuse* about the recent sentencing of yourself and many of our sisters in Brittany. To us also the good Lord sends his cross to bear. I'll write to you at the end of January about these troubles.

There is no trace of this letter that Sister St Thomas announced; so either she never actually wrote it, or it has not been preserved. When she wrote on 24 February, she addressed her letter to the whole general council of the congregation. She gave them an account of the heated argument she had with the parish priest and went on to ask whether it had been decided to give her a transfer to another community.

Her next letter on 26 February 1908 continues about the trouble with the parish priest. She writes:

Father Kelly called to see me; he is willing to make peace, on two conditions; that we take his house as from next June for a rent of £47.00 (£2,300 today) per annum; that he is given an assurance that we shall not speak about this dispute to any of the Catholics. As regards the first condition, I replied that I would have to consult my superiors in Saint Brieuc; to the second, I gave a categorical refusal.

Four days later, she wrote to the superior-general:

> As I informed you yesterday by telegram, we went to look at the house in question (she gives details of it). As you see, Father Kelly seems to want to backtrack a bit. I should like to know what the bishop thinks. I suppose that Father Kelly has written to him about me, as he has done to you. Please be so good as to provide me with a solution to this problem this week so that we may know where we stand.

When she wrote again on 9 March, she mentions a telegram that the superior-general had sent telling her to reject Father Kelly's demands. Her reaction was:

> It frightens me. We simply cannot continue to live here, if we don't take Father Kelly's house. Please send another telegram. I'll wait until I have received it before telling Father Kelly that we will not take his house.

At the elections of the 3 May 1908, for a new superior-general, Sister Marie Alvarez was elected to succeed Mère St Georges. In Sister St Thomas' first letter to her, dated 3 June, there is the first mention of the closure of the foundation:

> There is nothing new to report. Mgr Mostyn (the bishop) is no doubt, awaiting the result of the consultation about Father Kelly's school before writing to you. However well disposed he may be towards us, there is nothing he can do for us, and nothing for us to do here. Were we to leave now, our departure would be more honourable than it would be in a few months' time.

From now on, events moved with great rapidity; this was precipitated by the knowledge that they would not gain teaching posts in the new Catholic school there. On 11 June, Sister St Thomas wrote again:

> I forgot to mention that the lease for our house is due to expire on 20 June, and if we were going to leave, we would need to notify our landlady. What kept us going at Pembroke Dock was the hope of having a Catholic school here. There may or may not be one but, if Father Kelly succeeds, in establishing a school, it will not be for us. Mgr Mostyn's slowness to act confirms my opinion of him, he is trying to run with the hare and hunt with the hounds. Possibly you would render him great service in taking the initiative and deciding [to withdraw the sisters from Pembroke Dock]. Our pastor will be going to Palestine at the beginning of August; I should like our departure to be effected while he is away.

During the six to seven week interval between this letter and the next one, which was the last to be written from Pembroke Dock, Sister St Thomas must have been notified that the sisters were to leave and been given the instructions for the arrangements relating to their departure. In her final letter addressed to the superior-general dated 26 July, 1908, she wrote:

> Tomorrow the rest of the furniture will be sent off and we ourselves, will be leaving on Wednesday morning: Sister Marie Augusta and Sister Marie Desirée for Caernarfon, while Sister Mary Patrick, her sister, Sister Renée, and myself will leave for Plymouth and Brest. Sister Jeanne de Ste Angèle and Sister Anne de Gonzague will leave for the community at High Wycombe in Hertfordshire and Sister Rodolphe Marie for the community in Llanrwst. Sister Patrick O'Regan will leave for the USA. In conformity with the instructions on the card received from the general bursar, I shall leave my trunk at Carmarthen. [Sister St Thomas was to return to Wales as superior of the community in Pontypool from 1908 to 1921]. Two more days and St Mary's, Pembroke Dock, will belong to history.

From the 8 January 1904 till the 28 July 1908, St Mary's Convent, Pembroke Dock, had a total of ten sisters who worked there, and four of them lived there during the whole life of the community.

The foundation of St Mary's Convent, Pembroke Dock, seemed so promising at the beginning, in so many ways. The parish priest wanted the sisters to settle there; the people welcomed them; there were prospects for a parish school, where the sisters could teach. Their attempt at running a private school was not without some success, and there was a comparatively large Catholic population there, compared with that at Usk, Llanrwst, and some of the other areas where foundations were made. The exact nature of the difficulty with Father Kelly about a house is not stated in the correspondence. When Father Kelly vacated his presbytery for the sisters to live there when they arrived at Pembroke Dock, in January 1904, he probably rented another house perhaps for a number of years. Yet within nine months of their arrival there, the sisters had moved in to 49 Guyther Street, and Father Kelly was left with the lease of the house he had rented. Although we shall never know the true facts of this case, it is certain that the souring of relationships with the parish priest over the issue of his house, which they would not take, led in the end to the decision, that for the welfare of all concerned, it was best to withdraw the sisters from Pembroke Dock.

St Joseph's Convent, Pwllheli 1904–1920

THE FOUNDATION made at Pwllheli, in April 1904, was totally different in conception and realisation from all the others foundations of the Daughters of the Holy Spirit established in Wales. It owed its existence to Sister St Félicien Nicolas, herself an eighty-eight-year-old Daughter of the Holy Spirit. She seemed to have a special relationship with Father Julien Tanter, one of the priests who served in the parish there. She called him her "adopted son." The first mention of the possibility of a foundation at Pwllheli is gleaned from a letter written by Sister St Félicien to Father Tanter in January 1904. She writes:

> I have a request to make of you; having firmly made up my mind to buy a house in Wales; I see that there is no good to be done in France. So I thought I would ask you if you could find a suitable house for sale in Pwllheli. When you have found one, please let me know immediately and also name the price asked for it. I shall be so happy to provide for a foundation in Wales, and it is my wish to be near you, my dear Julien. Your 'second mother' as you call me, will be happy to end her days near her adopted son, and I think that the Daughters of the Holy Spirit will be able to teach the little Welsh children to know and love the good Lord.

Writing again to Father Julien on 27 February, Sister St Félicien apologised for all the trouble she was causing him. She blamed the sale of a house, which he had hoped to buy and which was bought by someone else, on the work of the devil. She asked him to rent another house for the sisters as soon as possible, and said that she wanted to come and conclude affairs at Pwllheli, before her life ended. She also said that it was of her own free will that she undertook it, the superior-general was leaving all the negotiations to her. The superior-general and her council were not so happy, however, with the idea of Sister St Félicien, who was an invalid, wishing to travel in person to Wales to undertake this mission. Her determination was such, however, that she persisted: "Dead or alive, I must go."

Sister St Félicien's determination and resolve was seen, eventually, by her superiors as an indication of the will of God, and when the doctors were consulted, they agreed to her undertaking the journey. So, on 23 March 1904, having recommended themselves to the protection of St Joseph, Sister St Félicien and the two experienced sisters, Sister St Philibert Le Hideux and Sister Marie de St Martin Hamayon appointed to look after her, set out on their long journey. They were accompanied by Jean Louis, one of the employees at the mother house in Saint Brieuc; he was to help with the transport of Sister St Félicien and her wheelchair. They travelled by train from Saint Brieuc to Paris, where the Sisters at Crillon gave them hospitality. The next day they took the train for Boulogne. After a rough three-hour crossing during which all suffered seasickness, except Sister St Félicien (who, as a native of Plouguerneau, must have been a good sailor) they arrived at Folkestone. From there they took a train bound for London where Father Julien met them. Then, they went by train to North Wales via Chester, where Sister Louis de St Yves was waiting to greet them and after another lap of the journey, to welcome them to the community at Llanrwst.

No house had as yet been found for them at Pwllheli, so they stayed at Llanrwst for about three weeks. Writing from there on 25 March, Sister St Philibert, who was to take responsibility for the new foundation, tells the superior-general:

> On Monday, Father Le Jeune will go with Father Tanter to Pwllheli to find a house for us. The Fathers have told us to leave it to them and not concern ourselves with it. So, this evening after Holy Communion, I placed everything in the hands of St Joseph, certain that this great saint will not let his month (the month of March) draw to a close without having found shelter for us.

A week later, Sister St Philibert who was able to report that there was another house which they hoped to buy, wrote:

> It is today or tomorrow that the house in which we are interested is going to be sold. Father Le Jeune has been to view it. According to him and Father Tanter, the house is spacious and in very good condition; it has outbuildings, a garden and fields, all enclosed. Let us hope that St Joseph will not let this house escape us.

The house they proposed to buy had been leased till December 1905, so if it were bought for the sisters they would still have to move into rented accommodation until the lease expired, unless other arrangements could be made with the sitting tenant. The tenant, himself, had wanted to buy the house at all costs, but there was a disagreement between him and the landlord, with the result that the landlord chose to sell it to the sisters. The fact that subsequently they were not able to move into it until December 1905, eighteen months after they bought it, was a cause of great suffering and inconvenience. Worst of all, it would mean that Sister St Félicien, who paid for it from her own patrimony, would never live in it.

The sisters moved into rented accommodation at South Beach. As Sister St Félicien was not very well, she asked for her niece, Sister Marie Félicien

Le Mao, to come from the Carmarthen community to help to look after her, and this request was granted. From their rented accommodation at South Beach, Sister St Philibert wrote to the superior-general, on 17 April:

> Here we are in Pwllheli; the house we have rented is quite near the sea and the view from it is superb. The contract for the house we have bought has not yet been signed because the owner is in London undergoing surgery. St Joseph keeps us waiting but it is a really good house that they have found for us. Father Tanter and Father Méreour are most kind to us. They have asked us to start giving catechism lessons in our small chapel. We have also been asked to see to the decorating of the little church. Caring for Sister St Félicien occupies two of us for the greater part of the morning, so we are going to need help. As for myself, my rheumatism has been so bad these past four weeks that I have aged and have lost as much weight as if I had been seriously ill.

The contract for the new house, called Plastirion, was duly signed. The house which the sisters rented was too far away from the church and when they rented it, the landlord made it a condition of tenancy that the sisters would not start a school there. This was a great disappointment, as they had hopes, as always when they started a foundation, of opening a school. Their search for other rented accommodation subsequently proved fruitless, so they were obliged to stay at South Beach. The landlord did agree to the sisters giving private lessons in their rented accommodation, and a few little girls had started private lessons with them. The parish was considered to be "one of the poorest in the world," in the opinion of Father Méreour.

> There is nothing more wretched than the poor little church building of corrugated iron, and yet this is where we are drawn to God. The two of us together (Sister Marie Félicien and Sister St Philibert) are scarcely able to lift Sister St Félicien who is growing so heavy now. The Fathers have found us a little maid; she is 14 years old, the eldest of 9 children. She seems intelligent, and is getting quite used to the sisters. As regards our timetable, from now on, we are taking it in turns to go to Mass because we cannot leave Sister St Félicien alone for too long. I am hoping that you will soon be able to send someone to help us. It is not without reason that I say this, and I know that if you could do so, you would send someone immediately. In the meantime, God will provide.

The superior-general was not long in sending reinforcement to the tiny community at Pwllheli. On 12 April, Sister St Philibert wrote to thank her for having sent Sister St Vincent de Paul Meheut:

> I want to write and thank you straightway for having sent us another Sister. She was most welcome, I can assure you, for we are growing

> tired. The doctor has just left, saying that Sister St Félicien, short of any unforeseen circumstances, will last a long while yet. Next week, we shall try giving catechism lessons to the children.

Sister Félicien, herself, had a great love of children.

As the months went by, the main problem for the sisters was the state of health of Sister St Félicien. On 8 June, Sister St Philibert wrote to the superior-general:

> For the past few days, Sister St Félicien has not been at all well; she seems to be in a lot more pain. Even so, on Saturday, we kept the 60th anniversary of her Final Profession.

Writing two days later, she thanked the superior-general for parcels which were sent to Pwllheli.

> We have just received the promised parcels. A thousand thanks from us and from the Fathers. The white vestment will be worn on Sunday, the Feast of the Sacred Heart, and Mass on that day will be offered for you and for the needs of the Congregation. Sister St Vincent de Paul and Sister Marie Félicien have started to learn Welsh. Father Tanter is giving them lessons. P.S. Since I wrote my letter, Sister St Félicien has taken a turn for the worse. She is still fully conscious and very edifying in her patient endurance. Father Tanter, whom she holds so dear, kept watch with us last night, and Father Méreour, another night. The sisters are admirable in their care of her.

Fourteen days later, on 21 June, Sister St Philibert wrote again, this time to announce the death of Sister St Félicien. She said:

> Sister St Félicien has just breathed her last, after three days' agony. What a peaceful death she had! It is her burial that is going to cause us difficulties; we are going to have to go miles to obtain the authorisation for it. I shall write to you again after the funeral. This is a sad time that we have to live through. I am so tired that I fear you may not be able to read my writing.

The account of the death and burial of this valiant sister was reported in an article in *La Colombe*, which was taken from the letter written on 24 June. The death and funeral of the first Daughter of the Holy Spirit to die in Wales was described in detail, and it illustrates the state of ecumenism, or lack of it in Wales, at this time.

> Sister St Félicien had a beautiful death. How she edified us during her cruel sufferings! What patience! What resignation! What gratitude for the services rendered to her! With what humility she asked our forgiveness! To this I replied that what we had done for her was no more than our duty, and that we asked her forgiveness for any failure

to treat her, as we should. During the two nights that she was laid out, the two priests kept watch with us. But for their presence we were alone, all alone, in a foreign country where we were scarcely known. Sister St Louis came from Llanrwst for the funeral; we were so glad that she did. Sister St Félicien's was the first Catholic funeral to take place in Pwllheli for centuries, knowing this, made us all the more apprehensive. Yet all went well, thank God. Father Tanter accompanied the body from the house to the church, walking behind the hearse, dressed as a clergyman. We walked behind him together with a few Catholics from the Mission. In the church, an impoverished catafalque, made of packing cases, draped with curtains and surrounded with greenery, looked quite pleasing. Father Méreour sang the Mass; the chants with musical accompaniment were beautifully sung. Father Jones from Caernarfon and the priest from Trémadec insisted on being present. There was not enough room in the church for all the onlookers who came through curiosity.

From the church to the cemetery, a distance of about half a mile, the route was lined with people. But there was not a discordant note, the men removed their hats; one could sense that people were quite moved by what was taking place. More than 200 children followed us from the church to the cemetery; they even climbed the hill, which leads to it (and it is steeper than the one up to *Bon Repos* in Brittany). As we climbed the hill, I said to myself "only the poor and the little children accompany her to her last resting place." These, it must be said, were the ones who were constantly in her thoughts. How many times did she not say: 'Do not forget the poor; clothe the children of the poor. It is for them that I came here.' She found her happiness in having these dear children come to her bedside where she would give them sweets and a few pennies. How these children wept for her!

Lest there might be disturbances as the funeral cortège made its way to the cemetery gates, the police had officers posted at our front door, at the door of the church and at the cemetery gates. (One wonders what kind of disturbance they expected!) But everything went smoothly and there was no trouble of any kind. When the cortège reached the cemetery gates, the police allowed only the Catholics to enter. I was quite upset on entering the cemetery. What a sad place it looked! Not a cross anywhere, only long grass that needed cutting. The coldness of the cemetery added to our grief, and as we left, our tears fell fast. You can have no idea how attached we were to Sister St Félicien. She would never accept anything unless I told her to do so, because she was anxious to set a good example for the sisters. All 3 of us have gained from being her companions. Her memory will always remain with the little community over which she will I hope keep watch from heaven.

Following Sister St Félicien's death, both priests strongly urged the superior-general to allow Sister St Philibert to remain in charge at Pwllheli; Father Méreour when calling on her in Britiany, and Father Tanter by letter. The latter urged sister's retention as "for the good of our mission and of the new foundation." He pointed out that the transitory state of affairs would be very difficult for a new superior unacquainted with what had been done so far, that shortly the community would take possession of their home, that the young sisters would learn from Sister St Philibert the different kinds of needlework necessary as a source of income, and that their superior's health was not really up to the long journey. He added that if Sister St Philibert were recalled to France, he would accept that decision as 'a manifestation of God's will, but that it would pain us deeply as we are very fond of her.'

Sister St Philibert did in fact remain at Pwllheli for another four years, of which there is some trace in the nineteen letters that she wrote during that time. In the first of these, dated July 1904, she queries why there had been no word from the mother house since Sister St Félicien's death. The silence may have been due to the deliberations that were taking place over the future of Sister St Philibert herself. "Forgive me", she writes

> if I have given you any grounds for complaint. Father Tanter tells me that you have promised that I would remain for some time at Pwllheli. For this I thank you for, as I have told you, I experience quite a special attachment to this poor and truly mission country. Things are not easy here however. We have no works apart from the 18 little girls who come to the catechism class and to learn how to sew. These children are very nice, but so ignorant of the Catholic faith. It is quite heartbreaking. I have bought a quantity of wool and crochet cotton so that we can begin making articles, which we hope to sell to some shops in Liverpool.

The next letter dated 5 September was written after the summer holidays, and in it she returns to the question of the house they have purchased. Mr Mitchell, the tenant, persisted in staying in it till the expiry of his lease, which was December 1905. " For our part," she writes,

> We go on addressing our fervent and continual prayers to St Joseph. I am still waiting for news about Sister St Félicien's inheritance, of which I hear nothing except what comes in letters by the Fathers, saying that the family are contesting the will. This matter, we now entrust to St Joseph.

The sisters hoped that Mr Mitchell, the tenant who occupied the house the sisters had bought, might have vacated the house by September, since the tenancy of the house they were renting would expire in September. To this end, she and Father Méreour visited Mr Mitchell with their request, but without success. The people of Pwllheli by now had begun to recognise the presence of the sisters. At first they were suspicious, but soon they were proud to have the sisters in their town. Church attendance was very poor in the Pwllheli mission. For example, on Sundays, the congregation, including adults and children, was only about thirty. Yet the two priests were apparently optimistic hoping that the seeds they were sowing would later reap a rich harvest, in what they called the "arid soil."

When she wrote to the superior-general on 8 November, Sister St Philibert had received a short visit from Mère Marie Angélina, the general bursar, and began her letter with thanks for the chocolates, which the superior-general sent to her. She writes:

> While she was with us in Pwllheli, she told me that I was to send Sister St Vincent de Paul to Aberystwyth for studies. The latter seems pleased at the prospect, provided that she is allowed to return to Pwllheli afterwards. On the strength of what Mère Marie Angélina has said I was able to reassure Sister St Vincent that she would return.

The greatest concern during the months after Sister St Félicien's death was the delay in taking possesson of Plastirion, the house they had bought, and because of this delay, they asked the landlady of their rented property if she would consent to them starting a small class in the house which they had rented. She said that she would give them her reply in a few days. If she consented to this, they would have their children as soon as they opened their doors. There were only five Catholic families in the parish but as there were eight or nine children in each that meant that they would have a considerable number of pupils.

From a reference in the letter which Sister St Philibert wrote three weeks later, on 28 November, it would appear that the landlady did finally consent to the sisters opening a class for Catholic children in their house, because she tells the superior-general:

> ...we are going to need a Sister to take the class until Sister St Vincent has passed her exam. The needlework class is going quite well. This morning we were asked to make 4 overalls by Wednesday. It is unfortunate that we are not very good at cutting out. How dearly I should like to be able to gather into a workshop all the poor girls who are so abandoned, but for that we would need to have a sister who is more experienced in dressmaking. [This was a dream to be realized later, by others, in the foundation at Abergavenny.] Your retreat is hardly over and here I am trying your patience with all my requests, but to whom can one have recourse, if not to one's mother? And one bit of

good news: our tenants have paid the 6 months rent they owed us. We have heartily thanked St Joseph for this, since heaven certainly had a lot to do with it.

When the class for the Catholic children had been opened, there were only two sisters in the community, and Father Méreour wrote to the superior-general on 3 December asking for a sister to teach this class. Two little girls, aged 7 and 9 from a well-to-do family, the Smalleys, attended the small class. There was also a little boarder whose father wanted her to stay with the sisters at any cost; while Father Tanter found another boarder who was 12 years old and came from Penmaenmawr. (These three pupils became the nucleus of their private school.) Two more ladies from Pwllheli came to ask for private lessons in music and art. Sister St Philibert pleaded for more sisters to help. She said:

> Having waited all these months to be asked for private tuition, it is hard to refuse it now. The two of us [Sister Marie Félicien and herself] are doing all we can but, even with the best will in the world, we cannot give what we have not got. Believe me, it is sheer necessity that compels me to trouble you with these requests.

The ongoing conflict with the tenants at Plastirion ended in Sister St Philibert sending in the bailiffs to remove them, but even this did not, at first, seem to make any difference. In her next letter written at the beginning of December 1905, she begins with good news about Plastirion.

> May God be praised for it! We have won our case: our tenants have been sentenced to leave the house on 31 December, and to pay the rent they still owe. They will also have to pay our costs…the only expenses we have incurred are the solicitor's fees.

This was not the end of their troubles: the tenant at Plastirion, not having found another place to live, had left all the furniture there, and the state of the house was deplorable. Immediately, they got workers in to do the most urgent repairs, and workmen also began digging the foundations for the mission school. This was to be a corrugated iron building to serve as a classroom, and Sister St Philibert intended, as a matter of courtesy, to write to the owner of the site to get his consent in writing.

Other sisters were sent to this foundation in due course, and in her next letter to the superior-general, she also gives information about the work of each sister. Sister Julie de Jésus was going to take the class of boarders and fee-paying pupils, Sister Antoine de Padoue the boys' class of the parish school, and Sister Marie Félicien the girls' class. She adds: "If you knew how we are longing to be able to gather in all those dear children. I need a sister to teach music and another for the housework."

As a response to these needs, Sister St Antoine Minoc was sent to Pwllheli in February 1905, and in May Sister St Vincent de Paul was recalled from Aberystwyth. Like all the foundations in Wales, the transfer of sisters from one convent to another often caused problems. While Sister St Philibert was delighted to welcome Sister St Antoine and the return of Sister St Vincent from her studies in Aberystwyth, a letter received on 5 May brought her news of the transfer of Sister Marie Félicien to the Carmarthen community, from where she had come to help care for her aunt, Sister St Félicien. Sister St Philibert lamented her departure since she was the only one who could speak Welsh, and the children of the poor only spoke Welsh.

This was a period of financial difficulties, and the superior was obliged to write to the general bursar for financial aid. She needed money to pay for the building which was nearing completion. At the time, the sisters were also meeting the costs of the education of forty poor children. She hoped that, with an increasing number of fee-paying pupils, she would not be obliged to borrow again the following year. She asked once again for more sisters, especially one for the school and another for housework. As superior of the community she said that her role was the oversight of all that went on both inside and outside the community. With only 3000 francs to pay for the building, and for their livelihood, times were hard. At this time too the religious prejudice that the sisters experienced in Llanrwst was once again going to make life more difficult for them. The Calvinistic Methodists and Baptists were furious when they learned that the sisters had opened a school, and several of them tried to stop the children from coming. This happened just at the time when the number of fee-paying pupils was on the increase.

The letter dated 3 March also gives a few items of news on the Mission, and of the results of their ministry in Pwllheli. Sister St Philibert spoke of the birth of a baby girl in the parish; of the reception into the church of a lady who had several children whom she promised to send to the sisters' school, and of a gentleman who was 'seeking his way', presumably he was thinking of joining the Catholic Church. Another young man of twenty four was under instruction, and one of the teachers from the High School had gone to London for her reception into the Catholic Church. A great spirit of unity existed among the sisters who were very zealous for the interest of the Mission. She also mentions the first funeral that the sisters attended since the funeral of Sister St Félicien; this time it was the funeral of a three year old child, and the sisters were very sad for the parents. She promised to get Sister Julie to write a letter to the sick sisters in the infirmary at the mother house, to ask for their prayers, and to keep them in touch with the work of their sisters overseas.

The community now numbered six sisters: two new ones having been sent to join it during the summer: Sister Elie de Ste Anne Bouvet from Usk, and the newly professed Sister Antoine de St Yves Lageat, who replaced Sister Marie Félicien in the Mission school. Sister Elie's state of health soon became a source of anxiety to her superior who, on 13 November, wrote to the superior-general:

> Last Saturday I went to Aberystwyth with Sister Elie because I did not want her to see a doctor here; in these parts people flee from what they think is 'consumption.' The doctor in Aberystwyth re-assured me about her.

In this letter, she also gives news of the mission. The departure of pupils for one reason or another was always noted. There was a note of sadness when pupils left the schools, while a note of joy greeted the arrival of new pupils. Five of the pupils in St Antoine de Padoue's class had gone with their parents to live elsewhere, and that left only fourteen pupils in her class. The other class taken by Sister Antoine de St Yves had sixteen pupils, as six others who were present at the beginning of the term had left with their parents to seek their fortune elsewhere.

In each foundation, the sisters kept in touch with what was happening in their native Brittany, and the Pwllheli foundation was no exception to this. One of the priests in the parish passed on to the sisters *The Universe*, a national Catholic newspaper published weekly, and in this paper they were able to read of the happenings in France regarding the secularisation of Catholic education. In one of her letters to the superior-general, Sister St Philibert wrote: "The reports it [*The Universe*] carries of what is happening in our country is almost beyond belief." Sister St Philibert was a little more positive about their apostolate in Pwllheli as time went on.

> Slowly, our labours are beginning to bear fruit... It gladdens us so much to see persons responding to God's grace. One has to live in a country like this in order to know how it feels to witness the workings of God's grace. I would never have believed it possible to experience, in a foreign land, joy such as this.

In August 1908, Sister St Philibert returned to France for good, and died there three years later. After her departure from Pwllheli, Father Méreour wrote to Mére Marie Alvarez, the new superior-general, as follows:

> The memory of Sister St Philibert will always remain alive among us, and especially among the children of the poor whom she loved so well.

She did well while she was here and will be rewarded for it in Heaven, if not on earth. It cost her to leave her dear Mission in Pwllheli, but I am sure that she was wholly resigned to the will of the good Lord with whom she intercedes and will continue to intercede for us.

Sister Julie de Jésus succeeded Sister St Philibert. She was not a prolific letter-writer and her letters to the superior-general are relatively few, not more than a dozen. It is from a letter dated 17 August 1908, addressed by Father Méreour to the superior-general, that we learn of Sister Julie's appointment. He wrote:

> Reverend Mother, I write to thank you for the trust and honour that you have shown me in asking me to present dear Sister Julie de Jésus to her companions as their new superior. I could not have had a more pleasant task, and it was made all the easier as I knew how the Sisters felt about her. They welcomed her with open arms and I might add, without manifesting any great surprise. The only person to be affected by her appointment was herself. I am convinced that she will make a very good superior and will fully justify the trust you have placed in her. To assist her in her work, she may count on my total support for as long as I remain in Pwllheli.

The first letter that Sister Julie herself wrote is dated 5 October 1909, and was addressed to the new superior-general, Mère Marie Alvarez. It begins with a lament:

> Another cross has been added to the ones heaven has sent me over the past few months: our dear Sister Olivier Joseph has failed her exams, with marks which do not offer much hope for the future. Is there any point in her continuing her studies? I do not think there is much hope of her ever succeeding, and the exam fees are so costly... Thank you for your kind words and for the prayers you have offered for the repose of the soul of my dear grandmother. With regard to the deceased, it had not occurred to me before now to ask you about a custom that has been established here. Since the death of Sister St Félicien, not only is she named in all our prayers, but we also have a Mass said for her every month. I should like to have the sanction of obedience for this. My companions join me in sending their best and respectful wishes.

Some fifteen months seem to have elapsed before Sister Julie wrote again, at the beginning of January 1911, and from her letter it is obvious that she was beginning to have some problems. She mentioned her difficulty with the community accounts, and asked for further particulars about what was required. A few weeks later, she received a reply which was not exactly what she expected. It was to inform her that Sister Marie Félicien and herself were to be transferred to the USA. Dr Johnson of Carmarthen had wished to open "a home for girls who are feeble-minded" in Carmarthen. The doctor was anxious that this home should be run by Daughters of the Holy Spirit and, as a first step toward this, she asked that two of the sisters from Wales should be sent to an American institute for the feeble-minded, which was on the East Coast of America and was called Waverley. The idea was to receive the necessary training to open such an institution in Carmarthen, where Dr Johnson herself worked at the mental hospital. One can imagine the surprise of such a request, coming at such an unexpected time. Sister Julie's reply was: "What I have to offer here and now is my good will and my devotedness for the service of the poor creatures to whom Providence is sending me."

Sister Marie Félicien was surprised and upset to receive this news, as she dreaded leaving her elderly mother in France and going so far away. When she learned that she would be definitely returning to England, she then decided not to inform her mother about her transfer to America. Sister Julie de Jésus and Sister Marie Félicien set out for America from Liverpool on 2 May 1911.

Sister Julie was replaced as superior of Pwllheli by Sister St Anais who, after two years at Pembroke Dock, had been a member of the community at Olney, in Buckinghamshire. Of the letters she may have addressed to the superior-general only two are extant, the first written the day after her arrival at Pwllheli. The first reads:

> I arrived yesterday evening in the new house you have designated for me, and went to renew without delay my promise of loyal obedience to what you ask of me. It is not without regret that I left Olney and Sister Marie Dominique whose health has not been so good of late, and my dear companions with whom I have always lived on good terms. My regret is all the keener as I feel how incapable I am of fulfilling the responsible task you have entrusted to me... I will however do all I can. Sister Antoine and Sister Elie were waiting to meet me at the station. The welcome I received from them and the other sisters was truly religious and I was touched by it.

On the return from America, Sister Julie was first sent as superior to Newton Abbot where the Daughters of the Holy Spirit were taking the place of the Sisters of the Presentation of Mary. Before long, however, the relationship between herself and the parish priest, Father Barney, became so strained that in August 1914 she was given her transfer. Her return to France was envisaged, but the outbreak of the Great War 1914-1918 made the superior-general decide that the journey might prove too risky, and Sister Julie received her transfer for Pwllheli, where the arrival of Belgian refugees was creating fresh pastoral and social needs. There is no further reference to the house for feeble-minded girls to be run by the Daughters of the Holy Spirit, so we can assume that the training was beyond the liking and capability of the two sisters, or that the superior-general decided against it, since it was not part of the founding charism of the congregation.

In the first of the four letters, which Sister Julie addressed to the superior-general between September and December 1914, she submits the arrangements she wanted to make to provide for the increase in numbers of children seeking admission to the two schools. She said that at that time, she had no sister to take the class of fee-paying pupils and that she could not take it herself. She asked whether Sister Marie Apolline McGlynne (newly arrived in Pwllheli, and meant for the Mission School), could take this class. Her request was granted, and she then tried to find someone to help. She asked for Sister Marie de Ste Barbe (still a postulant) who was recovering from an operation to come and help until there could be a more permanent arrangement. Sister Marie de Ste Barbe duly arrived in Pwllheli and was able to assist her sister, Sister Marie Apolline, as recommended by Sister Julie. On account of an epidemic, which was raging in Pwllheli at this time, all the schools had been closed. There were eight pupils in the fee-paying class, two of whom were boarders. The fees in the private school were £22 (£1,000 now) per annum. Since it was war-time, Pwllheli had its share of refugees, and sixty Belgian refugees arrived in the town.

As was the practice in all the foundations in Wales, each community contributed in some way to the welfare of those who fled the war-torn areas of Europe; many sought refuge in Wales. Among the Belgian refugees, the sisters had given hospitality to two boys and two girls. Sister Julie took responsibility for their education, and as she says in one of her letters:

> I taught them a lot of French and a lot of English, and of course their catechism and their prayers. It goes without saying that I insisted on their attendance at Sunday Mass. The parents seem to have taken this as applying to themselves as well; this Sunday 11 out of 17 Belgians were in church for the first time since their arrival here. We continue to pray for peace, in these troubled times, and think and pray for our own dear land suffering thr ravages of war.

Any letters that Sister Julie may have written during 1915 are no longer extant. But from the correspondence between the superior-general and Mother Marie Dominique, the provincial in charge of the communities of Wales and England, we learn about the sisters who were sent to help in the schools at Pwllheli. On 11 August 1915, the superior-general wrote to Mother Marie Dominique about a young sister who was being sent to

Pwllheli to help, either Sister Marie Apolline or Sister Marie de Ste Barbe. The superior-general wrote:

> I have written to Sister Julie de Jésus, informing her of the arrival of her new companion and specifying that she is to help in school. Thus the two teachers will have more time to give to their studies.

Ten days later, she wrote again to Mother Marie Dominique:

> We are giving to Pwllheli a musician and she is also capable of taking a class. We hope to be able to send another Sister who will help with the domestic work. So you see that with the help and direction from Sister Marie du Christ, the three teachers at Pwllheli should be able to give time to their studies.

On 14 February 1916, Sister Julie de Jésus wrote to the superior-general:

> I write to thank you for your kind letter and to make good the omissions you pointed out in my last letter. These were due not to forgetfulness, but to my reluctance to tell you about our small troubles, which would augment your regret at being unable to give us the help we need.

From now on, there seems to have been some problems in the community at Pwllheli, the exact nature of which have not been recorded, or at least have not been preserved. There are some hints of difficulty in this letter. She writes: "To deal with your questions in the order that you put them. I can tell you that my companions enjoy good health, thank God." She then goes on to write about the studies of the sisters. Sister Marie du Christ who was in charge of studies was obviously pressing Sister Julie to spare no expense. She writes:

> With regard to studies, I wrote as you advised to Sister Marie du Christ and she is of the opinion that our students should be given time to familiarise themselves with the set books before embarking on a correspondence course. In this connection, do you think that one such course would be enough for the two of them since they are both studying for the same exam?

Sister Julie then goes on to outline her own heavy timetable as follows:

> This term I have not two but eleven pupils for music lessons; you can imagine how little time that leaves me. This is my timetable on a typical working day: after breakfast I go to the kitchen where I remain until lunch time because I can give the maid only the most basic tasks to do, and even for those, I have to supervise her. At 2 pm I give French lessons to those who are studying for the Junior and Senior exams. Then I have pupils for music lessons.

She ends on a note which would seem to suggest that there is much happening in the community at this time for she ends her letter: "There is much besides that I could tell you but I have not the time to do so."

The extant letters from Pwllheli are fewer and fewer during the following years. Sixteen months elapsed between the writing of the letter just quoted and that of the following one. During this long interval, the superior-general, Mère St Georges, had died and been succeeded by Mère Marie Alvarez, to whom Sister Julie's letter, dated 25 June 1917 was addressed. She spoke of a number of difficulties. With increasing numbers of students to train for teaching, each community had been asked to contribute a sum of money to help with the training. Sister Julie queried why this sum could not have been taken from the money left by Sister St Félicien when she died. She gives an up-to-date account of the money that they had, and listed all the expenses they had to meet, including rates and taxes, fuel and travel expenses.

The next extant letter is dated 25 July 1919, and is addressed by Sister Julie to the superior-general. In fact this was to be the last year that the sisters would remain in Pwllheli. In the intervening two years since the last recorded letter, things had moved very quickly, because, from the opening paragraph of this letter, it seems obvious that negotiations had been going on about the future of the foundation which are no longer visible in the correspondence. The closure of the school had been decided. This sudden decision angered the parents of the pupils attending the private school, and they were going to demand a term's notice of the school closure. They did in fact keep the school open for a term, but had sent the notice of its closure three months before. The sad note in her letter referred to the information gleaned from the Director of Education and from other important sources in town, that the intake of pupils for the following September would have been the largest intake of pupils ever. Referring to the closure, she wrote:

> Everyone is against it. It is a real misfortune for the area, but they do at least want to keep us till the last date promised. Our situation is not, of course, a pleasant one but, if you allow us to remain here until Christmas, we would be able to leave a good impression behind us.

Events moved with great rapidity from this point, for on 1 January 1920, Sister Julie wrote to Mother Marie Dominique:

> Yesterday, I spent my whole day showing people around the house which was due to be auctioned at 2.30 pm, in town. As you will see from the letter I enclose, there was not a buyer for it; I think that the solicitor and auctioneer were asking too high a price for it. You ask me whether

> I got a good price for the sale of our non-transportable items of furniture. Here are the figures: in October, £19. 6. 6 (£380 now); in November, £33. 2. 6 (£650 now), in December, £10 .5. 8 (£195 now) totalling £62. 14. 8 (£1,150) or 1568 frs 30. I have received a kind letter from the superior-general from America with a reply to her many questions that troubled me.

Here again, there is a veiled reference to some kind of difficulties experienced by the community at this time, but once again, the nature of these difficulties is not featured in the correspondence.

When St Joseph's Convent, Pwllheli, closed its door for the last time, Sister Julie was sent to the community in Pontypool where she was given responsibility for the postulants. Sister Marie Apolline was sent to Ingsdon in Devon, and Sister Ste Catherine to America. The only connection thereafter of the Daughters of the Holy Spirit with Pwllheli was the fact that the 'Foundress' of the convent was buried there in the country of her adoption. On her grave is the simple inscription:

Sister St Félicien
Who died June 23, 1904
R.I.P.
Arwyl Iesu, Trugaredd **(Plate 26)**

St Joseph's Convent, Pwllheli, was one of the early foundations which did survive for a total of sixteen years. There was great hope for its success in the early years, and with the sound foundation on which it was established with the patrimony of Sister St Félicien, there are fewer references to financial problems, which were so prevalent in many of the other foundations. It would appear from the correspondence, however, that the schools which the sisters opened there, both the mission school and the private school did not really flourish over the years, and ultimately this was probably the main reason for the sisters leaving Pwllheli.

St Helen's Convent, Caernarfon 1904-1924

THE FOUNDATION at Caernarfon was the eleventh of those established in Wales between 1902 and 1904. With Llanrwst and Pwllheli, it formed the little cluster of communities in North Wales, known as 'the triangle.' The three sisters who arrived there in July 1904 were Sister Ange Augustine Morvan, the superior, Sister Eusèbe de Jésus Mevel and Sister Joseph du Carmel Jégu. Sister Ange Augustine's account of their arrival and the first days in Caernarfon appeared in *La Colombe*, 1904. It reads:

> We arrived in Caernarfon yesterday evening. Father Jones (the parish priest) was waiting for us at the station. From there we took a bus to go for a quick look at our future convent and to make a visit to the church, before reaching the presbytery where the good Father Jones provided us with a tasty supper. After this, he accompanied us to the house where we were to spend the night. Next morning our hostess, Mrs Conlon, took us to the church for the Mass, which Father kindly offered for the intentions of the new community. It was 26 July, the feast of St Anne. So our beginnings were placed under the protection of the Bretons' great patron, Saint Anne.

The sisters would have liked to call their new home St Anne's Convent, but that name had already been given to the convent at Llanrwst, so they chose to call it St Helen's Convent. St David and St Helen were the patrons of the parish.

There are no Annals extant for this foundation, so its history has to be traced solely through the correspondence of its local superiors with the superior-general of the time, and through accounts of the Welsh foundations published in various issues of *La Colombe*. (Archives, Maison Mère, Saint Brieuc, File G14 and File 8T14). There are approximately seventy letters written by Sister Ange Augustin during her time as superior of St Helen's Convent, Caernarfon. These deal with the problems of finding suitable accommodation for the community (for, as always, the sisters began in rented premises which were unsuitable), the necessary works as a source of income and apostolate, and the health of the sisters.

The first letter from St Helen's Convent to the superior-general is dated 15 August 1904, a few weeks after their arrival. It reads:

> The arrival of the 'White Sisters' [referring to the colour of their religious habits] in Caernarfon caused quite a stir, people would stand in the doorways to see us pass, but there were no unfriendly looks, no impolite words. This was, no doubt, because the good Father Jones had

been careful to notify people of the arrival of the 'nuns'. An article was printed in two local newspapers, and soon it was widely known that the 'Breton Sisters' had come to ask their brethren in Wales for hospitality that was refused them in their own country. One day, an old Welsh man told me: 'The Welsh and the Bretons are brothers.' We have no works as yet, for it is still the holidays and, as you know the English make the most of their holidays. It was not without sadness that I left the dear community of St Mary's at Monmouth, where I had spent such happy days. The Sisters had been so kind and helpful to me that I did not feel that I was an exile there. Yet, I had been called to leave all that behind and to set out for the unknown.

An event took place in the town at the beginning of September, which was very significant for the sisters, as they were soon to realize that they were not the only Bretons there. Caernarfon was the venue for that year's Eisteddfod. Some account of it, written by a Breton, appeared in *La Colombe*, and was entitled 'Le Congrès Panceltique'. Parts of it are reproduced in *La Colombe*, because of their relevance to the sisters and their new field of mission.

It was during the first days of September that the Eistedfodd began in Caernarfon. The Breton participants, who had arrived on the Saturday, went on Sunday morning to visit the Religious of the Holy Spirit (a Breton Order which has a house in Caernarfon). The three Sisters have been living here for a month or so. Their first days here were not easy for them, and their white habit aroused popular and not very welcome curiosity, and a certain suspicion. Were they ghosts? The Superior and one of the Sisters who are Breton-speaking soon dispelled these fears. It became known that they were from Brittany, that they spoke a language similar to Welsh, and soon a current of goodwill and sympathy surrounded them. Our compatriot, Théodore Botrel, who had been invited to the Eisteddfod, recited before an audience of more than 6,000 persons, a narrative poem in two parts, entitled *Les Barques de Granit*, and *La Chaine des Celtes* dedicated 'Aux Frères Gallois.' On this occasion, the Welsh went out of their way to prove to our dear companions, whom they consider their sisters, that being of the same race, the sisters should not look upon themselves as being in exile, but rather as being in their new homeland.

When they attended some of the Eisteddfod concerts, moreover, the sisters were pleased to find that they had been given seats among those reserved for persons of note, in between the Hon. Mrs Herbert and her daughter, Mrs Maxwell.

Father Jones, who met the sisters on their arrival in Caernarfon, was the only priest in the parish. There were two hundred Catholics in the parish. There is mention of his church in *La Colombe:*

> His chapel (i.e. church) in which we assisted at Mass is very small and drab, but Father is not without hope. He is convinced that little by little, the Welsh people will return to the faith of their fathers. To effect this conversion, he counts very much on the help of the OMIs (Oblates of Mary Immaculate) who have a Mission in Llanrwst and on the Benedictines from Kerbénéat who have recently settled in Carmarthen.

There are no indications in the correspondence as to where precisely the sisters lived for the first two years or so, other than that it was in rented property. This accommodation, as we learn from a letter written in those early days in Caernarfon, was damp and rather too small for all their needs. Could this unsuitable premises have hastened the untimely death of Eusèbe de Jésus Mevel, one of the first sisters in the foundation? When she arrived in Caernarfon, in July 1904, she was already suffering from the symptoms of illness, and had to return to France, where she died of consumption in January 1905.

Soon the sisters opened a private school or, perhaps more correctly, a class for private pupils; even though the house was unsuitable for such a venture. Sister Ange Augustin wrote to the superior-general on 1 January 1906:

> All our pupils are off sick or convalescent. Rightly or wrongly this is blamed on the school classroom being too small, and on the house being damp. It is also situated too near the county school, and so there is too frequent contact with the pupils there. These complaints are justified, up to a point, our premises cannot compare with the spacious ones occupied by the other (private) schools in the town.

In view of these difficulties, Sister Ange Augustin must have been authorised by the superior-general to start looking for other accommodation. In a letter dated 29 May 1906, she reports that she has visited two houses which were for sale or for renting:

> ...the first would not really be adequate for our needs, as for the second, not only would it be adequate, it would also allow for future development. Since, however, another party is interested in acquiring it, we would need to decide promptly whether or not to make an offer for it.

The "we" indicates that the general bursar was in Caernarfon at this time, since four days later she addressed a letter from there to the superior-general saying:

As Sister Ange Augustin has already told you, we looked at two houses, and it is true that the Sisters cannot remain where they are; it is the least suitable of all our houses in this country and restricts them in their works. This foundation has a future and will make good the sacrifices made for it.

However, nothing apparently resulted from these hopes, for writing to the superior-general on 23 July, Sister Ange Augustin tells her:

There is nothing settled about the new house; the owner is still opposed to our buying it… Mr Nee, our solicitor, works hard to try and find something suitable for us.

Hopes had risen again when Sister Ange Augustin wrote to the superior-general on 26 March 1907, reporting that

Mr Nee has found another place, more spacious and in better condition than the one we looked at last year. It is not freehold, but ownership is assured for 57 years. If you allow me to take this up, please let me know as soon as possible.

The letter written four days later, on 30 March, indicates that the response from the superior-general had been a negative one.

Although I am disposed to submit to the decision of the General Council of the Congregation, I am heartbroken at doing so. I beg you to allow me to plead once more the cause of my beloved Caernarfon.

Sister Ange Augustin was authorised to continue the search for the right house, but it proved unavailing. On 29 May 1907, she tells the superior-general:

…for two months now I have been searching to find a place for our private school, pupils are growing tired of waiting, we have lost four since Easter. It will be very painful to see the school ruined for want of adequate premises. But this is what is going to happen sooner or later.

Sister Ange Augustin's patient perseverance, however, did not go entirely unrewarded. On 17 June 1907, she wrote to the superior-general telling her that she had found a house to rent, which had fifteen rooms, including a kitchen, dining room and a laundry in the basement. The rent would be £36 (£1,800 per annum). The owner of the house was leaving Caernarfon for health reasons, and was selling off all his furniture, so the sisters decided to buy some of the necessary things they would need rather than having to buy them later on. In order to attract boarders, an advertisement was placed in the local newspaper. The house they were buying was well situated in the town centre and within a few minutes' walk of the station, which would be convenient for pupils travelling by train.

It was also conveniently situated with regard to the church, always an important consideration, wherever the sisters set up a foundation.

After the move, she wrote again on 6 August 1907.

> With your permission, I borrowed from Mr Nee the money to pay for our move. He is not well off; instead of giving us money, he is generous with his time and his services. It really is thanks to him that we are housed in this pleasant and spacious building in which we hope to develop our works. Not only has he secured it for us, he is also working to ensure that we may be able to keep it without an increase in rent. The owner of the house we have left, instructed his agent to write and tell me that he was very satisfied with the state in which we left the house.

By this time, there were five sisters in the community: Sister Ange Augustin Morvan, Sister Lucia Marie Nado, Sister Irene Le Flock, Sister Olivier Joseph Hamon and Sister Anne Françoise Allain. The one thing of which the community felt the lack after its move to its new home was a chapel with the reservation of the Blessed Sacrament. This lack was made good a little over a year later, as we learn from the letter, which Sister Ange Augustin addressed to the superior-general on 9 September 1908.

> We were so happy to have the Blessed Sacrament in the house during our retreat that we resolved to make every effort to obtain that we should have it permanently. But we have neither sacred vessels nor vestments. Perhaps the general bursar has some in reserve that she could let us have.

In her letter of 16 September 1908, she reported that the bishop had granted their request to have the Blessed Sacrament reserved in their chapel.

In addition to the private school, which the sisters established shortly after their arrival in Caernarfon, they were fortunate to find that a mission school already existed in the town. During the twenty years' presence of the Daughters of the Holy Spirit in Caernarfon, they taught, therefore, in two different schools: the mission or parish school and the private all-age convent school. Father Jones had founded the Mission school in 1876 in a small building adjacent to the church. The pupil attendance was about forty at the time when the sisters arrived, and was staffed by a head teacher and an assistant. They set their hearts on work in this school soon after their arrival. The first person to teach there was, in fact, a novice, Sister Sylvère Marie, and from what Father Jones wrote to the superior-general in July 1906, she acquitted herself very well. He wrote:

> I have a very high opinion of Sister Sylvère Marie, and she has taught well, but I am doubtful whether she can safely take on the serious charge of headmistress.

The post of headmistress was about to fall vacant, and both Father Jones and Sister Ange Augustin were hoping that a sister might fill it. Accordingly, on 14 July 1905, the latter wrote to the superior-general saying:

> I am sorry to add to your pre-occupations by asking you to designate a Sister who would be capable of filling the post of headmistress in Father Jones' school. The present one will be leaving on 1 October.

Her request was granted and the sister designated by the superior-general was Sister Lucia Marie Nado, who had begun teaching in the elementary school at Olney. Sister Ange Augustin was very pleased with the news, and she hoped that Sister Lucia Marie would be recognised as headmistress and would do good in her new post. This hope was realised, and for almost twenty years Sister Lucia's name became synonymous with the Mission school. But the appointment was a gradual process, as she had first to satisfy the schools' inspector that she was capable of filling the post envisaged for her by Father Jones and her religious superiors.

The first stage in this process of her appointment was recounted in a letter addressed to the superior of the convent by Mr Nee, one of the school managers, and dated 2 October 1905.

> I am pleased to inform you that at a meeting of the managers held on Monday last, Miss Nado (Sister Lucia) was appointed temporarily as headmistress of our little school. In accordance with arrangements made with the HMI, the school will be examined by him in about two months' time when, if everything is in order, and there is no reason to think that it will be otherwise, the appointment will be made permanent. There is in consequence of the foregoing a vacancy for a monitress or assistant mistress, and the Catholic managers would facilitate the appointment of another sister to fill this position. If you have anyone qualified to take the post, I would strongly recommend you to lose no time in securing it. As Sister Lucia is an Article 51 teacher, the salary will be £50 (£2,700 today) per annum, that being the maximum allowed by the county council, and we will endeavour to get £15 (£800) for the assistant, if appointed.

Sister Lucia's appointment, however, was not made as soon as anticipated. In the letter which Sister Ange Augustin addressed to the superior-general on New Year's Day 1906, she writes:

> You must be waiting with impatience to know the decision concerning Sister Lucia Marie. Only yesterday evening did I hear that the Inspector had postponed making the appointment, alleging that he did so on account of her accent; apart from this he was quite satisfied... The

Inspector has promised to come and visit the school again soon. But Sister will not be able to change her accent in a few weeks. I think that this is just a pretext.

There is no letter extant announcing Sister Lucia Marie's appointment as headmistress of the mission school, but from letters written during 1906, it becomes apparent that the appointment was made. On 9 November, Sister Ange Augustin wrote to the superior-general and told her that:

According to the Inspector who called to see it at the beginning of October, the parish school is being run very satisfactorily. Two of our Sisters, as you know, teach there: Sister Lucia Marie as head teacher, and Sister Olivier Joseph as assistant. They both have begun to study for their certificate.

Sister Lucia Marie took the exam for this in Bangor, in December 1907 and was successful in obtaining her certificate, while Sister Olivier Joseph was given her transfer in November 1907 and left for Pwllheli. Sister Gabrielle de Jésus Brajeul, in whom Father Jones recognised a competent teacher, replaced her. He was, therefore, very sorry to lose her, when in January 1910 she was selected to be head mistress of the Catholic elementary school in Bedford.

Once Sister Lucia Marie had succeeded in obtaining her certificate and since she had such a dependable assistant teacher in the person of Sister Gabrielle, it was decided that she should continue with her studies and prepare for the Diploma of Associate of the College of Preceptors. During the week of examinations, Sister Lucia Marie and Sister Irène Joseph, who taught in the private school, received hospitality from the Sisters of Nazareth in London. Sister Lucia Marie passed in all subjects and was awarded the Diploma of the College of Preceptors. Sister Irène Joseph passed in psychology, pedagogy and French. This, as Sister Ange Augustin explained to Mère Marie Alvarez, meant that she would not need to present these subjects, if she were to take the exam again. Writing to Mother Marie Dominique, the provincial, in April 1910, the superior-general advised that, as Sister Irène's discipline was good she should go to teach in the Mission school until such time as she obtained her Diploma. These two sisters were to work together in the school until 1919 (when Sister Irène was given her transfer for Newton Abbot.) They made a very successful team and as Sister Ange Augustin reported to the superior-general in May 1910:

The Inspectors, the Managers, in fact all who visit the school, are unanimous in saying how well it is run, what a good spirit it has, and what steady progress is made by the pupils. And it is quite true that the Sisters do not spare any effort when the interests of their pupils are at stake.

By 1909, the little old school building was no longer considered adequate by the authorities, and the Education Committee stipulated that large-scale repairs and improvements would have to be carried out as a condition for the school's continuing to receive a subsidy from public funds. The estimated cost of these improvements was so high that the bishop, Mgr Francis Mostyn, decided that the money could be better spent on erecting a new school building, and he undertook to find the greater part of the money for this. In 1910, the plans, which had been drawn up, received the approval of the Board of Education, and work on the buildings was begun. The formal opening of the new school took place on 16 October 1912 and was reported in the local press:

> A new Roman Catholic Elementary school at East Twthill, Caernarfon, was opened on Wednesday, the proceedings being presided over by the Right Rev. Dr Mostyn, Bishop of Menevia...the opening ceremony was performed by the Mayor, Councillor R. Newton, who was accompanied by the Mayoress. All the priests from the neighbouring parishes were present for the ceremony, as were members of the County Education Authority, and the school managers.

It is not difficult to imagine what a difference the new building made to the work of the two sisters who taught in it; not only did it do away with overcrowded classes, it also allowed for a greater intake of pupils, the number of whom soon rose from forty to sixty. In order to meet the ever more stringent requirements of the education authorities, the teachers were expected to be suitably, not to say fully, qualified. For Sister Lucia who already had two qualifications, the next step would normally have been the two-year course at a teacher training college, but the growing school of which she was the headmistress could not do without her, and it was not until 1924, when the sisters withdrew from Caernarfon, that she was 'free' to do her teacher- training. Sister Irène Joseph did her training at Newcastle from 1912 till 1914, during which time Sister Apolline MeGlynne replaced her.

At the beginning of December 1913, there was an inspection of the school, and the inspectors gave a fairly good report. They spoke of the "commodious well-lighted classrooms", the hard work of the teachers, of the highly creditable level of instruction, and the good progress made by those pupils who had spent some years in the school. On the negative side, they pointed out an inadequate supply of desks, inadequate staffing, and a lack of teachers with a knowledge of Welsh. The inspectors requested that the Board should be informed what steps the school proposed to take to make the staff comply with the requirements of the Code.

The private school, as already mentioned, had begun in a room of the rented house in which the community lived from 1904 until it moved to a larger house in 1907. Its first two teachers are named as Miss Black and Sister Irène Joseph (before she moved to the mission school). On 2 November 1905, in her letter to the superior-general, Sister Ange wrote:

> We have eight pupils in the private school, and four of them take piano lessons. Sister Joseph also has two young ladies for music lessons, and twice a week she takes the children in the school for a singing lesson.

The number of pupils fluctuated between seventeen in a good year to six in a lean year. They seem to have been grouped in two classes, one for the infants, a second for all the rest. The wide range of age and ability made the task of the sister who taught the older pupils a difficult one. So there are frequent requests in Sister Ange Augustin's letters for an extra teacher, for a more experienced or qualified one. These requests were made the more insistent as she had to deal with dissatisfied parents who found that they were not getting value for the school fees that they paid. But until there was a ready supply of sisters able and qualified to teach, the superior-general could only send sisters who, for the most part were young and inexperienced. On 9 September 1912, she wrote to Sister Ange Augustin saying:

> If the Sisters you have will not do, then the only thing is to take an educated English person 'au pair.' Mr O'Shea, a school teacher in Ireland, says that there is no shortage of educated Irish girls who would be delighted to spend a year 'au pair' in a convent school and learn French…

One of those who came to Caernarfon was Mr O'Shea's daughter, Maureen, the future Sister Pierre Elizabeth O'Shea who was later to be appointed as headmistress at the Catholic school in Abergavenny.

A month later, on 11 October, the superior-general wrote again to Sister Ange Augustin pointing out to her that:

> No, you will not have good capable teachers unless you cultivate, or make arrangements for others to cultivate, the aptitudes of the Sisters we can send you.

Sister Ange seems not to have replied directly to this admonition, but in her letter dated 26 December 1912, she tells the superior-general:

> In spite of everything, God's protection has been visible for, in spite of the lack of experience of our Sisters who teach in the private school and

of the one who gives music lessons, the number of pupils has not fallen, we still have 6.

Fewer fee-paying pupils meant a smaller income for the community. On 13 July 1913, Sister Ange informed the superior-general:

> I shall not be coming to Saint Brieuc this year, after all. The cost of travel incurred for the young Sisters, plus other unforeseen expenses, and the prospect of not having much money next year, make it a duty for me to cut down on travel expenses as far as possible.

Sister Ange did in fact go to Saint Brieuc during the summer of 1913, and while there she was given her transfer, and was sent to Moosup, one of the communities in America.

The school's fortunes improved a little at least with regard to the number of pupils, though the increase was due mainly to the presence in Caernarfon of Belgian refugees. The number of pupils in St Helen's Convent school in the years for which figures were available gives an indication of the poverty of their situation. In 1905, there were eight pupils; in 1906, there were also eight; in 1908 there were thirteen; in 1909, there were seventeen, in 1910 there were ten. These small numbers were only slightly augmented in the following years with a slight increase during the war years. In 1914, there were fourteen; in 1915, there were twenty six, and when the school closed there were about thiry pupils. During the fourteen years of its existence from 1905 till 1919 when it closed, some thirteen sisters taught in the school.

When she came to Caernarfon, Sister Marie Thomasine, who replaced Sister St Ange as superior, had just completed the sad task of closing the house at Monmouth where she had been since its foundation in 1902. Three members of that community were sent with her to Caernarfon: Sister Bernard du Sacré Coeur Cozanet, Sister St Vincent de Paul Meheut, and Sister Madeleine de Jésus Bachelot. They arrived in their new community in mid August 1913. Sister Thomasine's first letter is dated 19 August. She began it with an apology to the superior-general for not writing sooner.

> What shall I say to you about Caernarfon? The situation outside the community frightens me somewhat, but I trust that the good Lord who has laid this burden on me will, if I am deserving of it, give the grace to bear it according to his merciful and loving designs. Our Father, the Holy Spirit, whom I love to entreat, will I hope grant me his light, his counsel and the strength to do his work wisely.

Sister Marie Thomasine had a frail constitution and the strain, stress and fatigue of the previous months had taken their toll on her energies. Soon after her arrival in Caernarfon, she was forced to take a long rest. During this time, her aunt, Sister Albertine Le Breton, was sent from Carmarthen to help look after her and to replace her in community. For this, Sister Marie Thomasine was very grateful to the superior-general. On 30 October, she wrote again about her state of health:

> I am very happy to be able to tell you that I am really better and hope to be able to start giving lessons next week.

Before having to capitulate and take to her bed, Sister Marie Thomasine had been able to go out and make contact with some of the parishioners. This she recounts to the superior-general, in her letter dated 8 September 1913:

> Sister Lucia Marie accompanied me on my first visits to the parents of her pupils. Father Furniss, who replaced Father Jones as parish priest, had asked me to make the monthly collection of contributions to the 'Altar Society.' I had agreed to do so, since these visits would put me in direct contact with Catholic families and be a form of apostolate. Most of the families are very poor, and what is sadder still, not very interested in their faith.

In her last letter for the year 1913, dated 3 December, Sister Marie Thomasine wrote:

> The Catholic school re-opened for the new term with a record number of pupils about 68. Quite a few of those presenting themselves for the first time are protestants but that will not matter since they stand to gain from the religious instruction that they will receive with all the rest. God be praised for this increase! May He send us pupils for our private school; we have such great need of the income from the school fees. When I arrived I found just ten shillings in the community purse. Since then, we have been living on the money brought from our community in Monmouth; I spent £15.0.0 on food and one or two other small items, but there remain many bills to be paid. Since the community at Monmouth [now closed] has made some small savings, which are kept at the Mother House, will you allow me to ask Sister Marie Angélina, the General Bursar, to send us enough to pay what is owed here? Once that is done, we shall live as frugally as possible on what the community can earn. This week we are having an advert put in the newspaper, announcing the date of the term at our little school; and also the availability of private lessons in music, needlework, art, painting in oil and pen and ink. I am hoping to have pupils for the last of these which is an art form scarcely known here, whereas it was much in vogue in Monmouth. Sister Madeleine de Jésus is preparing to take an Infants class that we plan to start at Christmas. May I send for the little chairs

> and tables left in storage with the good Sisters at Troy House,
> Monmouth? All my companions, old and new, join with me in sending
> you the assurance of our respectful and filial affection.

She ends with a comment on the community itself, and the state of her own
health:

> I am happy to have nothing but good news to give you of our little
> community where each one takes her work seriously; where progress is
> made in the spiritual life, and where the Sisters get on reasonably well
> together. As for myself, I am back to my normal state of health but my
> good aunt has made it obligatory for me to take certain precautions. I
> am allowed to go out to Mass only twice a week, this on account of the
> bad weather and the rough paths.

The letters of Sister Marie Thomasine during the year of the outbreak
of World War I relate to staffing difficulties, the outbreak of the Great War
and the purchase of a house, called Cae Cristo. On 12 March, she wrote:

> I had intended writing to you earlier than this, but knowing that Sister
> Marie Dominique had told you about the difficulty, I preferred to wait
> and see what would happen. As the inspector had stated in his report of
> last December: neither of the Sisters in the parish school have any
> knowledge of the Welsh language, and there seems to be mounting
> pressure for appointing a teacher who could teach Welsh. As Sister
> Marie Dominique must have told you, I mentioned the name of Sister
> St Antoine de Padoue as being the only Sister who can save the situation.

On 19 March, she wrote again:

> I thank you for your comforting letter which I received this morning. I
> am afraid that I am unable to tell you anything definite about the
> situation because I do not know what the School Managers have
> decided, and I dare not speak about it to Father Furniss who does not
> like anything to be said about 'his' school by persons who are not
> directly concerned with it. Both he and Sister Lucia are off sick at present.

In her letter of 4 April 1914, Sister Marie Thomasine returned to the
question of a teacher who knew Welsh:

> You must forgive me if I return to the charge about a supplementary
> teacher knowing Welsh, for our parish school. It seems that if we
> cannot provide one, the education committee will appoint a Welsh-
> speaking Protestant to the post. The mayor who is the most influential
> member of the Committee has advised me to write and appeal to you to
> let us have, for our little school, the only Sister who knows Welsh.

Actually the sister in question, Sister St Antoine, did not know
sufficient Welsh to be able to teach in that language. After receiving the

letter of 4 April, however, the superior-general authorised the transfer of Sister St Antoine de Padoue from Pwllheli to Caernarfon. In June, Sister Lucia Marie tried to obtain official recognition of Sister St Antoine as a supplementary teacher, with a small salary, but she was not listed as such until 1915. In this same month of June, Sister Irène Joseph completed her teacher training at Newcastle and, to the great relief of Sister Marie Thomasine and Sister Lucia Marie, was able to return to her post in the parish school which had been filled in the interim by Sister Apolline, who was transferred to Pwllheli.

The next big event in the life of the community was the purchase of a house in Caernarfon. On 1 September 1914, Sister Marie Thomasine wrote to the superior-general telling her about

> a house which is perhaps, the only one in Caernarfon suited to the needs of our community and private school, and it is up for sale…I pointed it out to Mother Marie Dominique when she was here a fortnight ago. It is just seven minutes walk from the church and parish school; it has a large and well-kept garden. A short while ago, I had a visit from Mr Newton, a Town Councillor who is a friend of the owner of Cae Cristo. He had come to see about the accommodation for the Belgian refugees, but when I mentioned the house, Cae Cristo, he did confirm that it is up for sale. Another reason I have for asking you to consider the purchase of Cae Cristo is that the work is about to begin on building a hall for the Boy Scouts on the ground immediately behind our present house, and this will mean that we can no longer take the short cut across the field to get to church. You will be happy to know that the new school year began with a record number of pupils in the parish school. We are hoping that Sister Irene Joseph will soon be recognised as assistant teacher.

Sister Marie Thomasine gave further particulars about the proposed house in a subsequent letter of 21 September 1914. Mr Nee, their solicitor, was employed to carry out the negotiations for the purchase of the house. He tried to persuade the owner to lower the asking price from £20,000 to £15,000 (37,000 francs). The transactions went very smoothly and the house was purchasedf for 42,000 francs. Once again, the sisters had the problem of the rented house they occupied, and the lease had not expired. Fortunately for the sisters, the outbreak of the war brought Belgian refugees to Caernarfon, and they hoped that the house they were vacating might be taken over for the refugees.

The house, Cae Cristo, was duly purchased and the sisters moved in to it. They were very happy with this house, but they had difficulty in finding tenants for the rented accommodation they were vacating. "We like our new house," she wrote on 24 November,

> ...it has many advantages, which the other did not have. I am sending you herewith a letter from Mr Nee about taking out a mortgage with a view to completing payment for Cae Cristo. As you advised, we are praying to St Joseph to find us a tenant for our old house...our shortage of money does, at least, lead us to a stricter observance of our vow of poverty... With regard to the mortgage which you said we might take out, Mr Nee tells us to defer doing so until 12 May when the full payment falls due...

The letter of Sister Marie Thomasine to the superior-general, dated 20 May, records the financial problems which had to be endured during the war years. She wrote:

> Thank you for your generous and charitable assistance which will prove very helpful in our present financial straits. We really are in need... Mr Nee has used all the money we had to decrease the mortgage, more than I intended that he should because I like to keep a small amount by for urgent needs. I try not to worry about money matters but, finding myself penniless and with such debts, it is more than nature can do to refrain from worrying. May I recommend Sister St Vincent very specially to your prayer? Last Sunday, she learned that one of her brothers who are in the army, and the one to whom she was closest, was reported missing on the night of 22-23 April, the night of the infamous poison-gas attack. She is heartbroken and, although she entertains a certain hope she is close to murmuring against Providence.

The year 1916 saw the beginning of strained relationships between the sisters and Father Furniss, bringing about a situation which was to haunt them for the remainder of their days in Caernarfon. "The ordeal," as it was called, seemed to have originated in the animosity of certain influential persons who had tried to influence Father Furniss. Although there is no detailed reference to the nature of this problem, we learn that things suddenly came to a head in May of that year. In the letter which she addressed to the assistant superior-general on 18 May, Sister Marie Thomasine announced:

> I write to tell you about a situation which has just erupted and which beggars belief. I can only think that it must be the work of the devil, angered by what our Sisters are doing for the good of the souls of the children entrusted to their care... Yesterday the three Sisters who teach in the parish school were summoned to appear before a meeting of the Managers of the school and parents who accused them of a whole number of things. Sister Lucia responded to these accusations with

calm, while Mr Nee, our sole protector, once again gave proof of his devotedness to us. He is now going to accompany Sister Lucia to an interview with Mgr Mostyn. The Bishop has already been made aware of this situation (which had now come to a head) by the Belgian priest who was in Caernarfon last year and by Mr Nee who, last November went to speak to him about it. It is Mrs Farren who is mainly responsible for it, and Father Furness sides with her. Do please pray for us and ask the prayers of the members of the Council. The religious examination of the children is due to take place on 1 June. Although they have been well instructed, they may not be able to answer the questions put to them, if over-awed by Father Furniss.

In her letter of 21 May, she says:

Our little community has just lived through a terrible week, ending with the visit to Mgr Mostyn who had already received from Father Furniss a list of his grievances against us, among these that: we do not visit the poor and the sick; that we tend to favour Protestants; that we let the children play in the church, without reproving them for it, all of which is quite untrue. The Bishop noticed my emotion, which I was unable to hide. He told me not to worry and to leave everything in the hands of God. He is particularly concerned to find out whether the charge that the children are not being properly instructed in the faith, is well founded...There is much else I could tell you but, as our letters may be opened by the censor [war-time conditions] it is risky to tell you more. Our enemies have not disarmed, quite the contrary. We no longer know what to do...but we continue to place our trust in the Good Lord. This morning I accompanied Sister Etienne to the Justice of the Peace, in response to a summons she had received for coming to Caernarfon without any identity card... The meeting was far from being as stormy and as painful as last week's, everyone was so kind and helpful; yet they were not our own people.

The ordeal was to continue for the sisters, for when the bishop wrote to Sister Marie Thomasine on 1 August, he told her that he had seen the report of the religious inspector. He said that it was not as good as it should be, and he hoped that it would be better in the future. The bishop went on:

Father Furniss who does not seem to be satisfied with the work of the Sisters in Caernarfon, has asked me to come over to that town. I am telling him that I have already seen you and put before you all the complaints that he has made against you, and that I do not see what good I can do by going over to Caernarfon now. Let me beg you to do all you can to help in the Mission and to do anything that your priest wants you to do.

Sister Marie Thomasine was at the mother house in Saint Brieuc when she received this letter, and it was from there that she sent her reply to it on the 16 August. In her letter she refuted every allegation made in Father Furniss' report. She lamented the fact that Father Furniss announced it at all the parish Masses, as being "deplorable." She concluded as follows:

> I must apologise for writing so fully but I am sure that your Lordship would prefer to have the fullest answer to what I consider to be a very unjust criticism upon the work of the sisters. I am at all times most anxious that the members of our little community at Caernarfon should give to Father Furniss the greatest respect and assistance, but although we have earnestly tried, we have failed to win his good will.

She then lists a number of tasks which he removed from the sisters: the organist and the sisters who sang in the choir were asked to leave; Sister Marie Thomasine herself who was responsible for the Catholic Needlework Guild had this responsibility taken away from her. Lastly, the sisters who taught the children at Sunday school were removed.

> As I told you when I visited you in Wrexham, Father Furniss threatened us with the same fate as our Sisters in Pembroke Dock. I'm afraid he has since been trying to realise his threat. I have, in common with the Sisters, been caused much grief by the repeated insults and injustices we have experienced at the hands of Father Furniss, and again I appeal to your Lordship for protection. In conclusion, I can assure you, my Lord, that it is and always has been the desire of the Sisters and myself to help the priest in every possible way, and if your Lordship can advise me how to obtain a little appreciation and fairness in place of the resentment which is continually shown towards us, I shall be ever grateful to you.

Subsequently, the bishop paid a visit to the community, and it was a very acrimonious meeting indeed. Sister Marie Thomasine was forced to call in her solicitor, Mr Nee. Sister Marie Thomasine gave the superior-general an account of the bishop's visit in the letter, which she wrote to her on 9 September 1916.

> It was obvious that he had called at the presbytery before coming to us. He said that the transfer of Sister Lucia Marie and Sister Irène Joseph could only remedy the situation. I was indignant at the way he interprets things or, at least, gives credence to what is reported to him. When he stated that Father Furniss categorically denied all that I wrote (in my letter of 16 August) about his behaviour towards us, I could no longer control my indignation. I asked to be allowed to send for Mr Nee who came immediately. I envied the calm, wise and prudent way in which he spoke to the Bishop as he presented to him the report he

himself had made at the awful meeting of 17 May. One by one he refuted all the allegations brought against the sisters, and made it plain to the Bishop that this whole affair had been engendered by persons who were prejudiced against the sisters. He said that the removal of the sisters would be tantamount to condemning them and punishing them unjustly; nor would it change the situation.

With the help of Mr Nee, and in the absence of Sister Marie Thomasine, the bishop came to an agreement to leave things as they were for a period of six months, in the hope that given time things would sort themselves out for the best.

In the subsequent correspondence relating to the 'ordeal' of the sisters with Father Furniss, there was evidence of the beginning of a certain peace and a process of reconciliation between the two parties, even though the hurt would never be forgotten. In the first instance, when Mr Nee, their solicitor and a school manager, next came to the convent, he was able to assure Sister Marie Thomasine that their cause was won, for the time being, at least. He said that, speaking as a solicitor, neither the bishop or the managers of the school could demand the removal of the sisters whose innocence was proved. He said that given time and with God's help, all could be repaired. In her next letter to the superior-general, however, Sister Marie Thomasine commented :

> Humanly speaking, I do not see any possibility of peace being restored while things remain the same. Sister Lucia Marie, Sister Irène Joseph and myself are ready to submit, with filial trust, to whatever decision you may be inspired to take in our regard.

The next letter was written to congratulate Mère Marie Alvarez on her election as superior-general, in 1917. She also has encouraging news about the problem with the parish priest:

> May God be praised for the fact that the painful and delicate situation in which our little community found itself over the past few months, has begun to improve. Father Furniss seems to be much more kindly disposed towards us, and gave no hint of resentment after the Bishop's visit to us. Last Sunday when he had given the sermon, he went on to say that his duties no longer allowed of his taking the Sunday catechism class but that he thought he could count on parents sending their children to it, even though it would be taken henceforth by the Sisters. Given what has been happening, Sister Lucia and Sister Irène Joseph are vary reluctant to accept responsibility for this religious instruction... I put to them my point of view and told them that the Bishop and the members of your Council would advise them to over-

come their repugnance and to give this weekly instruction. The twofold victory was won by their generous acceptance.

There was no other letter till 26 December. In this letter, Sister Marie Thomasine mentioned that the situation seemed to be improving in their relationship with Father Furniss. With a view to encouraging the children to attend the Sunday school, they planned a party for them. Father Furniss even agreed to preside at the party. The sisters also planned to form a group of the Guild of St Agnes, which would allow them more freedom to attract the children away from what Sister Marie Thomasine called "the baneful influence of persons who are against us." Father Furniss agreed to this also and offered to give benedicton in the convent on the evening that the meetings were held. The bishop too showed a more positive attitude towards the sisters. The superior had received a letter from Mgr Mostyn, and was more than satisfied with the tone of his letter. She hoped that Father Furniss' improved attitude towards them would mean that he would not repeat his failed attempt to send them away from the parish. In this letter, too, she showed her concern for the sisters who were suffering from war conditions in Belgium and France and says that she had petitioned the King of Spain on their behalf.

The year 1917 proved a good year for the community and its mission. The ten long letters, which Sister Marie Thomasine addressed to the superior-general during the course of 1917, contain many positive notes. On 28 January she wrote:

> I am happy to be able to tell you that our situation continues to improve. We seem to have entered upon a period of peace and calm. We are going to make the most of our work for the good of souls in this dear Mission. The regular meetings of the Guild of St Agnes have begun and are well attended. The girls have asked if they could receive Communion on a Thursday, which is the day of their Guild Meeting, and the day on which Mass is celebrated in our little chapel. I cannot tell you how happy we are at seeing how God has made everything work out for his greater glory. We are now going to be able to become more actively and more directly involved in the Christian education of the young Catholics of Caernarfon... Sister Lucia Marie who runs the Guild of St Agnes, gives herself wholeheartedly to this... In directing us to Cae Cristo just before the start of the war, the good Lord surely intended that the wood from the trees in the property and the vegetables from the garden would be particularly helpful to us, now that things are in short supply.

26. Grave of Sister St Félicien, Pwllheli (p.174)

27. The Small Community of Sisters, Caernarfon (p.196)

28. Pen-y-pound House, Abergavenny (St Michael's Convent) (p.203)

29. St Michael's Convent, Abergavenny—The Needlework Room (p.205)

30. Gwladys Eileen Masters, Pupil at St Michael's Convent, c.1918 (p.213)

31. St Michael's Convent, Abergavenny (The Junior Convent School) (p.226)

32. St Michael's Convent, Abergavenny (The Junior Convent School) (p.226)

33. Provincial and Noviciate House, Woodbury, Reading, England (p.234)

34. Students aspiring to religious life, Apostolic School, Monaghan, Ireland (p.236)

35. Stained glass window in St Mary's Church, Carmarthen, a memorial to Sister Pierre Lazare (p.238)

36. Sister Mary Enda and her class, St Mary's School, Carmarthen (p.239)

37. A plaque unveiled in Carmarthen in tribute to the service of the sisters (p.240)

38. St Padarn's Convent School Extensions, Aberystwyth (p.241)

39. St Alban's Secondary School, Pontypool (p.246)

40. Hillgrove Convent, Pontypool (p.247)

42. Sister Brendan Downing, provincial charged with re-organisation and renewal in the province (p.253)

41. St Michael's Convent School, Abergavenny. Prefects on the lawn at Glancibi Grange (p.248)

43. Blaenafon—St Felix Presbytery 1986-95

49. The Blaenafon community (p.258)

47. Sister Imelda and her class at St Michael's Convent, Abergavenny

48. A school outing to the seaside, St Mary's RC School, Carmarthen 1954

44. The St Alban's Convent School Old Girls' Association on the steps of the entrance to Park House

45. St Alban's Convent School, Pontypool—the school netball teams

46. St Alban's RC Elementary School, Pontypool—Sister Callista, "football coach" and her team

Relations with Father Furniss continued to improve. Indeed he stated at a school managers' meeting that he was completely satisfied with the sisters, that the school was well run, and that the religious instruction was as good as he could have expected. At this time they had welcomed some more pupils to their private school, and Sister Thomasine wrote to the general bursar and asked if she could have some desks from the Tenby convent which was about to be closed. They had already received the altar from there, and it had been erected to replace the temporary altar, which they had installed on their arrival. She adds:

> We thank you for having thus enriched our poverty, thereby enabling us to increase the glory given to God and to acquire fresh graces for ourselves and for the young people who come to us... God, perhaps, allowed us to go through such a painful trial only to bring us to the goal he destined for us. Our present works, would they have seen the light of day if we had not been shaken by the storm?

Subsequent letters give news of the staffing difficulties in the private school. In July, Sister Marie Thomasine received word that Sister Philomène de St Jean Belanger, who had been sent to Caernarfon in 1916, was to return to America. In her response to the superior-general she wrote:

> Since this wretched war drags on and on, I was hoping that the dangers it represents for travel would have been a reason for allowing us to keep Sister Philomène... I quite understand how difficult it is for you to find someone to replace her and I wish that I could help by telling you that we could manage without another teacher next term. Such, unfortunately is not the case. We have at present 20 lovely children in the reception class. It behoves us to make adequate provision for these young pupils who represent the future of our school. I am very grateful to you for allowing us to keep Sister St Osithe, though she has more than she can do with a class of the older ones whose ages range from 7 to 17. And the older ones have to prepare to take their examinations. Last week, Father Furniss gave the children of the Guild of St Agnes a written exam in religious knowledge. He was so pleased with the results that he is thinking of sending the best scripts to Mgr Mostyn. On 29 June he examined the children in the parish school and had, I think, reason to be pleased with the results.

By the year 1917, the suffering that the sisters endured because of the breakdown of relationships with the parish priest was still foremost in their consciousness, or at least in the mind of the superior, but in her letter of 20 November 1917, she was able to write:

Having supported us in the cruel trial which almost destroyed our poor little community, you will be interested in the news I have to give you today. As you already know our pastor had reverted to a more favourable attitude with regard to us, yet we wondered how far we could trust the sincerity of it. But now we are certain that his eyes have been opened to the truth... and he is now meeting with a lot of opposition from the persons with whom he once seemed to side... At the Sunday Mass, a fortnight ago, he spoke with an eloquence we did not know he had, about the duty of parents to give their children a sound Christian education.

The following day he received word from Mgr Mostyn summoning him to Wrexham. There he learned that he was to be transferred to Barmouth.

The reaction of the sisters to this move was one of fear for the future, as they wondered whether they would have to recommence the struggles of the past. But their fears soon gave way to trust. Father Furniss spoke highly of them to his successor, Father Brunton. It seemed as if he was trying to made amends for his failings. He asked for forgiveness from the sisters for his misunderstanding of them. He said it had taken him three years to get to know the people of Caernarfon and that had he known sooner, of certain situations, much heartache could have been avoided. Father Brunton was a young priest who had been ordained to the priesthood only two years earlier. He was well loved and appreciated in Llandudno where he was a curate. The sisters undertook to help him in every way that they could, and would try to assist him in doing good.

Sister Marie Thomasine's next letter dated 4 March 1918 seems to be a reply to one from the superior-general setting out plans for the transfer of sisters who were engaged in teaching, transfers which she resisted. She wrote:

I am not opposed to your plans, yet as you rightly say, they would affect the interests of the Mission here and its school. I went to speak to Father Brunton about it; he listened calmly and attentively. When he had heard all that I had to say, he told me he did not think it would be possible to change any of the Sisters in the Catholic School, but that he would reflect on the matter. Yesterday, I met him again, only to find that his reflection had not led him to change his mind... He thinks that the Education Committee would be only too pleased to have the way opened to the appointment of secular teachers selected by them, as has been done in Bangor. As for our private school, if you wish to take Sister Ste Osithe for Newton Abbot, I am prepared to accept that; however, it would be necessary to find someone to replace her who is capable of preparing pupils for their Senior Oxford examinations.

Her next letter to the superior-general, dated 23 April 1918, mentioned the Great War, which was coming to an end. The little private school re-opened for the summer term with a change of teacher. Sister Pierre Angélina replaced Sister Osithe, because the three most advanced pupils, who were Belgian, had been requested to leave town, together with their families. There was still need for more personnel to help in their apostolate. She said that the three sisters in the parish school, Sisters Lucia Marie, Irène Joseph and Antoine de Padoue, had discovered that after all, they had no cause for anxiety, as a result of the change of parish priest. They were, however, concerned about changes in the educational system, with the proposed new education act. They hoped that they would not be affected by this, and that they could continue to work in peace and harmony with everyone concerned with education.

When Sister Marie Thomasine wrote on 15 August, 1918, she mentions that there were many things she would need to tell the superior-general, but there was also some good news:

> I feel really ashamed that my wishes for your feast will not reach you in time. Rather than make excuses I will simply ask you to attribute this to overwork, which brought many things about which I should have liked to tell you. The good news is that Sister Lucia and Sister Irène Joseph have been awarded a scholarship, which entitles them to follow the 4-week Summer School in Bangor—all expenses to be paid by the Education Authority. The same letter notified Sister Lucia of a rise in her salary. She was so surprised at this that she asked Mr Nee for an explanation. He told her that the Education Committee was giving this in recognition of the discipline, the regular attendance of pupils, the favourable reports from the Inspectors and the care taken of the school buildings.

The armistice of 11 November 1918 having brought the war to an end, the superior-general lost no time in going to visit the communities in Belgium and the North of France. Having heard of this, Sister Marie Thomasine expressed the wish that she would then visit the sisters in England and Wales, which she did during the month of June 1919, before going on to visit the communities in the USA. During this visit the superior-general decided that the private school would have to close. This was probably not very welcome news for the sisters, but the numbers in the private school had always remained low, and there was no guarantee that this would change, after its fifteen years in existence.

There is only one letter for the year 1921, and from it we learn that Sister Marie Thomasine had been called to leave Caernarfon. She was not the only superior to receive a new call. With the coming into force of the 1918 Code of Canon Law, which set a limit to the length of a superior's mandate in one and the same community, several changes had to be made. On the 18 September, she writes about her transfer:

> Through you, the Divine Master has just given me a share in his cross. I want to accept it with all the love and generosity that I can. But I was not expecting it, not for the present, at least. The burden you lay on my weak shoulders, though different, will be no less heavy than the one I bear at present. I shall try not to dwell on my physical and emotional capacity for it, rather I intend to comply with the designs God has for me or at least show my willingness to do so. There can be no need to tell you that the separation will prove a very painful one. Friends of the community, with Mr Nee at their head, wanted to write and tell you of their fears for my health (once I leave Caernarfon). I have managed to dissuade them from doing this since I don't want to go against the designs of Providence in my regard. I thanked them for their interest in my well being, and I intend to try out the somewhat better health I have enjoyed while in Caernarfon. Unless I receive any instruction to the contrary, I shall leave for Aberystwyth on Monday.

Sister St Lazare, who was superior of Aberystwyth since its beginnings in 1903, replaced her. So for her too the uprooting was very painful. The community she left was a sizeable one of 14 to 15 sisters: its works were well established and thanks in part to the sisters who had studied for their degrees at the University College, the community enjoyed a favourable reputation. In coming to Caernarfon, Sister St Lazare found a small community of five sisters **(Plate 27)** whose only remaining 'work' was teaching in the parish school where they met with not a few difficulties. Of the twenty extant letters, which Sister St Lazare exchanged with the superior-general, fifteen of them were written during 1924 and relate to the almost inexorable train of events, which led to the closure of the convent and the sisters' departure from Caernarfon.

The problems leading up to this were connected with the supply of sisters for the parish school, and the growing pressure for them to be able to teach Welsh. The trouble with the education committee and school managers began in 1923, when it was decided by her religious superiors that Sister Lucia Marie, who had been head teacher at the school since 1905, should go to college and study for her teacher training certificate. On 4 October 1923, Sister St Lazare wrote to the superior-general:

> You are no doubt expecting to hear about the first of the formalities
> that have to be completed for Sister Lucia Marie. On Saturday, I went
> with her to announce to Father Brunton the decision you have made in
> her regard. His immediate reaction was one of shock and dismay. Then
> he regained his composure. And I came away leaving Sister Lucia Marie
> to discuss with him the event which would have such important conse-
> quences for them both. Sister Lucia returned to the community at half
> past four in the afternoon. She told me that Father had said to her:
> 'there is only one thing left for you and that is to obey your superiors;
> I am more ready to accept the trial of your leaving the school than that
> of losing the convent through closure.'

The next letter Sister St Lazare wrote to the superior-general spoke of
the sequel to the decision to send Sister Lucia Marie to train in London.
Father Brunton had informed the school managers that Sister Lucia was
resigning from her post, but explained this in such a way that it met with no
opposition.

Sister Lucia began her training at Cavendish Square, London, in
January 1924. Sister Ste Athanasie was sent from Pontypool to Caernarfon
to replace her, and then followed the formalities for her appointment as
head teacher. Sister Lucia Marie, who was very successful in her post as
head of the school, was obviously taken away at a very important time for
the school with the advent of educational legislation. After the first few
weeks, Sister Ste Athanasie wrote herself to the superior-general on 10
February saying:

> I was very fearful of having to replace Sister Lucia Marie and for a long
> while I thought and, I admit, hoped, that the School Managers and
> Education Committee would turn me down. Yet the good Lord must
> want me to be here since he permitted that my application for the post
> was accepted.

It was undoubtedly an unwise decision to take Sister Lucia Marie from
the school where she was successful at such a critical time. After Sister Ste
Athanasie's unpleasant experience teaching in the Catholic school at
Blaenafon already described in an earlier chapter, it would appear to have
been an unwise decision to send her to a school where there had been so
much difficulty. Unfortunately, she was to experience further difficulties
when she arrived at the Catholic school in Caernarfon. On 24 May, Sister St
Lazare wrote to the superior-general:

> As you know the state of the school at Twthill (the parish school) makes
> it less than engaging for poor Sister Ste Athanasie. From her very first
> week there, she realised the extent of her duties, which she does her

best to fulfil, but her strength is not always equal to this harsh task. The inspector has been to visit the school for a second time, and I need not tell you how much Sister Ste Athanasie suffered during the visit. He spent two whole hours there, listening to lessons given by the two sisters (Sister Jeanne Egide, an inexperienced teacher was the other teacher). It is a struggle against tremendous odds to try and improve this poor school, where there are now only 19 Catholics out of a total of 96 pupils, from the lowest class in Caernarfon, and whose bad behaviour is ruining the very name of our works.

On 15 July, Sister St Lazare wrote to the superior-general about the inspector's visit:

> Once again it is another letter from Caernarfon for you... Father Brunton has asked me to send you this copy of the Inspector's report on the school which was sent to the Board of Education. Mr Williams, HMI, reports on visits made on 8 May and 11 June 1924. His report stated: *This school cannot now be regarded as efficiently conducted. The new head teacher, who assumed charge on the re-opening of the school after the Christmas holidays, seems quite unequal to the duties of the post. She is genuinely anxious for the success of the school, but she is unable to engender the requisite response in the children.*

The superior-general acted as soon as she received the report, for in her next letter, dated 25 July, Sister St Lazare wrote to the superior-general:

> Father Brunton is waiting to receive the promised letter before starting to look for new teachers. So please, send him a letter which will put an end to his lingering hope of the Sisters' remaining here...

Given these problems in the school, and given the fact that the community now numbered three sisters, the superior-general and her council decided on the withdrawal from Caernarfon of the remaining sisters. On 3 June, 1924, in response to a letter received from her, Sister St Lazare wrote:

> Your instruction to close the house did not surprise me in the least. I have for a long time prepared for this eventuality. I communicated to Father Brunton the content of your letter; understandably he was very upset by it. As we talked about the closure, he suggested that perhaps the private school could be re-opened, thereby ensuring that the sisters would remain in Caernarfon.

There was no turning back; steps for the closure went ahead and Bishop Mostyn was advised of it. Sister St Lazare wrote to the superior-general on 11 June 1924:

Father Brunton has not yet heard from the Bishop and so cannot yet do anything on his own initiative. He wants to write to you, but I have given him to understand that there really is no hope of our re-opening the private school. He is overwhelmed by the prospect of seeing his works disappear and of being left alone in the Mission. He has just received Sister Ste Athanasie's resignation and Sister Jeanne Egide will hand hers in at the beginning of August. My niece, Yvonne, has accepted a post in Bedford, so everything seems to be moving towards the end of our time in Caernarfon.

Then on 17 June, she wrote again:

I have no more definite news to give you, though everything is quietly going according to your wishes. The Inspector came back to visit the school again on 11 June. The bishop has written to Father Brunton notifying him of our departure and instructing him to start looking for teachers to replace us. Will you allow me, now that Mr Nee is acquainted with our situation, to deal with the sale of Cae Cristo? When we spoke about selling it, he said: "You paid £1,500 for it;. I'll give you the same amount." The advantage of a direct sale, as I see it, is that we would receive payment immediately, and before we leave in September. In the meantime, we plan to sell our vegetables as they become ready for picking. The garden is in very good condition and producing a good crop of them.

The superior-general herself wrote to Father Brunton on 1 July 1924, to inform him of the closure of the convent. She wrote:

In the present circumstances it is impossible for Sister Ste Athanasie to remain in the school, and it is just as impossible to replace her… I have instructed Sister St Lazare to make Sister Jeanne Egide hand in her notice in time to be free by the beginning of September. I cannot allow her to remain alone in the school; besides her salary would not be sufficient for the upkeep of the convent.

As things turned out, even though the two sisters had handed in their notice, they had to return to school for the first week of the September term because Father Brunton had not been able to find replacements for them.

Mr Nee, who had been a great friend of the sisters throughout their time in North Wales, and who was a school manager and the solicitor of the sisters, proceeded to buy the convent, and he paid a visit to the mother house in order to finalise negotiations for the purchase. On 27 August, Sister St Lazare wrote:

> Mr Nee has arrived from Saint Brieuc, delighted with his journey and with the successful outcome of the negotiations. I have just seen Father Brunton; he promises to do all he can to speed things up. He is counting on the new head teacher's arrival for the 8 September. She is an MA. Everything has now been packed and will be sent off tomorrow, except items destined for Aberystwyth which will be sent later, since they include our beds.

In her last but one letter from Caernarfon, Sister St Lazare wrote on 4 September:

> You are, no doubt, waiting for news of our last days in Caernarfon. Sister Ste Athanasie arrived back last Saturday and was here, with Sister Jeanne Egide, to start the new school year. This they did to Father Brunton's great satisfaction. Last Thursday we sent off the loads (of furniture) from Cae Cristo, 91 in all. There were 50 for Pontypool, 30 for Abergavenny, 11 for Newton Abbot; the rest between 20 and 25 will go to Aberystwyth. Mr Nee has kindly arranged for these to be transported by rail. He just cannot do enough to help us.

The last letter of Sister St Lazare from Caernarfon was written on 8 September,1924. She wrote: "We have just received your letter telling us of the place which providence has marked out for each one." The transfers were as follows: Sister St Lazare herself was destined for Newton Abbot, Devon; Sister Ste Athanasie was transferred to Olney, Buckinghamshire; Sister Jeanne Egide to Carmarthen, and Sister Marie de Pontmain to the USA.

Sister Ste Athanasie left on 8 September 1924; Sister Jeanne and Sister St Lazare on 13 September for Pontypool. "From there I shall go to my new post on Monday or Tuesday. When I have acquainted myself with all that you expect of me there, I will write and tell you frankly what I think of it."

So the Daughters of the Holy Spirit left Caernarfon and North Wales; the Convent at Llanrwst had been closed in 1909, and the one at Pwllheli in 1919. In the foundation at Caernarfon, they had, once again, sown in tears, though not in vain.

In their joint pastoral letter issued in February 1986, over a century and a half after the departure of the sisters from Caernarfon, the Archbishop of Cardiff together with the Bishops of Menevia and Wrexham had this to say to the people of Wales:

> At this time we should thank God for the amazing growth of our Catholic community, from 940 two hundred years ago to 7000 one hundred ago, to more than 150,000 in 1986. During Mass today, let us recall the wonderful people who went before us: our families, and friends, our

religious, our priests and bishops... Those who went before us died in the hope of what we celebrate today. We are reaping the harvest they planted and cared for... While we pray for God's blessing on our future efforts, let us pray too for those who made such valiant efforts in the past.

CHAPTER EIGHT

1906: The Twelfth Foundation in Wales

St Michael's Convent, Abergavenny

> Our beloved Congregation now has another 'Dovecote,' the twelfth, in the hospitable land of Wales. It was opened on 23 April 1906, in a delightful little town, by the name of Abergavenny, Monmouthshire.

THIS NOTICE APPEARED IN *La Colombe* (1906), AND REFERS TO THE foundation of St Michael's Convent, Abergavenny. The arrival of the first sisters in Abergavenny had been preceded by long-drawn out and delicate negotiations between the Daughters of the Holy Spirit, the Honourable Mrs Herbert of Llanover, and the Bishop of Newport, the Rt Rev John Cuthbert Hedley, OSB.

It was the ardent wish of Mrs Herbert that a community of the Daughters of the Holy Spirit should live in her property in Abergavenny, known as Pen-y-pound House. Mrs Herbert had been responsible for the establishment of a number of the foundations in Wales already, as we have seen, and she was most anxious to have a community of the Daughters of the Holy Spirit in the vicinity of her own home. Rather than hand over Pen-y-pound House to the sisters, however, she decided to donate it to the bishop of the diocese, who would then lease it to the sisters. Representing the superior-general in these negotiations were Mère Marie Angélina, the general bursar, and Sister Thérèse du Saint Esprit, superior of St Mary's Convent, Monmouth.

In a letter which she wrote from Usk, dated 18 October, 1904, the general bursar tells the superior-general:

> Sister Thérèse must have given you a detailed account of our visit to Bishop Hedley at Llanishen, and I am hoping that he will reach an agreement with Mrs Herbert this week, about Abergavenny. He strongly advises that we should not take any steps before the official act of donation to the trustees, of whom he will be one, has been drawn up. He seems to like the sisters and to take a great interest in them. Sister

Thérèse says that it is going to require tact on our part, if we are going to be able to manoeuvre between the priest at Abergavenny and Mrs Herbert. [There was some disagreement between Mrs Herbert and Father Wray, OSB, the parish priest of Abergavenny].

After the general bursar's return to Saint Brieuc, Sister Thérèse was left to continue these negotiations which were proving far from easy, as revealed by the six long letters which she wrote to the superior-general during 1905. Three of these letters were written from Mrs Herbert's London house in Mayfair, where she stayed while the solicitors were drawing up the contract relating to Pen-y-pound House (Plate 28). When, at last, the final draft of this was submitted to the superior-general, the following stipulations formed the essential clauses of the agreement. At least five sisters were to live in the house. They would be required to visit the poor and sick Catholics of the Abergavenny mission, under the direction of the bishop and of the priest in charge of the mission. They were to be ready to undertake and pursue charitable works that were in keeping with the spirit of their congregation, and intended to promote the good, especially of young school-leavers in Abergavenny, and that of the diocese in general. They were allowed to have a day-school for girls over the age of fourteen years of age, for adults and non-Catholics, but they would not be allowed to open a boarding school. They could, however, take in a few young girls, though not from the Diocese of Newport. They could give private lessons in French, music, drawing and embroidery, even to girls under fourteen who would ask for it, provided it took place outside the school hours of the mission school. Under the terms of the contract, the trustees of Pen-y-pound House would hand the house over to the sisters, free of all rent and other charge, except for rates and taxes, for a period of ten years. The contract could be renewed after that period, provided both parties were in agreement. The three trustees were: John Herbert Hedley, Bishopof Newport, L. Bodenham Lubienski and Robert L. Hunter. The contract was approved and accepted by the Congregation of the Daughters of the Holy Spirit, and signed by the superior-general at Saint Brieuc on 30 March 1906.

A little over three weeks later, on 23 April 1906, the first Daughters of the Holy Spirit arrived in Abergavenny to take possession of their new home. They would have liked to have had it under the patronage of St George, since it was opened on the Feast of St George, but it was the wish of Mrs Herbert, their benefactress, that it be called St Michael's Convent. This was not only because she had a special devotion to the great archangel, but also because for centuries his name had been linked with Abergavenny and one of its surrounding hills, Skirrid Fawr, also known as the 'Holy Mountain' or 'St Michael's Mountain.' The sisters therefore, could not do otherwise than acquiesce with Mrs Herbert's choice of name. The main sources for tracing the history of this foundation is the correspondence of its first superior, Sister Thérèse du Saint Esprit, with two superiors-general, and also articles which appeared in *La Colombe* from time to time. (Archives, Maison Mère, Saint Brieuc, File 12G 16 and file 8T 16).

Sister Thérèse was a prolific letter-writer, sending forty-four letters to the superior-general, during her superiorate at Abergavenny. The first of these dated 23 April, the day the sisters arrived in Abergavenny, recounts Sister Thérèse's experience on that day.

> Dearly Beloved Mother, according to your wish, I came to Abergavenny today, 23 April, with dear Sister Paul de la Providence whom I had asked to accompany me on my first visit to the parish priest, Father Wray OSB. We were dismayed at the frosty reception he gave us. He told us that he could not give us recognition, since he did not know who we were, from where we came, or what we planned to do in his Mission. This must have been due to the Bishop having forgotten to notify Father Wray of our coming to Abergavenny, and the works we hope to do here. I have written to tell the Bishop of the reception we had, and to ask him to smooth out our difficulties. Prayer is the only means to which we can have recourse at present. On the other hand, we have reason to thank providence for all the good things we found in the house on our arrival, and which Mrs Herbert had arranged should be placed there for us. She even had the kindness to send us a telegram from London to welcome us to Abergavenny. Thank you for your prayers to which we are indebted as also those of our Sisters, for the ability to accept with resignation the pain of today. I must stop writing now, as it is past midnight.

This rejection of the sisters by Father Wray was to be a source of great suffering on the part of the sisters for almost twenty years. Indeed there were strained relationships between the two sides till the death of Father Wray. At one point, it almost led to the sisters leaving Abergavenny. They were not allowed to start a school, which was always their chief aim in each foundation, and they were not allowed to teach in the parish school till 1932. The first five sisters who composed the community were: Sister Thérèse du Saint Esprit, the superior, Sister Paul de la Providence, Sister Béatrix Marie Savidan, Sister Félix Cécile Clery and Sister Agnès de Jesus Gaonach. In a spirit of faith and courage, they began to earn their livelihood soon after their arrival in Abergavenny. They soon had requests for private lessons. In her letter of 6 May, Sister Thérèse wrote to the superior-general:

> Mr Tainly, a very influential man and a good Catholic, says he will send us his five young ladies for French conversation lessons; what is more, he says that a lady friend of his wants us to educate her 3 daughters, but for the present we have no Sisters able to teach in English. As for myself, I am spending the greater part of my time in the kitchen because Marianne, our maid, knows hardly anything about cooking. Dear Father Wray seems satisfied with your letter. I asked him to come and bless the house, but he has not yet set foot in it. We have bought a piano for 400 francs; we shall also need a mandolin. I have ordered some music for the piano lessons, materials for painting and artwork, also books for the French lessons.

The first task of the sisters with regard to accommodation was to convert the shed (**Plate 29**) into a workroom for the needlework classes. It needed new flooring, a stove for the winter and a window large enough to let in the light. But in order to do this, Sister Thérèse thought it would be wiser to consult Bishop Hedley, and even Mrs Herbert. One of the first tasks also was to make an inventory of all that Mrs Herbert had supplied for the sisters by way of furniture, and send it to the superior-general. She spoke of the great generosity of Mrs Herbert in providing for all their needs. The housekeeper, aged eighty-two, had stayed on at Pen-y-pound House when the sisters arrived there. She was very helpful in introducing the sisters to various aspects of life in Abergavenny. Mrs Herbert had also allowed the gardener to stay on, as there were extensive grounds belonging to the property.

Six weeks elapsed before Sister Thérèse wrote her next letter, dated 21 June 1906, during which time the general bursar had visited the community. In the brief report of her visit she wrote:

> The Sisters are still in the process of settling in, nevertheless the Holy Rule is faithfully observed and charity reigns in the community. Each of the Sisters brings to the arranging of the house and to the preliminary tasks her entire good will and all her energies.

Sister Thérèse wrote to the superior-general three days after the departure of the general bursar to thank her for the visit. She said:

> I do not want to put off any longer the expression of my heartfelt gratitude to you for having arranged that our dear Mère Marie Angélina should visit us. Her sound advice, her wise counsel strengthened our souls and cheered our hearts, which sometimes feel discouragement.

Mrs Herbert invited their visitor to Llanover, where she entertained her, and spoke about the work of the sisters in Abergavenny, and of any further needs, to which she was happy to respond. They had thirty hours a week over and above the needlework of which they had more than they could do. Soon a request was made for more sisters to help in their apostolate. They needed an extra four sisters, and in response to this need, the superior-general sent four more sisters in July, only three months after the arrival of the five pioneers. These were: Sister Louise de St Yves Corre to visit the poor and the sick, Sister Léon Marie Cosson for the needlework, Sister Octavie du Carmel Ollivier for the French lessons and Sister Marie Philomène Clery as bursar.

When the sisters first arrived in Abergavenny, they were pleased to find that there was a group of Catholic ladies already working for the poor of Monmouthshire. Sister Thérèse mentions this too in a letter to the superior-general:

> Last Sunday for the first time the meeting of Catholic ladies was held at the Convent. There are 22 of them, and they work to help provide clothing for the poor in Monmouthshire. Our Sisters have offered their services for cutting out and making up garments. The meeting was presided by Mrs Bleiddian Herbert, the daughter-in-law of the Honourable Mrs Herbert. It was she who served the tea and provided all that was needed for it. All went well, with God's help, but what a long day it was!

An unusually long interval between this letter and the next one must have been due to the illness of Sister Thérèse during the summer, to which she alluded in her letter of 11 November 1906. By this time, the sisters were already well accepted, and the people were beginning to take a personal interest in them. One of them wrote her a kind letter having heard of Sister Thérèse's illness. This letter, which came from a Fred Daniel, was printed in *La Colombe*, 1906. It read:

> I wish to send you something to make you strong, but I do not know what you would like, so I send you a £1 (worth over £50 today), and will you please buy whatever you like for yourself. Surely, you will have trouble enough being wrongly turned out of your own country and being 'foreigners in a strange land' without the additional trial of sickness… I should like to write to you in French but alas! I cannot speak a word of your beautiful language. With kindest regards to your community, and hoping to hear soon of your complete restoration to health.

When Sister Thérèse next wrote to the superior-general on 11 November 1906, she gave news of her state of health, which by this time had improved. She also spoke about their work, and in this letter we have the first mention of the sisters taking in pupils. She wrote:

> I send you my heartfelt thanks for your last very kind letter. The health of the Sisters remains good apart from a few colds. As for myself, I have quite recovered from my illness and am able to attend to all my occupations, as before, thank God! It is now over 6 months since we arrived in Abergavenny, and we have more or less settled in. Everyday we make new acquaintances, and I dare hope that the number of our pupils will increase. We visit poor Catholic families regularly, once a month. Sister Louis de St Yves has entered on her notebook the names of about 100 families that she has visited over the past 3 months. I sometimes send Sister Marie Philomène with her, so as to be able to tell Mrs Herbert that there are two Sisters who visit the poor. I visit them myself whenever I can. We receive a warm welcome from these poor unfortunates, and I think that we shall do a lot of good among them. They began telling us their troubles as soon as we started to visit them. There are about 800 Catholics in Abergavenny but only about 300 come to church.

By this time, news of the sewing workshop was also encouraging. It was attended by girls of between 9 and 14 years of age, but the sisters could take them only from 7 o'clock in the evening. The older girls worked in the printers or in the laundry. The younger ones were at school, which they were obliged to attend until they completed their fourteenth year. There were forty-six of them on the books. They were taken in two groups because the room could not hold all of them at the same time. She said that Mrs Herbert had supplied them with quantities of unbleached cotton and of cotton fabric for the girls to sew. Mrs Herbert felt that the girls would come to the class more readily if they were able to make something for themselves. These sewing classes, which were organised for these poor girls three times a week, were very much appreciated in the town. A protestant lady so admired the work the sisters were doing for these girls that she offered her help if it was needed.

The community Annals for the year 1906 describe the first annual Christmas treat that was organized for these girls. Mrs Herbert and her daughter, Mrs Maxwell, were so pleased with the work done by these girls that they wished to reward them by giving them a Christmas party and a Christmas tree every year. A splendid pine tree was brought from Llanover estate and laden with all kinds of gifts. These remained on display for the two days on which the parties were held. The private school pupils had the honour of the first party and the first choice of gifts. They put all their heart and soul into singing 'Que J'aime Ce Divin Enfant' and into reciting little verses 'Pins and Needles', 'Pussy and Little Mouse'. On the second day the thirty older girls sang, with great feeling and ardour, the Welsh National Anthem, 'Hen Wlad fy Nhadau'. This group enjoyed themselves as much as the other children had enjoyed themselves the previous day. Mrs Maxwell and Mrs Vaughan graced the occasion with their presence.

The following summer, Mrs Herbert provided another treat for the girls; this too was duly recorded in the community Annals. It was announced immediately after the Christmas party. When the day arrived, three carriages turned up outside the front door of the convent. The fifty-three children and the sisters who were waiting there, set off in triumphant mood for their destination. At Llanover plenty of surprises awaited them. The lady of the manor had planned a day which she succeeded in making most enjoyable to them. They stepped from the carriages, and wended their way along the beautiful pathways of the property. The children had never seen anything like it before. They were particularly delighted with the boat trip across the lake. Their appetites having been sharpened by the fresh air, it was with ill-disguised haste that the young people sat down to the table, prepared out of doors, and laden with the delicious food prepared for them, to which they duly did honour! After such a feast, the need to express gratitude made itself felt, and they did themselves credit by their well-read compliments and their singing, in English, French and Welsh, which earned them the approbation of Mrs Herbert, and of all present. The games and races went on until evening, and it was not without regret that the sisters and the girls got back into the carriages to return to Abergavenny. The account of the day recorded in the Annals ended:

> Even so, we were pleased to have been able to contribute, for a day, to the happiness of our poor young girls whose life-experience is one of privation, and we were glad thus to have earned more of their trust and affection, all of which, given time, should enable us to do all the good we hope.

There are six extant letters, which recount *inter alia*, the rapid growth in the number of girls attending the evening sewing classes and the problems arising from lack of space. Sad to relate, there is also mention in the next letter about the continuing problem with Father Wray. On 14 January, 1907, Sister Thérèse wrote:

I send you herewith our accounts for 1907. We have been able to make some savings, thanks to the generous kindness of Mrs Herbert who paid the taxes and gas bills for us, as also the gardener's wages. If we had had to pay all these expenses, we would not have been able to do so from our slender income. The cost of the maintenance and repairs of this large house amounts to quite a considerable sum each year. As of now, we are caught in the crossfire between Mrs Herbert – who wants us to organize a sale of work, the proceeds of which will be for improvements to the sewing room – and Father Wray who is opposed to this. Bishop Hedley is due to come to Abergavenny in the spring, to administer the Sacrament of Confirmation. I intend to speak to him about this difficulty and to ask him what ought to be done. It is a great relief to know that our mother visitors will be soon coming this way. In the meanwhile we pray and keep quiet so as not to draw any more fire!

Twelve days later the asssistant general arrived, accompanied by the general bursar. They spent two days in the community, and carried out the canonical visitation, on 26 and 27 January. At the end of the visit as was the custom, the assistant general wrote her report:

The house is well kept, and governed with piety, prudence and regularity. Mutual trust exists, and our dear Sisters are very devoted. Good is being done: the poor, and the sick are visited, and seventy girls and young women come to the community of an evening, to learn how to sew. Regrettably, the space available for these classes is inadequate, and it is hoped that it will prove possible for this work to be housed in a more spacious room, or better still, in a proper workroom. Such is the wish of the Superior who will do what she can to bring this about. The Sisters have a goodly number of lessons in French and the fine arts, and there is no shortage of needlework to be done.

The need for a more spacious workroom for the sewing class was realised when Mrs Herbert gave £35 (£1,700 in today's currency) to acquire a larger room. In order to raise funds for the furnishing of it, a bazaar was organised, and advertised as follows in all the country houses, in the town, and among the sisters' acquaintance and pupils:

A Grand Bazaar will be held on Saturday 27 June 1908, at the Convent in Pen-y-pound House, Abergavenny, for the benefit of the new workroom. The Honourable Mrs Fitzmaurice will open the Bazaar at 3 o'clock. The following are among the ladies who have consented to hold stalls: The Honourable Mrs Herbert of Llanover, the Honourable Mrs Maxwell, Mrs Williams, Ty Clyd, the Honourable Mrs Bleiddian Herbert, the Misses Findlay, Mrs G. Vaughan of Glen Trothy and others. Admission free. Open from 3 to 9 pm.

In the letter she wrote to the superior-general eight days after the event, Sister Thérèse said that the bazaar was a great succees, and earned for them the sum of 700 francs. An interesting detail in the written account of the bazaar refers to the fact that the sisters from the convents at Monmouth and Usk sent some of their needlework to be sold for them at the bazaar. The sale amounted to 150 francs, which was given to the two communities providing the needlework. She then goes on to say that Mrs Herbert was going to have the desired improvements made to the workroom—the architect's estimated fee was 900 francs. The Herbert family also gave a great deal of help with the sale. Following this event, Mrs Herbert provided transport for the sisters to go to Llanover and spend the afternoon there; a pleasant occasion but, during their visit, Mrs Herbert told them that she wanted her gardener back and that the sisters would have to find another one. Sister Thérèse ends her letter with a further reference to the disagreement between Mrs Herbert and Father Wray. She wrote:

> It seems that eight years ago, Father Wray had a disagreement with the Herbert family, and so it has remained. This is our heaviest cross; it sometimes becomes a very heavy one. Fortunately, the Sisters prove good Cyrenians and help me to bear it all. We are very happy in community.

Work began on the room destined to be the new workroom for needlework. By 30 August it was ready for use. The sewing classes began on 14 September in the new spacious workroom, and everyone was delighted with it. At this time, too, there was a Eucharistic Congress held in London, and Mgr Morelle, by then Bishop of Saint Brieuc, came to take part in it. We learn from a subsequent letter that he also managed to make a fleeting visit to a few of the sisters in Monmouthshire: Mrs Herbert invited him to Llanover, where he was the guest of the Herbert family. The superiors from the Brecon, Monmouth, Usk, Pontypool and Abergavenny communities went to visit him at Llanover. The Congress proved a great success—the protestant press was full of praise for the Pope's Legate Cardinal Vanutelli, and the congress itself drew crowds of admiring spectators.

The early years of the sisters at Abergavenny, thanks to the great generosity of the Honourable Mrs Herbert, were free of money worries. In this, the foundation was indeed fortunate when we consider what other convents had to suffer in this regard, as we have already seen in previous chapters. The sisters at Abergavenny, as elsewhere, had to deal with the inevitable language problem, their inadequate knowledge of

English, and the lack of qualified sisters to undertake the work demanded of them. Studies were undertaken without delay. As early as 1907, Sister Marie Béatrix obtained her ALCM (Associate of the London College of Music), and other successes were soon to follow. The community had the help of domestic staff, as we have mention of Marianne in the kitchen. There is a reference too to a little maid, Anne Marie Trottin, who had gone to France for her holidays but whose father did not allow her to return to Abergavenny.

In her letter of 1 October 1908, Sister Thérèse writes:

> There is much work to be done in this big house where we now have 2 lady boarders (teachers from the intermediate school). We have written to Marie Le Men, offering her the same conditions as Anne Marie Trottin had. If she does not accept, I don't know how we will manage during the winter, with 5 or 6 fires to be lit every morning, and the cooking and the garden. From now on, since we have to pay a gardener, we try to do as much as we can ourselves. Our Sisters are engaged in some very intricate needlework for Mme Tavier in London. The sisters have had no holiday at all, and these past few days, they had to get up at 5 am so as to try and get the work finished on time. The trousseaus they are making are really quite splendid.

After having agreed to come, Marie le Men had written to say that she had changed her mind. However, Sister Thérèse did eventually find a maid from France, as she wrote:

> …our little maid arrived on Wednesday together with one from Roscoff for Sister Amélie des Anges at Brecon.

Sister Thérèse sent her next letter, dated 1 October 1908, to the superior-general with Sister Marie Philomène who was going to Saint Brieuc. In it, she gave an update on their work and ministry. She spoke of their private lessons, and of their first needlework class to be held in the new workroom on 29 September, the Feast of St Michael. It was exactly two years since fifteen girls had atttended their first class. By now there were seventy girls attending, thirty of them were Protestants, but they took part with the Catholics in the readings, prayers and hymns which preceded each lesson. The sisters saw these lessons as a serious form of apostolate, for the spiritual formation of those who attended. Sister Thérèse then asks for an extra sister to help with the sewing and the housework, as the sisters were very tired with all the work they had to do.

There is a vivid description in the community Annals of the Christmas party of 1908, which was held in the new workroom. The annalist's account provides a delightful picture of the setting, as well as of the hosts and their young guests:

> The Christmas tree, sent from Llanover, was the focus of the celebration held in our new workroom named after St Michael. At 3 pm, ninety-three children and young girls gathered for the party, which they well deserved. The little girls sang and recited while the older ones from the printers, Protestants for the most part, entertained the honourable ladies present with their fun and frolic: 'Perrette and her Milkpail'. The good Mrs Herbert of Llanover who was in France at this time, delegated her daughter-in-law, Mrs Bleiddian Herbert to represent her. This excellent lady was only too pleased to contribute to making others happy, as were the members of the excellent Findlay family. With great satisfaction they watched the young people enjoying themselves at the tastefully decorated long tables, laden with good things. After the tea, it was time for the Christmas tree which, adorned with crackers, birds, flowers and gifts, stretched out its long branches as if to say: 'I'll not forget anyone.' And indeed no one in this joyous gathering was forgotten. An hour later, back in their homes, the children were telling of the lovely time they had had.

The sister promised for the sewing class, Sister Jeanne de St Joseph Coadou, duly arrived, on 8 January 1909. With the addition of this extra sister, it was decided to start a daytime dressmaking class, which was within the norms for such classes. To begin with, the sisters would take, as apprentices, girls of over 14 years of age who had left the Catholic school. Sister Thérèse wrote to a retailer in London, who sold articles made by religious communities, to ask him if he could supply them with orders. In this way, they would not deprive the Abergavenny shops of their custom.

When the convent at Usk closed in 1909, Sister Aline returned to France, and Sister Thérèse sent the 1908 community accounts with her, together with a letter. On 15 January 1909, Sister Thérèse was able to record that the year ahead was likely to be a good one for private lessons. On 15 January, Sister Octavie gave her first French lesson in a private school, which was non-Catholic. Because of their exclusion from the parish school, the sisters tried other avenues of apostolate. The headmistress in the non-catholic school there was very well disposed towards the sisters. She had written to all the parents, asking whether they had any objections to the sisters giving French lessons in the school. Only six families out of a total of forty had objected to this. It was three months before Sister Thérèse wrote her next letter to the superior-general, and the reason was undoubtedly because of the pressure of work. We do not hear any more in the correspondence about these lessons, and we can assume that they presented no problems, but were phased out as the sisters took in more private pupils for their own convent school.

Writing to the superior-general on 13 April 1909, Sister Thérèse begins by alluding to the long interval between this letter and her previous one: She wrote:

> Throughout last term, we were very busy, so all our Sisters are really tired, and the Easter break is welcome. Yesterday, we went for a long walk; today the Sisters are writing their letters. Next week, it will be back to work. Our daytime sewing class began on 22 March, with two apprentices, one a Catholic the other a Protestant. They have committed themselves to working with us for two years. We are not going to pay them anything but the work they do will, I hope, help us to meet our expenses. Moreover this will be a form of apostolate, enabling us to work for the good of the souls of these girls who are so exposed to worldly influences, once they have left school. In this connection, we have many consolations: Sister Louis through her visits to the poor has had the joy of bringing back to the church numerous persons who had not approached the Sacraments for years. Father Wray seemed very pleased on Sunday. He said that this year and last year he had not seen so many Catholics make their Easter duties, since his coming to Abergavenny.

There are no letters extant for 1910, nor are there entries in the community Annals for the years 1910 to 1918, other than the reports which Mother Marie Dominique wrote at the end of the canonical visitations which she made in April 1910 and in June 1913. These two reports are very similar: both reports speak positively about the community and its works. The needlework classes were continuing to grow. The sisters had started to give lessons during the day as well as the evening classes. Five girls were enrolled for the daytime class, and one hundred for the evening classes. The private lessons in French and the fine arts were numerous. The sisters continued their visits to the sick and the aged, bringing them material help and words of comfort and consolation.

Sister Thérèse's next letter addressed to the superior-general is dated 25 January 1911.

> I have just finished our accounts for 1910 which I send herewith. As you will notice, our receipts were not as high as the previous year; this is due to a decrease in the number of French lessons, 800 francs less. Fortunately, the lessons in music and art go some way to compensating for this. In the workshop, sewing lessons keep us busy as ever, with more Protestants than Catholics. Our five little boarders are very good; we take them to Mass every morning **(Plate 30)**. The Sisters are not

very strong and have a lot to do; I think that when one is not very robust, physically, the spiritual life is not so vigorous. My responsibility weighs heavily sometimes on my shoulders, yet what is this as compared with all the worries and concerns that you have at the present time?

Just one month after this letter was written, we read of a flu epidemic, which affected all the community, and the five boarders of which there is mention at this time. It was noted:

Our community has been like a hospital: our five boarders and all the Sisters except Sister Béatrix Marie have had the flu and they are not yet over it. Each of your daughters at Abergavenny works from 6 am till 9 pm. The sewing classes for the poor entails a great deal of work: cutting out, shaping, tacking etc., for each one. You could not take either Sisters Louis de St Yves or Octavie du Carmel (referring to their proposed transfers to another foundation) without having to cease the visits to the poor, or sending away our boarders, or ceasing to give the French lessons that we still have. The Sisters' health is not particularly good; I am strong, thank God, and able to help with the washing and ironing, also the cleaning etc... Were I not able to do this, we would have to employ a char woman. Forgive me for writing at such length; I am not very good at expressing myself in a few words.

The following letter, dated 13 November 1911, is the first of eighteen letters which Sister Thérèse wrote during the next three years to Mère St Georges who had been re-elected as superior-general:

I am afraid that I have not written to you for a long time, but that is because I was waiting for news of the little postulant whom the priest at Wrexham proposed sending to us, to replace Anne Hogan. Sister Léon's niece has arrived, accompanied by her uncle Father Corson from Ploubalay. He stayed with us for two and a half days and celebrated Mass in church on each of the three mornings that he was here. Father Wray was very nice to him; yes, our Reverend Father is improving! I know that there are many invalids at the Mother House nowadays and that my dear Sister Guillaume Marie (her sister) is one of them. I know that all her spiritual and corporal needs are provided for and that she has the consolation of your frequent visits.

In January 1912, an unexpected event took place. The sisters woke in the early hours of a bitterly cold Sunday morning to find water pouring down from the third floor to the ground floor. They had to turn off the water at the mains, mop up and do without any water for the remainder of the day. They realised that they would have to do considerable repairs to the house during the spring months, and the superior asked permission from the superior-general to undertake this. The accounts for the previous year were satisfactory. When she wrote to send the accounts for 1911, she said:

> This term is not so good and we are making a novena for the intention of an increase of requests for private lessons. It will please you to know that I am at present instructing four persons, men and women, in the Catholic faith.

Once again, as happened so often during those early years, the Honourable Mrs Herbert financed the necessary repairs to Pen-y-pound House. Sister Thérèse wrote:

> Today, I am pleased to be able to tell you that Mrs Herbert is going to pay for these. She instructed her steward to notify us of this, and when he came to see us, he said: 'I am going to do my utmost to ensure that no more rain, no more water, gets into your house'. We had recommended this matter, during March, to dear St Joseph; the outcome has been far beyond our expectations. May the good Lord be blessed for this and may he repay our debt of gratitude to Mrs Herbert.

In the midst of their own financial difficulties, the sisters were always ready to help others, even their own congregation. One occasion was when the sisters learned of the sufferings and difficulties endured by the sisters during the expulsions, and the fines they incurred for non-compliance with the laws. In her letter of 21 May 1912, she wrote:

> Having heard from Father Corson that you are at Ploubalay, I hasten to address our Pentecost wishes to you there. We know that you have frequently to go before a court and to pay unjust fines; in so far as we can, we share in this harassment. Our community has some small savings at the Mother House, these as well as the small income from my patrimony, are, as you know, at your disposal. Do make use of them; we should be so happy if you did.

The sisters always hoped, since their arrival in Abergavenny, to have a private school, but as we saw the terms of the contract for their occupancy of Pen-y-pound House did not allow them to have a day school for children, under fourteen years of age. Undaunted by this stipulation, however, the sisters still did not lose hope of such a development, and when Bishop Hedley came to Abergavernny on 16 May 1912 to administer the sacrament of confirmation, Sister Thérèse asked him if the sisters could start a school for Protestant pupils, since they did not want to compete for pupils with the parish school. "I am thinking of asking him for permission to start a fee-paying school for protestant pupils," Sister Thérèse noted in one of her letters at this time. "We shall never get into the Catholic school while Father Wray is still alive."

In her letter of 7 July 1912, Sister Thérèse wrote to tell the superior-general that her request to open a private school was turned down by the bishop. She also said that the number of requests for private French lessons was on the decrease, but there was no shortage of sewing to be done. Attendance at the evening sewing class was still very good. The devotedness of the sisters responsible for this class, and their visits to the poor, earned them the appreciation and good will of many in the town, though they also had their enemies. The next letter dated 19 July and following so soon after the previous one, was prompted by the notification that Sister Ste Octavie, who gave private lessons, was to be given her transfer. These lessons and the few boarders they had at the time, provided their main source of livelihood. This news filled Sister Thérèse with real dismay. In fact, in a letter of 28 July, we learn that Sister Ste Octavie was not moved from Abergavenny, and Sister Thérèse duly thanked the superior-general for allowing her to stay in the community. It is interesting to note that perhaps on account of the two main works of the community, there were only two transfers during the first six years of its existence; and these were of sisters whose placement lasted a few months only.

Sister Thérèse wrote to the superior-general on 29 October 1912, as follows:

> The venerable Mrs Herbert sent for me last Saturday to say good-bye before she left to spend the winter at her London house. Today, her steward came to tell us that she had been taken ill. They sent for the doctor from London and for one of the Abergavenny doctors. They say she is a little better, though not out of danger; she must be at least 90 or 92 years of age. When I saw her last Saturday, she enquired after your health, that of Mother Marie Angélina and of Mgr Morelle.

However, less than one week later, she wrote again to convey the sad news of Mrs Herbert's death, after barely a week's illness. She was suffering from influenza, complicated by pulmonary congestion. Sister Thérèse wrote:

> She had the benefit of receiving the last sacraments and of being assisted by Father Maxianus of Kerbénéat, as well as her three sons. Her daughter, Mrs Maxwell, has not been able to summon up the courage to look at her mother dead. Poor Mrs Maxwell, she loses a great deal in losing a mother.

The family asked that the sisters should keep vigil in the mortuary chamber to pray, night and day, for the repose of the soul of the deceased until her funeral took place. The requiem Mass was celebrated in the banqueting hall, transformed for the occasion into a chapel. Sister Thérèse wrote to the communities at Pontypool and Monmouth (the community at Usk had closed by this time) to ask them to send a deputation to the funeral. Mrs Herbert was buried at Llanover in a grave next to her mother's grave. Sister Thérèse noted:

> In her death we lose a great benefactress. Having known her for almost ten years, (since Sister Thérèse first arrived in Monmouth in 1902), I feel sad at her death, even though she could be exacting at times.

Things were to change for the sisters after the death of Mrs Herbert. Shortly after her death, Sister Thérèse received a letter from the tax collector informing her that the solicitor of the late Mrs Herbert had notified him that the family were no longer going to pay the rates and taxes for Pen-y-pound House. The interest on the bequest to the community would just about suffice to meet this considerable annual expense.

Much of the subsequent correspondence dealt with the aftermath of negotiations about Pen-y-pound House following the death of Mrs Herbert. The community had a visit from Mère Marie Alvarez, the superior-general, and Sister Marie Dominique, the provincial, in June 1913. While they were there, they met with Mrs Bleiddian Herbert who told them that it was required by English law that every community should have a certain degree of financial security. The Herbert family solicitor said that the interest on the legacy made to the sisters by the late Mrs Hebert would not be sufficient to make them financially viable. Moreover, as the family did not want the sisters to become dependent on them, they asked that the mother house should be answerable for the sisters, in a case of necessity. Sister Thérèse requested the superior-general to write a letter undertaking responsibility for the community, which she could show to Mrs Bleiddian Herbert and Mrs Maxwell, one from which they would see that the sisters were financially independent. This would also serve to reassure the trustees of Pen-y-pound House.

The next move was an attempt to gain independence from the trustees, and so it was decided to look into this. On 26 August, Sister Thérèse wrote to the superior-general:

> I have just received the letter which I am forwarding to you herewith, it is from Mrs Herbert's solicitor. What a good thing it would be, if we ceased to be under the control of trustees, and if the Congregation were to have the ownership of our house in Abergavenny. In proposing that the lease be made permanent, the executors of Mrs Herbert's will seek to ensure that they no longer have to pay for major repairs (to Pen-y-pound House.) Were this to be the case, and having the 1000

francs interest on the legacy, with which we could pay the rates and taxes, we would by the help of Divine Providence be able to manage without their generosity. What we must really try to obtain from Mgr Hedley is that he revokes his prohibition to start a school. We are, it is true, beginning to disregard it since we have 12 children promised next September. Among these are two little boarders, the children of Dr Dwyer, from Ireland, who is living six miles away from Abergavenny, at Beaufort, where there is no school and no Catholic church. I have not the courage to refuse these two young souls the opportunity of learning about their religion.

There was a rumour that Bishop Hedley was very much an invalid, that his heart condition was deteriorating, and that, when he was no longer bishop, the diocese of Newport would be merged with that of Menevia. If and when this happened, it was also rumoured that the Benedictines would no longer be in charge of the diocese, and Father Wray might well be given his transfer. Sister Thérèse writes:

> We await in peace all that may be, in God's good time. I shall be writing to Mr Hunter that I have communicated to you what he proposes and that you will let him have a reply as soon as possible.

At the beginning of December, Sir Arthur Herbert wrote to say that he had succeeded in investing the money his mother left the community at a 5% rate of interest. Bishop Hedley and Mr Hunter had not yet notified her of any new decision with regard to the house. She wondered whether they would not make any changes until 1916 when the present lease was due to expire. On 28 December 1913, she wrote again:

> Greetings and good wishes for the New Year. Once again the celebrations of Christmas which, in England, entails a great deal of extra correspondence to be done, is over. But all the numerous gifts which kindly providence arranged that we should receive have not yet been consumed. Over and above all these treats, on Christmas Eve, Lady Herbert of Llanover came in person to hand me an envelope containing £50 sterling (£2,250 in today's currency) and a letter which read as follows: 'My sister, my two brothers, Sir Arthur Herbert and Colonel Bleiddian Herbert and I (Sir Ivor) agreed that we should contribute £12.10.0 for the maintenance of the community in which our late mother took such an interest. It is now my pleasure to hand over this money to you and at the same time to ask you to continue to pray for the repose of the soul of my dear mother, as also for the intentions by which we are united.

The annual Christmas tree party initiated by the Honourable Mrs Herbert continued after her death, and the party for Christmas 1913 is recorded as follows:

> Yesterday we had the Christmas Tree Party for our girls who attend the sewing class. The ladies Herbert from Llanover, from Coldbrook, from Trebencyn honoured us with their presence. Our girls, 83 in all, were thrilled with the pretty gifts and with the abundance of good things that there were to eat. All the garments that they made since September were displayed in the room which had been decorated for the occasion. After the party they were allowed to take these garments home with them.

There is only one letter extant for each of the next two years, the one for 1914 was written in January, the one for 1915, in November. There is no mention in the Annals as to the life of the community during this long interval. In the letter dated 16 January 1914, Sister Thérèse gives various items of news about members of the community, and about the financial situation in the community, and the work of the sisters:

> Sisters Basilien and Yves de St Joseph came from Pontypool for a week during which they helped Sister Ste Octavie to prepare the term's work for her small class. I send you herewith our accounts for 1913. As you may notice the interest on the legacy and other providential gifts increased our income, but every year our house stands in need of repairs. At present the 'grande salle' needs to be repapered and to have its window replaced. Outside, the fruit trees are now very old and produce little fruit, and so need to be replaced. Will you allow us to incur these expenses? Next August I shall have the happiness please God, of seeing you. Then I shall be able to talk to you about all these matters.

In her letter of 20 November 1915, Sister Thérèse announced the death of Bishop Hedley who had died on 12 November, from a heart complaint. His burial took place in one of the cemeteries in Cardiff. Three sisters from the community attended the funeral. Father Wray, the parish priest, reported that Mgr O'Reilly, the vicar general, and private secretary to Bishop Hedley, had been appointed vicar capitular, and that it was unlikely that the new bishop would be a Benedictine. Undoubtedly, this was wishful thinking too on the part of the sisters, since their Benedictine parish priest and a Benedictine bishop remained less than sympathetic to their educational plans for the foundation at Abergavenny. The last of the letters from Sister Thérèse to the superior-general, is dated 11 February 1916, and it contained the news they were waiting for with regard to the successor to Bishop Hedley. She wrote:

> This morning I received word of the appointment of an archbishop to
> succeed the late Mgr Hedley. His Holiness Pope Benedict XV has
> elevated the diocese to the rank of an archdiocese with its see at
> Cardiff. The one chosen to be archbishop is Mgr Bilsborrow OSB,
> formerly Bishop of Port Louis. We shall no doubt need to get in touch
> with the new prelate before the end of the year, in connection with the
> contract, leasing the house we occupy. Will you be so kind, dear Mother,
> to indicate the line we should take when the time comes?

The following year, another death was reported, this time within the congregation. On 31 May 1916, the death of Mère St Georges was announced; a great loss to the congregation. What a work-load she carried, including negotiating for the future survival of the congregation with the French government, appearing in court on numerous occasions and having to pay fines for the non-compliance of the members of the congregation with the unjust educational legislation! As we have seen in this study, she also negotiated and supervised the twelve new foundations in Wales, and entered into personal correspondence with the superiors of each community. She was succeeded as superior-general by Mère Marie Alvarez.

During the Great War years, there are few extant letters from Sister Thérèse to the new superior-general. There are four extant for the year 1917, none for 1918, one for 1919, and 2 for 1920. Most of these letters concentrate on the question of the parish and convent schools. In her letter, dated 7 July 1917, she touches on the question of the parish school. "Father Wray," she says,

> is having great difficulty with his school. The head teacher has been
> very ill and has been confined to bed for several weeks. I doubt that she
> will ever be able to take up her post again, even if she does recover, and
> the Education Committee has not a single qualified Catholic teacher to
> give as a replacement for Mrs Hadfield. I am wondering if the time has
> come for us to take on the Catholic school. As I had occasion to write to
> Mother Marie Dominique, I put this to her a fortnight ago. She replied
> that she could not see any Sister free at present to take this post to
> advantage. To fill it, we would need a qualified English Sister who is
> prudent, firm and without inhibitions about teaching in front of other
> members of staff: all three teachers share the same room where they
> have pupils of different age-groups. The infants only have a separate
> room. If we were to have the Catholic school, this would make it easier
> for us to start a secondary school later on, when we have qualified
> Sisters to staff it.

The problem relating to their inability to gain posts in the parish school was to continue for many years more, and is mentioned in subsequent correspondence.

The situation at St Michael's Convent at this time was promising. The number on roll was forty-five pupils, but there was no room for more at the time. The sisters therefore had started a private school, as allowed by their tenure of Pen-y-pound House, although there is no extant letter referring to how this was achieved in the face of the unlikely support of the parish priest or bishop. Presumably, the sisters kept to the letter of the agreement made about their residence in Pen-y-pound House, where it was stated that they could run a school for pupils over the age of fourteen years. The number of requests for private lessons in the fine arts continued to increase, and the needlework classes flourished. On 16 October 1917, she wrote:

> We were very pleased with the number of pupils we had to start the new school year, 48 in all, which is as many as our two small classrooms will hold; we had to turn away three others. In case Sister Félicien's health does not withstand the winter, I have arranged for Miss Sullivan to come and help her. She is the young woman who replaced Sister Félicien when she went to France for her profession, some two years ago. Miss Sullivan is happy to come back to us. She is going to study French and do some housework, as well as helping in class.

For the year 1918, there is nothing in the correspondence nor in the community Annals, other than the report written by Mother Marie Dominique after the visitation she made from June 13 to 15, 1918. It reads:

> The works show signs of development and God's blessing visibly rests on this little community. The good superior governs it with wisdom and prudence, and our Holy Rule is observed with remarkable piety. The number of pupils shows a notable increase. The pupils seem to love their teachers, and in so far as I am able to judge, are making good progress in their studies. The same holds true for the lessons given in music and art. Visits to the sick, sewing lessons and religious instruction of the poor children are also well carried out, and good is being done. The rooms that are used as classrooms are totally inadequate, and it will be absolutely necessary to remedy this as soon as times become less insecure, the war proving a hindrance to various undertakings.

Once the First World War was over, the superior-general who was beginning her visitation of all the communities in the English-speaking world, came to Abergavenny, where she stayed for three days, from 30 June till 2 July 1919. She gave a favourable report on the community and its works. The sixty-nine pupils on register in the private school made a good impression on her. She records the numbers involved in the various works. In addition to the sixty-nine pupils in the school, there were ninety-two taking piano lessons and eleven art lessons. The house, she noted, required more repairs and did not provide adequate space. She also recommended that the superior should be seconded in the work of visiting the poor by a sister who knew English and who had been professed for a number of years.

In the autumn of the same year, the superior-general began her visitation of the Daughters of the Holy Spirit communities in America, and it was to one of these that Sister Thérèse sent the letter of 26 December 1919. In this letter, she says that Father Wray had died in March of that year (thirteen years after the sisters had come to Abergavenny). She writes:

> There is so much that I need to tell you and which it is impossible to write in a letter. With the death of Father Wray last March, a new era has begun for our works. His successor, Father Wilson, counts a great deal on the help of the Sisters for the Mission. He says that he is anxious to see us replace teachers in the school, as and when they retire. He asked me whether we had enough qualified sisters to replace all four teachers in the school. Their salaries would represent an annual income for our house of about £450 (£10,000 today).

She then goes on to say how necessary it was that they should add new buildings to the property in order to cope with the growing number of pupils. The new archbishop and the trustees were of the same opinion.

The decision of the superior-general about the renewal of the lease of Pen-y-pound House was that they should try to get a long-term lease, since their hope of owning it did not materialise. They did, however, get a lease that was renewable every 99 years. More important still, they got permission to open a secondary school and boarding school. She also mentioned in her letter a conversation which she had with the Abbot of Ampleforth, who was superior of the Catholic mission, when he came to Abergavenny the previous October. She wrote:

> In my conversation with the Abbot, he said: 'I consider that your remaining here will be for the good of the locality, for the Abergavenny mission, and especially for your Congregation itself. If your Mother House has money to invest, the best way for it to do so, would be to use it for building a convent school here.'

From this conversation, it could be surmised that the ordeal about which she wrote in previous letters may have centred on the possibility of the sisters withdrawing from Abergavenny, as they were unable to get posts in the parish school, and were not free to open the school of their choice. She wrote:

> Three times in succession, we have made the Novena of the three Hail Marys, and it was at the end of them that we were notified of the 3 Trustees' decision concerning the lease of our house. Now we are invoking the Holy Spirit to enlighten you, so that it will be his decision that you make with regard to the proposed new building. Now it is time to prepare the Christmas tree and party for the poor girls who attend our sewing class, 72 in all. The local aristocracy, Father Wilson and Father Exton will also come to it.

A week later, on 2 January 1920, Sister Thérèse wrote to the superior-general to announce the news that the deputy head of the parish school had resigned, although she would remain in her post till the following March. She said that she had taken it upon herself, in accordance with what she understood to be the wish of the superior-general, to give Father Wilson, the successor to Father Wray, Sister St Apolline's certificates with a view to her applying for the post. In November 1920, the head teacher was due to retire. Sister Thérèse was very hopeful that, at long last, a sister would be appointed to the parish school. Sad to relate, however, the sisters were to be disappointed once again, as Sister St Apolline was not appointed to the vacant post.

Sister Thérèse's next letter indicates she had been to London, accompanied by Sister Marie du Christ, to meet with the solicitor who was one of the trustees of Pen-y-pound House. They had an interview with Mr Hunter, of Gibson & Hunter. According to this letter, it seemed as if the possibility of the sisters receiving Pen-y-pound House was still on the cards for she writes:

> I shall wait till I have received the Act of Donation that he promised to send, before I give you a resumé of what was said at the meeting. In the meantime, I plan to see Colonel Herbert and tell him about our interview with Mr Hunter, so as to have his opinion about it. Then we shall have to have an appointment with the Archbishop. Let us hope that he will give us a favourable answer. I know that you are praying for this intention.

The sisters were also hoping to get the authorisation to open a boarding school, which Mgr Hedley as one of the trustees had expressly forbidden.

The above is the last letter that Sister Thérèse wrote as superior of the community at Abergavenny. Her next one, dated 12 September 1921 was written from Pontypool, where she had just arrived as the new superior.

> The sacrifice God asks of me through you made hearts at St Michael's bleed. I hear you say: 'At Pontypool too you will find generous souls dedicated to working for the good of souls.' I know this but I feel absolutely incapable of directing and governing such a numerically large

community, and I wonder are you really aware of my incapacity for this. I am willing to try, but the good Lord will have to play the greatest part. The one great advantage of Pontypool is that of having the Blessed Sacrament in the house. Please pray that I may live constantly under the gaze of Jesus in his sacramental presence, and under his divine inspiration.

The transfer of Sister Thérèse to Pontypool as superior was felt not only by the sisters at Abergavenny, and by herself; the Herbert family also had something to say about it. Two of them did not hesitate to write to Mgr Morelle, now bishop of Saint Brieuc, and to the superior-general, objecting to the move. In her letter to the former, dated 18 March 1922, the Honourable Mrs Herbert of Trebencyn wrote as follows:

> The Convent of the Daughters of the Holy Spirit at Abergavenny was founded, as your Lordship knows, by my mother-in-law, and she requested that Sister Thérèse du Saint Esprit be appointed the superior of the Convent. Some six months ago, changes were made and Sister Thérèse was sent to Pontypool. As the only Catholic among the wives of Mrs Herbert's three sons, I am the one who sees and hears what goes on in our small parish; and so it is that I notice with keen regret, what a difference the change of superior has brought among all who take an interest in St Michael's School and Convent. Through her tact and admirable *savoir-faire*, Sister Thérèse was able to sort out many problems and difficulties. I write this confidential letter to your Lordship in the hope that, if there were any possibility of a change being made in the course of this year, your Lordship would think of us and, if possible, give back to us the good superior whom the Honourable Mrs Herbert of Llanover, knowing the difficulties to be met with in our small parish, wanted to have as superior at St Michael's. If in writing to you like this, I am guilty of indiscretion, I beg your Lordship to forgive me. P.S. It goes without saying that Sister Thérèse is completely unaware of my writing to you.

Mgr Morelle replied to this letter saying that he understood the disappointment of the Herbert family at this unavoidable necessity. The rigorous requirements of the new Code of Canon Law meant that the mandate of a superior had to be limited to a specific number of years in any one community.

The requirements of the new Code of Canon Law made it virtually impossible for the major superiors of the Congregation to send Sister Thérèse back to Abergavenny. A few months later, they did appoint as superior someone whose gifts were more like those of Sister Thérèse than were those of her immediate successor, Sister St Thomas d'Aquin. She had been superior at Pontypool, before coming to Abergavenny. Accustomed to the spacious rooms at Park House and to the large convent school there, she found it hard to settle within the cramped and narrow confines of Pen-y-pound House and missed the schoolgirls, many of them boarders, in a school, which she had seen grow from strength to strength. In June 1922, the assistant general came to make the visitation of the community at Abergavenny where she found much to commend, other than the acute lack of space. In her letter to the superior-general, she wrote: "Sister St Thomas is not at all at home here…" A few weeks later, she was recalled to France and appointed superior of the community of Rostrenen, in Brittany.

Sister St Thomas was replaced as superior of the community at Abergavenny by Sister Amélie des Anges Le Bihan who had been superior at Brecon since 1905. She too had to make the sacrifice of leaving a community, a parish and a locality where she had devoted herself to the growth and development of St David's school and community from small and unpromising beginnings. At St Michael's too, her mandate proved a time of further growth and consolidation, especially of the convent school. Some idea of this is afforded by short entries in the community Annals and by six letters, which Sister Amélie wrote to the superior-general between 1922 and 1928. In her first letter, she thanked the superior-general for agreeing the plans for an extension of the school. There was a pressing need for a playroom, a dining room and a dormitory.

Sister Amélie undertook the necessary negotiations for building the extension. Colonel Herbert was in agreement and spoke to the bishop to seek his approval. In the autumn term of 1922, there were ninety-seven pupils on the registers, and there was need for a room in which to play on rainy days. The next step towards making more adequate provision for the growing number of pupils is indicated by a brief entry in the community Annals, dated 23 December 1922:

> Purchase of a small house and a piece of land adjoining the convent, obtained through the intercession of *La Petite Thérèse* [St Thérèse of Lisieux]. The very devoted Lady Herbert has given us £140 (£3,700 today), to help furnish the house.

Even though this house with its three bedrooms, two downstairs rooms and kitchen helped to ease the shortage of space, the need for a playroom and more classrooms remained acute.

In the letter, which she wrote to the superior-general on 1 January 1924, Sister Amélie says:

Now that the site has been acquired by our Congregation, I hope that we shall be permitted to build on it. The contractor tells us that the building we envisage will cost £1,900 [£52,000 in today's currency]. We have 106 pupils on the school register this term. If, as we hope, divine providence enables us to maintain these numbers it will not take us long to repay the loan we are going to have to take out for the building. Lady Herbert came to view the little house and liked it very much. Six boarders and two Sisters now sleep there.

Presumably the permission to build was obtained without much delay since a March entry in the Annals states: "Father Hilary Wilson blessed the first stone of the building to be erected on the ground we purchased." This building seems to have been completed without any undue delay, and in September, the annalist was able to note: "Blessing of the school building followed by that of five crucifixes to be hung, one in each classroom." Eventually this building, with further extensions in subsequent years, was to become the junior school of St Michael's Convent School (Plate 31). These new classrooms must have eased the overcrowding in Pen-y-pound House, and made it possible for the community to occupy a little more space for their prayer-life. In October of that year, the convent chapel was blessed and Mass celebrated there for the first time by Father Hilary Wilson (who was about to leave Abergavenny). In November, another Benedictine priest, Father Rylance, replaced Father Wilson.

There are no letters for the year 1925, but as the community Annals record, the first months of it were marked by three particular events. On 1 February, there was an unexpected visit from one of the general councillors of the congregation who stayed with the community for two days. In March came the sudden death of Sister Léon Marie who had been a member of the community since its beginnings in 1906. She was buried in Llanfoist Cemetery, in a village just outside Abergavenny. In April, there was a canonical visitation made by a general councillor. In her report, she wrote that the works of the community were progressing well. There were about a hundred pupils on roll. The poor were being visited regularly, as stipulated in the foundation statutes. The sewing class also continued to flourish, and was well attended by a large number of girls. Since the last visitation, significant material improvements had been made to the buildings, with five new classrooms, a playroom and a music room. From this report, we see that nineteen years after their arrival in Abergavenny, the sisters remained faithful to the conditions of the contract that brought them there.

By the year 1926, the parish priest, Father Rylance OSB, was beginning to look to the sisters for financial assistance. On 26 January, Sister Amélie wrote:

> Father Rylance has called to see me. He too is finding it difficult to make ends meet and asked whether, by way of contributing to the work of the parish, we could provide the services of our sister organist *gratis pro Deo* and whether we could make an annual offering for the Mass he celebrates once a week at the convent. I replied that I would ask you to authorize my so doing. I very much hope that you will, because Father Rylance is very devoted to us.

Father Rylance, however, was transferred two years later to a parish in Preston, as moves were set in motion at this time to transfer the parish of Abergavenny from Ampleforth Abbey to Belmont Abbey, a move which only finally took place in 1978. Father Placid Smith OSB from Ampleforth replaced Father Rylance as parish priest of Our Lady and St Michael's, Abergavenny.

The next canonical visitation by the superior-general took place in October 1929, and lasted for three days. The written report at the end of the visit was as usual a favourable one. The visitor commented on the various works of the sisters which, since the foundation of the community, concentrated on the same areas of apostolate. She praised the spirit of charity and unity that existed among the sisters. The numbers attending the needlework classes remained steady; eighty in number, girls who came from poor homes. The convent school numbers were steadily increasing. There were one hundred and seventeen pupils on register, of whom seven were boarders. Thirty-one of these took lessons in the fine arts. Once a month, benevolent ladies from the town met at the convent to work for the relief of the indigent poor. A sister presided at these meetings. The building and outhouses were well maintained. The report ends with a prayer: "May the Immaculate Heart of Mary continue to bless this community and to obtain for it the grace of doing much good around it."

The community was always affected in one or other way by a change of superior. In January 1930, Sister Amélie des Anges was given a new mandate and, to the keen regret of the community at Abergavenny, left there to go as superior to the community at Aberystwyth. The sister appointed to replace her had been a member of the Abergavenny community since its beginnings in April 1906. This was Sister Béatrix Marie, whose main occupation had been the teaching of music and art. Her correspondence with the superior-general records the gratifying development of the sisters' educational work and affords glimpses of some of the community's joys and sorrows during the years of her mandate.

On 23 April 1931, the community celebrated the silver jubilee of its foundation. It was an occasion of great rejoicing for the community, which by this time was well established in the town, and the ecumenical impact of the presence of the sisters was notable. Most of their dealings were with non-Catholic pupils and parents in the town and the surrounding areas, and they were thus able to break down any remaining prejudices against Catholics. To mark the silver jubilee, "a Mass of thanksgiving for all the spiritual and temporal favours required was offered, and a beautiful new statue of St Michael was placed in our chapel." This statue was paid for by the widow of Colonel Herbert of Trebencyn, who wished it to serve as a memorial of him. One month later Sister Arsène Le Cleck, who had been headmistress in the private school for six years, returned to France, and was replaced by Sister Lucia Marie Nado.

The year 1932 saw the sisters' hopes of obtaining a teaching post in the Catholic school finally realised: Sister Imelda Kelly was appointed as teacher in charge of the infant class, as from 4 April 1932. The long wait of twenty-eight years for an opportunity to minister in the parish school had finally come to an end, and the joy of this achievement must have been very great. A source of even greater joy came later that year when, on 1 November 1932, Sister Elizabeth O'Shea took up her post in the parish school, as head teacher of Our Lady and St Michael's Catholic School, Abergavenny. Due recognition was given to devoted prayer for this outcome. It is noted in the Annals:

> The hope of obtaining the headship of the Catholic school seemed fading when thanks to the intercession of St Michael and St Thérèse of Lisieux, the victory was won.

At this time there were one hundred pupils, twenty of them Catholics, in the convent school. Throughout the summer holiday period, of that same year, the community had workmen in, and the annalist records:

> Central heating is being installed; the rooms and hall redecorated. The boarders' dormitory is being transformed into a class-room [it had just being decided, for whatever reason, not to take any more boarders] and the boarders' refectory into a community room where the community library had been installed. A sixth class has been formed and an extra sister, Sister Mary Ita McCann, arrived to teach in the convent school.

In October 1933, the annalist reported the death of Lord Treowen in his home in Llanarth. As was the custom when a member of the Herbert family died, the sisters "took it in turns to pray by the body of our generous and regretted benefactor." The Annals continue:

> The Annual Celebration with Christmas Tree and Party took place in the convent as usual, despite the recent bereavement of the Herbert family and of the community. To cancel it would have entailed great disappointment to our poor children. The Christmas party went as planned and great was the enjoyment of those attending, both children and adults. This party was one of the highlights of each year, and the children looked forward to it for months beforehand, and talked about it for days afterwards.

The convent school went from strength and was highly regarded by pupils and parents alike. In 1934, the pupils from the convent school gave a concert at the town hall for the first time; it was reported in the local press on 2 November as follows:

> St Michael's Convent School, Abergavenny, gave their first public entertainment, at the town hall on Wednesday and the school deserves praise for doing so well. The programme was an interesting and varied one, and all departments of the school from the tiny tots to the most senior scholars contributed. The school achieved a standard of success that was beyond expectations for a first effort and the successful result of their work has laid the foundations for future successes. During the interval, Lady Herbert of Coldbrook, who presided, traced the history of the Convent School since it began at Abergavenny twenty eight years earlier. From a small infants' class at the beginning, it had grown into a large school catering for pupils up to school-leaving age. She praised the educational philosophy of the sisters who took a personal interest in every individual pupil, and moulded them with a character and integrity, which served them well for the future.

The Mayor of Abergavenny, who proposed a vote of thanks to Lady Herbert, emphasised the high standard of education that was given in the school and pointed out that it was entirely self-supporting and did not receive a single penny from the government. The proceeds for the concert of £17.00 was used to buy the *Encyclopaedia Britannica* for the school library, and a rocking horse for the kindergarten.

The following year, it was the turn of the children in the parish school to go public, and they did great honour to their school. They gave a perfect performance of the play composed by the Honourable Mrs Roche, entitled *And With The Children*. Mrs Roche was present for the performance and was very appreciative. Present in the audience also were the chief inspector of schools and one of his colleagues. Both expressed their appreciation for the efforts of the children, praising especially their enunciation. The Mayor, in his address, also complimented the children.

In May 1935, when the next canonical visitation took place, Sister Béatrix Marie discussed with the visitor the possibility of an extension to the school building. Her request was granted. Before the end of 1935 the construction of three new classrooms, a cloakroom and a laboratory was begun. A brief entry in the Annals for 1936 reads:

> In February, Forms III and IV take possession of their new classrooms; the laboratory is almost finished. In July for the very first time the school was approved as a centre for The Oxford Local Examinations. Of the ten candidates for these, nine were successful.

The following year saw more building being undertaken, this time for the benefit of the community. In April 1937, work began on the construction of a new chapel with bedrooms above it. The chapel was beautifully designed, and spacious enough to hold a hundred people. In October, Sister Marie Béatrix, after thirty one years at Abergavenny, was asked to make the sacrifice of leaving to go to Brecon, as the new superior there. She was replaced by Sister Clarisse Joseph Hamon from Ingsdon whose mandate proved a short one since, less than a year later, her failing health made it necessary for her to retire to France.

In May 1938, the superior-general made her canonical visitation of the community. This would prove the last official visit until the end of World War II. Her written report was again very favourable and gave an outline of the apostolate of the sisters at this time. Having alluded to the excellent religious spirit, which she found among the sisters, she outlined the nature of their apostolate. She wrote:

> The works are carried out with great dedication, between them the two schools have 226 pupils who give satisfaction, by their attitude and their religious readiness to learn. Their teachers are unsparing of their time and energies. Since the previous visitation, beautiful classrooms have been built for the private school, and a new wing has been added to the old house; it contains the present chapel and bedrooms for the Sisters who now have plenty of space. The poor and the sick are still visited regularly; the sewing class is still well frequented. May the Holy Spirit, our Divine Father, continue to bless ever more abundantly all the members of this dear community. May he render their zeal fruitful and always remain for each one, 'the soul's delightful guest.'

The community was soon again assigned a new superior. Sister Marie Henri, who at that time was headmistress at Ingsdon Convent School in Devon, replaced Sister Clarisse Joseph. Her eighteen months superiorate at Abergavenny coincided with the outbreak of the war and the first year of hostilities. Despite the extra cares which this brought, she made the time to record in the Annals how the war affected the community and schools. Her entry for September 1939 notes:

> The private school begins the new term with 150 pupils, of whom 20 are evacuees from Birmingham, accompanied by a schoolmaster and a school mistress.

As the war went on, the sisters lost all contact with their families in France. An entry in the Annals notes:

> …we lose touch with the mother house and with our families. From now on we live with incessant alerts of air raids, especially during the night. Life becomes very wearing, but we do not become disheartened because we have abandoned ourselves wholly to the all-wise providence of our heavenly Father. Every evening before we retire, we entrust to the Heart of Jesus our fate and that of all who are dear to Him.

There were occasions of joy too in the midst of the terrors of the war. In August 1940, three of the sisters of the community together with two other sisters from Pontypool celebrated the silver jubilee of their religious profession. It was a truly family celebration, in an atmosphere of piety, holy joy and delicate sisterly affection. In the words of one of the jubilarians, it proved to be a heavenly day amid the sadness and sorrow of war. The examination results were also excellent that year. All the candidates, with the exception of one, obtained the coveted 'Exemption from the Matriculation Examination of the London University.' The sisters always praised God for having so generously blessed efforts that were made even more laborious by the effects of the war. Despite, and indeed partly on account of, the war the number of pupils on the school registers increased each year.

In August 1941, a meeting was held at Pontypool, of the superiors of the English Province. At the meeting, fourteen months after all communications with the mother house had been severed, it was discerned and decided that a provincial superior should be appointed; and that a noviciate should be established in the province. Once the apostolic delegate, William Godfrey, had obtained from Rome the authorisation to open a noviciate, Sister Marie Henri was chosen to be the one responsible for it, and this meant another change of superior; she was replaced by Sister Lucia. We shall return to this development in the next chapter. For the remainder of the war years and right up to the golden jubilee of the sisters in Wales, both St Michael's Convent School and Our Lady and St Michael's parish school flourished.

CHAPTER NINE

The Golden Jubilee of the Province and the State of the Congregation in the 1950s

HAVING LOOKED IN SOME DETAIL AT THE FOUNDATIONS OF THE TWELVE communities of the Daughters of the Holy Spirit settled in Wales during the first four years following their exile from Brittany, and the difficult beginnings they experienced, we now move on some fifty years to the Golden Jubilee of the Province of Wales and England. The period from 1906, when the twelfth foundation in Wales was established, until the celebration of the Golden Jubilee, was a period of consolidation of those foundations destined to survive the difficult beginnings. During the next twenty years, as already recounted, seven of the original foundations were closed. Six foundations were made in England during this time, indicating that the development and future of the congregation was destined to be mainly in England rather than Wales. During the second half of the twentieth century, in effect, all but one of the new foundations were made in England.

The two most recent foundations leading up to the jubilee year were the opening of a Juniorate in Ireland in 1949, as a centre for recruiting candidates for the congregation. The second foundation was the opening of a Provincial House and Noviciate at Woodbury, near Reading, in the same year. The account of these two foundations is preserved mainly in a *Lantern Lecture*, produced by Sister Aloysia Saunders at the time of the jubilee celebration (Archives, Provincial House, Northampton). In this, she says of the two foundations :

Both came into being at the hour marked by Providence, and judging by the trials they met and overcame were kept in being by the same providence.

The outbreak of two world wars cut off further recruitment of sisters from France, from whence practically all the sisters had come in the early years of the sisters' presence in Wales. It was the very moment when more help was needed to cope with the growing numbers of pupils and the influx of evacuees into the schools run by the Daughters of the Holy Spirit. The sisters, it was felt, must henceforth be self-sufficient and draw vocations to the congregation from areas where convents had been established over the years. A small number of past pupils from Pontypool and Bedford, in particular, joined the congregation, and this, together with some candidates from Ireland where, as we saw, contacts had already been made through the schools, led to the formation of communities more international in character. In fact, it is on record that as early as 1909, Sister Ste Barbe went from Carmarthen to Ireland in search of postulants.

The need for a noviciate in the country became a vital necessity; the only problem was where it should be. In fact, the first noviciate of the Daughters of the Holy Spirit was established in Wales during the Second World War, when communication with the congregation in France was difficult. During the war, when the government commandeered every square foot of house-space, and the communities of the Daughters of the Holy Spirit had their share of evacuees, the purchase of new property was impossible. So it was decided to use one of the existing properties owned by the sisters, and St Alban's Convent, Pontypool, was chosen for the establishment of the noviciate. Those in authority at that time carved out a suite of rooms under the roof in one of the wings of the convent, a part that could be isolated more or less from the main school departments. This was to serve as a noviciate, a house of formation, for future Daughters of the Holy Spirit, from 1942 till 1949. On 1 March 1942, the first four postulants began their formation. One of these four had already taught for two years in the convent school, but as she did not inform the other members of staff of her decision to become a member of the congregation, they were more than surprised to see her emerge from her enclosure a few days later, and appear in the convent chapel, which was also used by the school, dressed in a black dress and a black veil.

It was not an ideal situation for a noviciate, and when the plan was laid before the local bishop, he agreed to the arrangement on condition that it was only provisional, and that a suitable house should be acquired as soon as peace made it possible. When the superior-general of the congregation visited Wales after the war, she was very interested in the project. Like the bishop, however, she saw the drawbacks of having a noviciate installed in a large and noisy school, and urged the provincial superior to purchase a house especially for the purpose, where the novices could enjoy the enclosure enjoined by canon law, with the necessary quiet and recollection their training demanded.

House hunting began with its normal accompaniment of alternate hope and disappointment, till at length at the close of a novena made to Dom Jean Leuduger, at last Woodbury 'swam into our ken.' This property (**Plate 32**) was situated in beautiful woodland surrounded by miles and miles of farmland, about seven miles from the prosperous town of Reading in Royal Berkshire. The necessary preparations were made, and on 3 August 1949, Woodbury became the Provincial House and Noviciate of the Daughters of the Holy Spirit. So Wales, which had become the cradle for the formation of future members of the congregation for a number of years, saw this 'work' of the congregation move to England. Sister Jeanne du Calvaire and Sister Marie Henri, two of the first sisters to graduate from University College, Aberystwyth, were appointed as Provincial Superior and Novice Directress, respectively.

It was also recognised at this time that, if the noviciate were to be successful, it must be able to attract candidates for admission on a more regular basis than the very few who had up till then joined the congregation and received their formation through the medium of French, in the noviciate at the mother house. The Second World War brought complete upheaval. Sisters from France were not forthcoming; the convent schools were bulging with evacuees and other new pupils. In addition, the war years witnessed drastic and far-reaching changes in the educational system itself. The Butler Education Act of 1944 with its establishment of a tripartite system of secondary education: grammar, secondary modern and technical schools for all, demanded considerable changes to the existing arrangements of schools.

If the convent schools were to be retained under the new educational requirements, their staffs would have to be doubled, even quadrupled, and well trained. Where were these additional teachers to come from? The pioneering Daughters of the Holy Spirit, those who had borne the burden of the day and its heat, were growing old. There was no generation of trained younger sisters to take their place. Initially, recourse was had to lay teachers, but where it was necessary to employ a large number, the salaries to be paid were ruinous for the finances of the convent schools. Besides, it was often difficult to get lay teachers, even at a price, since teaching in a convent school did not, in those early days, carry with it the right to a pension.

For years the question of a foundation in Ireland, a country that provided religious sisters in large numbers for so many religious congregations, was mooted, from time to time, but always turned down as being unnecessary. After the war, it aroused new interest. It was in fact seen as a vital necessity to help provide candidates for the newly established noviciate in Reading. The new venture was placed in the hands of Sister Geneviève who left the Brecon community to go house hunting in Ireland. The Irish bishops were approached on the subject since their authorisation would be necessary to establish a foundation in Ireland. This was usually without the success one hoped for; an understandable reaction when one considers that Ireland was full of convents and full of religious sisters, so the bishops were rightly cautious in admitting the need for new ones.

The initial difficulties were so great that it is on record "that any other but a Sister Geneviève would have given up the task as hopeless." She was obviously the type of person who never takes 'no' for an answer. She clutched at every straw of hope, and at length was rewarded by the promise of nothing less than a castle, Magheramena Castle. A visit, however, revealed the castle to be wholly inappropriate, described "as a desolate ruin in a desolate waste". It was in a bad state of repair and too isolated to be of practical use, so it was relegated to the limbo of lost causes. Then came a moment when the whole project hung in the balance. The superiors were sadly considering its abandonment when a new gleam of hope shone out; strong, steady and firm. It came from no less a source than the Bishop of Clogher, resident in Monaghan. The quest was reinforced by Sir Shane Leslie who offered the sisters a temporary lodging in one of the houses on his estate **(Plate 33)**, until such time as they could procure premises more suitable for the work they had in view.

It was, then, at Glaslough in County Monaghan, amid ideally beautiful surroundings on the edge of the village, and within the perimeter of the Leslie Family Estate, that the sisters settled in 1947, and soon received the first group of candidates desirous of joining the Congregation of the Daughters of the Holy Spirit. Within a few years, the bishop himself had found and invited the sisters to a larger building in the town of Monaghan, a stone's throw from the episcopal palace. The sisters therefore left

Glaslough, where they had been very happy, and went to the new foundation in the town of Monaghan. The original building was enlarged, and a small maternity wing added, as well as a business hostel for girls and women. The establishment of the maternity wing marked the first time that the Daughters of the Holy Spirit took up the second most important work of the congregation, nursing, and this was to lead in subsequent years to the training of nurses in the province. For the next quarter of a century until its closure in 1973, a large number of vocations (**Plate 34**) to the noviciate in Reading came through this juniorate, and later to the noviciate at Clapham Park, Bedford, where the provincial community and the noviciate moved in 1958.

The foundation in Ireland, like the noviciate in Reading, was to have an effect on one of the foundations in Wales. In order to provide sisters to run this new foundation in Ireland and the Provincial House and Noviciate at Reading, it became necessary to close one of the existing foundations and the axe fell once again in Wales, on St David's Convent, Brecon, where, at that time, there was a flourishing convent school. Negotiations began for its closure. Rather than close this school, however, the bishop of the diocese was fortunate enough to find another religious congregation to take it over. So it was that the Congregation of Ursuline Sisters of the Roman Union took over St David's Convent School, Brecon.

The Daughters of the Holy Spirit left Brecon after forty-five years, in 1948, as described earlier. This is how a sister who lived through the experience described the closure of Brecon:

> It was the sap of Brecon that was asked to feed the new shoot [foundation in Ireland]. As in all pruning, the operation was painful, bitterly so, not only to the sisters themselves whose lives had been bound up with Brecon for so many years, over thirty years in the case of one sister, but the bishop of the diocese, who could only with the utmost difficulty, be persuaded to give his consent to their going. It had to be. Brecon's life-blood was needed elsewhere. If you care to visualise it as such it was God's magnificent regard for its long years of patient toil in his cause, that it should blossom into the Provincial House and Noviciate and into the Juniorate in Ireland.

Another comment on the takeover of the school by the Ursuline Sisters recognised the difficulty of the departure from Brecon.

> They [the Ursuline Sisters] have entered into our labours and reap where we have sown. They can never know how hard that sowing was. But God, who sees all, recompenses all. Does he not tell us that 'both he who soweth and he that reapeth shall receive wages, that both may

rejoice together' (John 4:6). We have then an assured hope that in the new 'life' at Woodbury, and its continuation under the Ursulines, Brecon will in heaven shine out as one of the most precious jewels of the congregation, especially in those members who valiantly gave so many devoted years to its service.

The Golden Jubilee celebrations were held in the Provincial House in Reading. The superior-general, Mère Marthe de Jésus, accompanied by one of the general councillors, Mère Jean de Jésus, and by Sister Ildefonce Marie, who in March 1902 was one of the three very first Daughters of the Holy Spirit to set foot on English soil (she was a member of the first community to be established in England at High Wycombe in Hertfordshire), attended the celebrations. All the superiors from the different communities were invited to represent their communities at the jubilee celebration on April 1952. Even the celebrations of such a joyful occasion possessed its cloud of sadness, for on the very day that Sister Pierre Lazare, superior of the community at Carmarthen, was due to travel to Reading for the celebrations, she was taken ill and was unable to come.

The Golden Jubilee was a simple affair. There was a Mass of thanksgiving celebrated by the chaplain of the provincial community, followed by a celebratory lunch and entertainment provided by the novices and postulants for all the guests. Since the sisters had only been in the area for some three years, and as they had no apostolate among the people of the region, the event was not open to the local population. The necessary enclosure for the postulants and novices was thus respected.

Subsequent History of the Four Remaining Foundations

BY THE TIME the sisters celebrated the Golden Jubilee of their foundations in Wales and England, there were only four of the original foundations in Wales still in existence: Carmarthen, Aberystwyth, Pontypool and Abergavenny. As the congregation moved on from the jubilee celebrations, we consider the development of these foundations, until two of them were finally closed. Three of these had flourishing convent schools at the time. In Pontypool, there was St Alban's Convent School, which by now was a boarding and day school. There was a community of nearly thirty sisters at that time, although the number was reduced by the departure of the novices and postulants and the sisters in charge of their formation. The community at Abergavenny similarly ran a flourishing convent day and boarding school,

St Michael's, which had grown so much over the years that it was situated on two sites. In addition, three sisters taught in the parish primary school, and there was a community of nearly twenty sisters at that time. In Aberystwyth, St Padarn's Convent Boarding and Day School was the main work of the sisters, as their effort at setting up a parish school for the Catholic children had, as we have seen, a short history. The community was also enlarged by sisters who, after a break of some twenty years, returned to study in the university, to meet the needs of the increasing educational legislation of the government in post-Second World War years.

Carmarthen Convent

THE FIRST of these four foundations to close was St Winefride's Convent, Carmarthen. By 1952, the community had centred its apostolate in the school and parish. Three of the sisters taught in the parish school, and all five did parish and pastoral work in the parish and in the town. As mentioned earlier, Sister Pierre Lazare was unable to attend the golden jubilee celebrations at the provincial house. In fact, she died two days after she was taken ill. She was a woman of great vision, in the words of one who knew her "she was at least half a century ahead of her time." She was well known throughout the town by catholics and non-catholics alike. It was estimated that

> she had taught the grandchildren and even the great-grandchildren of that generation, and knew intimately the history of every family in the parish. [*St Mary's Newsletter*, Carmarthen, Vol I Issue 2, November 2000].

The whole town mourned her passing. A new Lady Altar and a stained glass window (**Plate 35**) were erected in the church as a memorial to her. On the window were the words:

> To the glory of God and in loving memory of Sister Pierre, Ma Mère, who died 23 April 1952.

The altar and window were erected by parishioners and friends. In the records of the Passionist Priests who served St Mary's Parish, Carmarthen, Sister Pierre was described as

> a wonderful influence for good, and she generously supported and not infrequently inspired the work of the clergy. Many Passionist communities of St Mary's through the years had reason to be grateful

for her assistance both spiritual and temporal [Taken from the Archives of the Congregation of the Passionists, Carmarthen].

An entry in the community Annals, the testimony of a sister who knew her well, perhaps best sums up the greatness of Sister Pierre Lazare. It reads:

> Sister Pierre Lazare returned to God without being able to enjoy in this life the visit of the superior-general who arrived the day before from France to celebrate the golden jubilee of the foundation of our houses in this country. She had spent 44 years of her life in Carmarthen. Her simplicity, her uprightness, her artistic and poetic gifts and her goodness showed itself in many ways: tolerance for others, compassion for the sufferings of others, and generosity to those in need. She showed so much love, simplicity, and a natural goodness that she became the confidante of all those who suffered and who needed consoling. All this was the result of forgetfulness of self, which she practised to a heroic degree, and it all came from a deep faith and union with God. She was loved and respected by all the people who knew her. At the request of parishioners and non-catholics, Masses were said for the repose of her soul for nearly two months following her funeral. She died after two days of illness, and now she rests in the cemetery, beside the church and the school she loved so much and which she served so well.

It was a cause of sadness too, that Sister Pierre Lazare had died before the celebration of the golden jubilee of the foundation of St Winefride's Convent, Carmarthen, which was held on 4 August 1953. On this occasion, Bishop Petit celebrated a pontifical Mass, and expressed his deep appreciation for the work of the sisters in the school, the parish and the whole area.

Sister Pierre Lazare was replaced as superior by Sister Gabrielle de Jésus who only stayed for one year at Carmarthen, before she was transferred to Bedford convent. Sister Maurice Joseph, who had been headteacher in St Alban's Primary in Pontypool, replaced her, and was superior there from 1953 till 1958. Sister Mary Enda (**Plate 36**) was appointed head teacher in St Mary's Catholic School on the retirement of Sister Pierre Lazare in 1948. Incidentally, she was one of the four first novices to make profession in the newly established noviciate at Pontypool. She remained in Carmarthen till 1959, when she was appointed head teacher of St Joseph's Catholic Primary School in Newton Abbot. She was replaced by Sister Mary Andrew, who was head teacher from 1959 till the sisters were withdrawn in 1970.

During the years leading up to the withdrawal of the sisters from Carmarthen, life was very peaceful and uneventful at St Winefride's Convent. The school prospered, and there was an increase in the numbers on roll. Three of the sisters continued to work in the school, but all the sisters were involved in ecumenical and social activities, as well as home and hospital visiting. These were also the years of great change in the congregation with the implementation of the requirements of Vatican II, as we shall see in the next chapter.

On 30 April and 1 May 1970, Mère Jean de la Trinité, the superior-general, made her canonical visitation of the community and wrote in her report:

> This will be the last canonical visitation of the superior-general to this dear community of Carmarthen. The Daughters of the Holy Spiirt will have worked here for nearly 70 years as 'missionaries,' sent by Mère St Georges. The country will long keep the memory of those who have passed this way, like Christ, doing good. May God bless the sacrifices of the three sisters in the community, at present, for the people of Wales.

The people of Carmarthen were saddened by the news of the forthcoming departure of the sisters. The parishioners and friends of the sisters organised a farewell tribute on 28 June, to mark the closure of the convent at 7 Picton Place **(Place 37)**. The provincial and all the sisters who had worked, at one time or another, in Carmarthen were invited to attend the closure. The story of the arrival of the sisters in 1903, their contacts and work among the people was movingly and lovingly narrated by Miss Eileen Jones, the sister of Miss Isaure Jones, the newly appointed head teacher of St Mary's Catholic School. The school children dramatised some of the highlights of the early days. Mrs Morris, Brynmyrddin, gave a very beautiful address. In it she sketched the role that the 'White Sisters' had played in the history of Carmarthen. Her husband was a nephew of Miss Abadam, who was instrumental in bringing the Daughters of the Holy Spirit to Carmarthen.

The last day of the school year, 10 July 1970, was also the last day for Sister Mary Andrew and Sister Mary Hilda, the two last sisters to teach in Carmarthen. There were farewell speeches from staff and pupils and tokens of gratitude, and the sisters gave a little party to the school children in the afternoon. As happened in Brecon, when the sisters left there, the departure of the sisters from Carmarthen did not mean the end of the road for religious in Carmarthen. The Passionist Fathers, who had served in Carmarthen even before the arrival of the sisters, invited the Sisters of the Congregation of the Cross and Passion from Bolton in Lancashire to come and replace them. The last entry in the Annals of the community mentions the arrival of these sisters on 15 August 1970.

> On 14 August, Bishop Langton Fox visited the community to bid the sisters farewell. On behalf of the parishioners and clergy, he thanked the sisters for the work they achieved throughout their sixty-seven years in Carmarthen.

The last brief entry in the Annals simply records:

> Sister Hilda, Sister Imelda and Sister Mary Andrew leave Carmarthen for their new communities, thus bringing to a close the life of the Daughters of the Holy Spirit in this corner of Wales.

Aberystwyth Convent

BY THE nineteen fifties, St Padarn's Convent School had survived the decision to close it, which, as we saw, was considered as a possibility when the future of Brecon convent was discussed. The sense of relief for the community was very great, so in a new spirit of zeal for their work, the sisters set about gaining recognition from the Ministry of Education during the 1950s. In fact at this time the sisters were still optimistic enough, according to the Annals, to hope that they would one day have a Catholic primary school in the parish, in addition to the convent school. Although they did not achieve this, it was realised in a different way some years later.

The sisters applied for recognition from the Ministry of Education for the convent school in May 1950. The school was inspected, and the good news that the school was recognised as efficient reached St Padarn's Convent Day and Boarding School in August 1950. Some recommendations were made in the inspectors' report to the effect that a new science laboratory and assembly hall were needed. Plans were soon put in hand to meet these requirements. In May 1953, excavations for the new building began, but in the summer of that year the superior was transferred to Bedford convent, to be replaced by Sister Lucia Marie. The latter did not enjoy good health, but she saw to the completion of the building **(Plate 38)** before she was transferred to the Pontypool community.

The number on roll during these years fluctuated. For example in September 1959 there were 212 on roll, but by September 1964 there were 112 in the junior school, with only 35 in the senior school. As the numbers decreased in the senior school, it was decided to close the senior department as a first phase in the negotiations to make St Padarn's a voluntary-aided Catholic primary school serving the parish and surrounding areas.

Discussions began with the local education authority, and in April 1963 a meeting took place between the diocesan and the education authorities to pursue this project. In 1964, 'Brendon', a boarding house across the road from the convent, was sold, as it would no longer be required, for the sum of £6,500 (£85,000 today). Negotiations of this type take a long time, but by 5 August 1965, an entry in the Annals states:

> Today, we learned from an article in *The Cambrian News*, [the local newspaper], that we have been given aided status.

It was signed by members of the Cardiganshire Education Authority. News of their intention regarding the school was made officially in a notice signed by the bishop of the diocese and two other signatories, and this was published in the press on 19 October 1965.

The senior department of St Padarn's Convent closed at the end of the summer term 1965. The pupils who were in the school when it was closed gained admission to the local grammar school or, in the case of boarders, to schools near their homes. In order for the premises to meet the standards required by the education authorities, certain conditions had to be fulfilled, and Mr G.R. Bruce, the county architect visited the school on 8 April 1968 to report on the progress of the updating of the premises in accordance with the requirements of the Department of Education and Science. Following this visit, on 28 April, came the official news of the granting of aided status as from the 1 May 1968. The number on roll on 30 April was 162 pupils. On 2 May, the official certificate from the Department of Education and Science was received by the school, and the sisters who taught in the school received their first pay packet from the Local Education Authority. On 21 June, the refurbished premises were blessed by the parish priest.

Sister Imelda Kelly was head of the junior school after the closure of the senior department, a post which she held for two years. Sister Anne Quin was appointed head in 1967, and she was the first head to manage the school when it received aided status. She remained as head of the school till her retirement in 1985. As there was no sister to replace her as head, the first lay head was appointed. He was Mr Douglas Grant who had been the deputy head till his appointment as head teacher.

Meantime, other parts of the property needed reorganising for different uses. By November 1977 plans were ready, and the first and second floors of the old dormitory block were turned into self-catering accommodation for students of the university. Mr Mervyn Jones, accommodation officer for the university, and Mr Eirwen Jones, technical adviser on accommodation, were consulted. Both were strongly in favour of the project. A new private nursery school began on 1 September 1977, in the old school hall which had been adapted to fit the needs of a nursery. Mrs M. Sallop was appointed as supervisor and Mrs Lloyd as her assistant. An entry in the Annals of the community noted that the private nursery opened with ten children aged three to four years of age.

On 3 October 1977, the work on the old dormitory block was completed and there were ten beautiful modern self-catering flats, which were rented out to university students. The first ten students to take up residence in Padarn House, as it was called, were all from overseas, and registered students of the college of librarianship. Three were from Malaysia, three from Indonesia, two from Kenya, one from Rhodesia and one from Canada. The sisters still had the oversight of the nursery and the self-catering flats. They lived in the old vicarage section of the property, but soon that was too large for the few remaining sisters in the community. So the next decision was to sell the whole property except the school part, which was finally leased to the diocese in 1998. It was decided to buy a small house for the remaining sisters. It was very difficult to sell the property since it was attached to a school, but eventually they succeeded in finding a buyer. Meantime a semi-detached house (Dolgadfan, 5 Loveden Road) was bought, and the sisters moved there on January 1995. At the time of writing, there are only three sisters in Aberystwyth, one working in the Family Centre, and the others playing a full part in parish life. The school is flourishing, serving the children of the parish and other parts of the region.

Pontypool Convent

To CROWN the work of fifty years in Pontypool, an inspection of the convent school was applied for, so that the status of the school as a grammar school might be settled. The inspectors came in force to inspect the school. Shortly afterwards, Sister Dominic Cusson, the headmistress, received the joyful news that the school was there and then placed on the official list of recognised schools, from the Minister of Education herself, Miss Horsbrugh. A great *Te Deum* of thankfulness went up from the hearts of all, and the event was duly celebrated. In that same year, when Mère Ste

Mélaine, the superior-general, paid a visit to the community, the only one of her generalate, she was struck by the motto inscribed on the great stained glass window over the main staircase in Park House, *Tout vient de Dieu* (Everything comes from God), and in subsequent reference to Pontypool, she never failed to quote these words, which she had never forgotten. An entry in the Annals noted:

> They echo the truth of God's blessing on the house for fifty years and his ever-watchful providence, for 'Tout vient de Dieu'.

In 1953, the beloved Mother Marie Albertine returned to Pontypool as superior of the community (She had taught science in the convent school some years earlier). She set about the celebration of the golden jubilee. This celebration took place on 3 October 1953, exactly fifty years to the day since the sisters' arrival in Pontypool. Sister Josephe Marie and Sister Maurice Joseph, who had served so many years in the community, were invited to attend the celebration. The day of celebration began with Mass sung in the Gregorian chant. Father Cahill, the parish priest, presented the sisters with a beautifully inscribed sanctuary lamp for the chapel, in recognition of their contribution to the parish. Mrs K. Price, the elocution teacher, in memory of her mother, Lady Percy Thomas, lately deceased in Cardiff, presented a thurible and stand, inscribed with her name. The entry relating to this event ended with the prayer: "May the incense which goes up from it, symbolic of our prayers, bring down from God many blessings on the donor." A statue of Our Lady in stone was also erected on the front lawn of the convent to mark the jubilee.

During the following years, the school flourished, until in 1959 new plans for the future of St Alban's Convent appeared on the horizon. An entry in the Annals for 1959, points to this forthcoming change:

> A complete changeover of schools is in progress. The provincial superior and her council have decided to present the property and school to the diocese in view of the changes brought about by the 1944 Education Act. The burden of supplying catholic secondary modern schools has been so great that the sisters felt obliged to do something about it to show our goodwill. The plans to transform this building (the convent school) into a secondary modern school with a grammar stream for the catholics of the valley have been approved by the Ministry of Education. It remains to implement them in the near future.

Further reference to the reasons for this change will be mentioned in the next chapter.

This was a significant moment in the history of the community because it meant considerable upheaval in many ways. The school year ended on a note of great joy, however, for finally the sisters had finished paying the debt owed on the junior school, which was completed in 1954. This debt which hung over them for five years was always a source of worry, and the sisters had often to deprive themselves of the necessities of life in order to meet payments. The sisters who taught in the convent school for nearly half a century were transferred to other convents. Sister Dominic Cusson who had been headmistress of the convent school for forty-five years was transferred to the community in Monaghan, Ireland. Sister Peter Dominic and Sister Marie Athanase who taught English and French respectively retired to the Provincial House, Clapham Park, Bedford, which had been established in 1958. The following year Sister Lucia Marie, whose three year mandate as superior ended that year, and whose health was giving cause for concern, retired to France on 3 August, accompanied by Sister Louis Eugène who also taught French in the convent school, and by Sister Françoise de Ste Anne who retired from her teaching post in the parish primary school. Sister Marie de Ste Barbe, who was in charge of the boarders and Sister Agnès du Calvaire were transferred to the sisters' retirement convent in Olney, a former convent school in that area of Buckinghamshire.

The first stage in the re-organisation was to close the junior section of the convent school, since the proposed secondary modern school was destined for pupils of secondary school age. So on 16 July 1959, only five years after its official opening, the convent junior school closed. The senior school continued for another five years, with 188 pupils on roll on 10 Septemebr 1959. These numbers remained fairly consistent, despite the fact that it was to close when the new school opened. On 3 July 1960, another aspect of the reorganisation of the school took place. The two senior classes from St Alban's Primary School moved into the empty premises of the junior convent school.

An entry in the community Annals for 18 November 1962, spoke of a joyful occasion which linked the convent with its past history. It read:

> By special permission of the Ordinary (the bishop), a christening took place in the convent chapel this afternoon. Mr Richard Hanbury-Tenison, descendent of the Hanbury family who owned Park House since the sixteenth century, is married to a Catholic. Their third child was born on 22 October 1962, and as it was the first of their children to be born in England, they wished the child to be baptised in the chapel here. Father

Cahill, the parish priest, performed the ceremony, and the child was baptised William Hanbury-Tenison.

During the early sixties, there were twelve sisters in the community. Three of these taught in the parish primary school, and four taught in the convent school and other sisters, some retired, gave their services in many different ways as cooks, sacristans, or with general household activities. Life in the convent school was often far from peaceful with massive excavation bulldozers and lorries bringing building requirements for the new building, which was to be erected in what was popularly known as 'the wood.' But 'wood' it would be no more, for in the place of the ancient trees emerged a new building containing a large assembly hall, two laboratories, a domestic science room, a needlework room, a typing room, woodwork and metal work rooms, and a large gymnasium. As the new school was scheduled to open in September 1963, the convent senior school closed for the last time on 16 July 1963, and the existing pupils at the time were offered places in the new school, if they so wished.

On 3 September 1963, the new St Alban's RC Secondary School (**Plate 39**) opened with 420 pupils from all the surrounding areas, in the eastern and western valleys of Monmouthshire. Five sisters taught in the new school; three of them for the first time in the voluntary maintained sector of education, and the other two were already teaching in the senior part of the all-age Catholic schools in Pontypool and Abergavenny, and moved automatically with their classes into the new school. There is an entry in the community Annals on 1 October 1963 as follows:

> These three sisters (those who had only taught in convent schools previously) received their first pay cheques from Monmouthshire Education Authority, receiving £127.10.0, £122.10.0 and £59.18.7 (£1,700, £1,600, and £775 respectively, in today's currency).

The official opening of the school took place on 8 June 1964. It is recorded as follows:

> The official opening of St Alban's RC School took place at 2.00 pm this afternoon. The school was formally opened by Archbishop John Murphy of Cardiff. The Rev Raymond Davies OSB Chairman of Governors introduced the Archbishop. Other speakers were: Mr T.M. Morgan, Director of Education for Monmouthshire, and Mr Leo Abse, Member of Parliament for Pontypool.

Between 1963, when St Alban's opened as a secondary co-educational school, and 1968, the sisters continued to live in the rear section of Park House which was kept by the sisters for their residence, and not handed over to the diocese. However, as time went on, it became evident that their accommodation was unsuitable. So in 1967, they visited a house for sale, called 'Hillgrove' which was situated on the opposite side of the road from St Alban's Catholic Church in George Street. This house had been, in fact, a former convent founded by the Franciscans, who had charge of the parish, as a convent for the Sisters of Mercy in 1865. The house by then was in great need of repairs, which were carried out, and on 19 March, the feast of St Joseph, the sisters took up residence there. St Alban's Convent then passed into the history books. As the private residence of the sisters, the house **(Plate 40)** was simply called 'Hillgrove', the name it had when it was bought. This was to be the home of the sisters in Pontypool for the next thirty-three years. Four of the sisters continued to teach in St Alban's Comprehensive School (the status it had acquired by this time), and two other sisters taught in the parish primary school.

The sisters became fewer and fewer over the next twenty years. They continued their teaching apostolate and were involved in parish and pastoral activities of various kinds. But the falling numbers of sisters and the reorganisation that took place in the province, as recounted in the next chapter, meant that when a sister reached retirement age there was no other sister to replace her. The last sister who taught in the comprehensive school left there in July 1990. The last sister to teach in the parish school left in July 1996. The word 'convent' seems to be indelibly marked in the minds of the people of Pontypool, who to this day speak of St Alban's Comprehensive School as the convent, and parents are still heard to say: "My son/daughter has gained a place in the convent for September."

During the millennium year, the final page in the history of the Daughters of the Holy Spirit in Pontypool was written. Since there were only three sisters left in the community, it was agreed to amalgamate the Pontypool and Abergavenny communities, and the choice of location fell on Abergavenny to be the future home of the sisters. Hillgrove house had to be sold, and this sale took more than a year to complete. The sisters from Pontypool transferred to the convent in Abergavenny on 15 February 2001. The sale of Hillgrove was completed on 21 February 2002.

Abergavenny Convent

THE SECOND half of the twentieth century was a time of great change and development for St Michael's Convent School, Abergavennny. The growing numbers in the convent school in post-war years had necessitated the purchase of a new property on the western side of the town, about a mile away, called Glancibi Grange (**Plate 41**). Archbishop McGrath of Cardiff came to bless the new property, and the senior school moved there in September 1945. The junior and senior schools were separate from then on, each with its own headmistress. An entry in the community Annals at the beginning of the school year September 1946 stated:

> The two schools open with large numbers of pupils, especially in the senior school. Glancibi is already hardly large enough.

The next step in the growth of the school was the application for recognition by the Ministry of Education. The year 1950 was a year of celebration for, in August of that year, both junior and senior schools were recognised as efficient by the Ministry of Education. Among the recommendations proposed by the inspectors was the need to build a new assembly hall and a science laboratory for the senior school, and within two years an action plan for their implementation was set in place.

One entry in the community annals during this period shows that the support of the Herbert family was still very much a reality. The entry for 28 June 1952 reads:

> Death of Lady Helen Herbert of Coldbrook. This lady was the wife of Sir Arthur Herbert, second son of the Honourable Mrs Herbert of Llanover. Lady Helen was what you might call 'a great lady.' Her life was devoted to works of charity. She was always ready to help anyone in need. She was a constant visitor to the homes of the poor and sick, as well as to the hospital, where she brought comfort to many a sick person. She was a great benefactress of our convent and whenever we approached her in any financial difficulty, we were sure to receive the delicate and kind assurance 'Remember I am your friend.'

Negotiations for the building of the new extension to the senior convent school proceeded, and plans were drawn up. These plans were approved on 16 December 1954, and the new building started. This was soon completed, and on 16 December 1954, there was the official opening of the new school block with its spacious assembly hall, and a state-of-the-art science laboratory. As the school grew in popularity, more and more pupils sought admission. A house in Avenue Road, called 'The Lindens,' had been purchased, to accommodate about a dozen boarders. Soon, however, the boarding accommodation was inadequate, and the next development was to build a new boarding school as an extension of Pen-y-pound House. The contract for this building project was signed on 30 November 1954, by Rev Mother Marie Amélie, Mr J. Duggan and Mr A.J. Denbury. As soon as the new boarding building was completed, The Lindens boarding-house was sold, and all the boarders accommodated in one building.

On 23 April 1956, the sisters celebrated the golden jubilee of the foundation. It was a private celebration concentrating solely on the religious aspect of the event. The main emphasis was on thanking Almighty God for all his watchful care of the community over fifty years. A Mass of thanksgiving was celebrated in the convent chapel for the special intention of the Honourable Mrs Herbert, the great benefactress of the sisters and the person they regarded as 'the foundress' of the convent in Abergavenny.

The death of Sister Félicien on 7 May 1957 was an occasion of great sorrow for the community. She was the able secretary of Sister Marie Amélie who was superior at that time, and who at quite an advanced age had the full responsibility for the building of the new boarding school. Sadly, the strain of the death of Sister Félicien, coupled with responsibility for the new building, was too much for the superior, and, three weeks later, she was struck down with paralysis, and had to return to France. The boarding building was completed, and the boarders took possession of the very modern and roomy premises.

St Michael's Convent Junior and Senior schools were by now flourishing, and waiting lists of those seeking admission were beginning to build up. Yet, as we saw earlier, plans were in hand to open a voluntary-aided Catholic school in Pontypool serving the whole of Monmouthshire except the Newport, Monmouth and Chepstow areas, which were served by St Joseph's Comprehensive School in Newport. The development at Pontypool was to be linked with the future of St Michael's Convent School. The Catholic pupils of secondary school age were to be transported by bus daily to the new school in Pontypool, once it opened. The result of this was the decision to close Glancibi Grange, the senior convent school, at a time when it was flourishing.

St Michael's Convent Old Girls Association, at their meeting on 31 December 1962, expressed their shock and sadness that such a change could ever involve the future of their well-loved school. It was bad enough to find that many of their old teachers were no longer at the convent. The Annals record their dismay:

> Those present expressed unanimous regret that the coming year would be the death knell of a flourishing school.

It was decided that the junior convent school, which was unaffected by these developments should remain open, and the junior school from then on became the chief apostolate of the sisters, in addition to that of the sisters who taught in the parish school.

On 12 July 1963, Glancibi (the senior school) closed its doors for the last time, to the great regret of parents, pupils and the sisters themselves who taught there. The community Annals note:

> The labourers of Glancibi field will have furrows to trace elsewhere.
> We pray that their work may be abundantly blessed.

In September of the same year, when Glancibi should have opened for the new school year, an entry in the Annals notes: "We feel lost without Glancibi." The next move was to sell the property, which was concluded on 20 January 1964.

The junior school opened in September 1965 with 130 pupils on roll, but just two years later, the numbers had gone up to 200. The school was to continue to grow and develop for seven more years, until it was decided to close it in line with the reorganisation and renewal movement, which will be related in the next chapter. Events succeeded one another with great speed, and in July 1971 St Michael's Convent Junior School closed its doors for the last time. On 30 June, shortly before the end of term, the parents of the pupils, at the time of closure, held a farewell buffet supper at the convent, and gifts from the parents were presented by the Mayoresss of Abergavenny and by Mrs Margaret Herbert to all the members of the teaching and the catering staff. Mr Robin Herbert, the great grandson of the 'foundress' whose children were pupils in the convent school at the time of its closure, spoke on behalf of the parents:

> As a parent I am sure I am only voicing the view of all those present when I say that we shall all miss the educational foundations which have been laid in this school. I am personally delighted not only that the order is going to keep a house in Abergavenny, but also that some of the sisters are going to continue to teach in the Catholic school in the parish. This will provide a vital link with the town.

The mayor too added his words of appreciation to those of Mr Herbert. The mayor said how pleased he was to be present to express the town's appreciation of the work of the school. He said that the business and social life of Abergavenny had been enhanced by the presence of the convent school.

When the junior convent school closed, part of the school premises was refurbished to provide a residence for the sisters who remained in Abergavenny. The rest of the building was converted into four flats, which were sold on completion. While this project was taking place, the sisters continued to live in Pen-y-pound House, the older part of the convent. On 5 October 1971, work began on the refurbishment of the junior school premises, and on 26 February 1972, the sisters moved into what was now to become the future convent of the sisters at 151 Park Crescent. The last sister who taught in the parish school left in July 1996, when she was transferred to the convent in Luton. The sisters continued to be engaged in educational and pastoral work, and visits to homes and hospitals continued to be a central part of the apostolate of the community.

The remainder of the convent property, Pen-y-pound House and the boarding school, was put up for sale, and interest in its purchase was shown by the Inner London Education Authority (ILEA), to provide a field centre for London secondary schools. On 12 January 1972, six members of ILEA spent several hours inspecting the property, and on 22 April, an inspector from County Hall, London, visited the premises. Shortly thereafter the property was bought by ILEA. When ILEA ceased to exist, the property was purchased by the Royal Borough of Chelsea, the present owners of Ty Morfydd (the current name of the centre). Money from the sale of the property was placed in a charitable trust called The Peny-y-pound Trust to benefit the needy of Abergavenny and the Archdiocese of Cardiff. In this way, the generosity of the Honourable Mrs Herbert and her great love of the poor will live on. She could scarcely ever have imagined when she decided to bring the Daughters of the Holy Spirit to Abergavenny in 1906, that her gesture of generosity would have such long-lasting repercussions for her native land.

CHAPTER TEN

The Second Vatican Council and its Aftermath: Re-organisation, Change and Renewal

WITH THE ADVENT OF THE SECOND VATICAN COUNCIL AND THE cultural and sociological changes of the nineteen sixties, the era of the 'works of the Province' as they were known, was soon to come to an end. To understand the changes in religious life after the Second Vatican Council, it is necessary to see how religous life was affected by Vatican II, the twenty-first ecumenical council of the church in its two thousand years of history, and one of the most epoch-making councils yet. For one thing it was the first council which did not issue anathemas against any individual or group of individuals. The vision of Pope John XXIII, when he summoned the council, was rather to renew and update the church, to open the eyes of the church to the needs of contemporary society, and to bring the church more in line with the needs of the world, which was in a state of tumult and profound change. The old traditional order, which had maintained stability in society since the sixteenth century, was, in the words of the poet Tennyson, "yielding place to new."

The Council issued sixteen documents for the universal church, dealing with all aspects of the church, and it is significant that only two of these documents are entitled "dogmatic" pronouncements. It was essentially a pastoral Council. The church itself was to be the sacrament of the world. One of the sixteen documents was addressed to religious orders and congregations. Entitled *Perfectae Caritatis, Decree on the Up-to-date Renewal of Religious Life*, it was published on 28 October 1965. This Decree dealt with religious life in all its aspects, and its "adaptation to changed conditions of the time."(Article I). It laid down certain general principles for the implementation of this renewal. Among the main recommendations was the need for religious to return to the original inspiration of the founder or foundress of the congregation or order, and to judge the relevance of their apostolate in the light of their founding vision. There had to be a serious return to the gospel and the following of Christ, "the supreme rule." (Article 2(a)).

Religious should be central to the life of the church, and promote the church's initiatives and undertakings in biblical, liturgical, dogmatic, pastoral, ecumenical, missionary and social matters. (Article 2(c)).

Religious were also required to receive the necessary human and intellectual formation to evaluate the contemporary world, and to understand its people (Article 2(d)).

The mode of government of the religious orders and congregations should also be examined using the same criteria. (Article 3).

This last prescription was in itself revolutionary, since the hierarchical structures had stood the test of time. For apostolic religious in particular, authority would be regarded from now on more as the communion of the members and the leadership, rather than the strict hierarchical structure it replaced.

There were some concrete changes recommended by the Council to bring about renewal. In Article 3, it is stated:

> For this reason, constitutions, directories, books of prayers, of ceremonies and such like should be suitably revised, obsolete prescriptions being suppressed, and should be brought into line with the synod's documents (Article 3).

This last recommendation was a major task for religious, and the process took many years before constitutions were rewritten and submitted to Rome for approval. Another far-reaching, perhaps revolutionary, recommendation regarded the dress worn by religious. It was stipulated that this too should be updated, and "suited to the time and place and to the needs of the apostolate. The dress of men and women, which is not in conformity with these norms ought to be changed." (Article 17).

Sister Brendan Downing **(Plate 42)**, who hailed from Cork, Ireland, was the provincial superior of the Daughters of the Holy Spirit during and after Vatican II. Like Pope John XXIII, she was a woman of vision, a gift so greatly needed at a time of transition. She read the signs of the times as recommended by Vatican II, and moved the province in a way that was inevitable, if unexpected; a way in which many Daughters of the Holy Spirit at that time preferred it did not go. A return to the founding vision of the congregation made it obvious that working in Catholic secondary schools, among the poor, and not so poor, seemed much closer to the original vision of the Daughters of the Holy Spirit, which was the education of poor children and the care of the sick, than the more privileged education of the rich in fee-paying convent schools. At this time, the Daughters of the Holy Spirit had a total of six private schools, three in England and three in Wales.

The sisters, however, beginning as we have seen, from extreme poverty and the hardships of their origins, had spent half a century building up these convent schools and paying off the considerable financial debts incurred by the necessary building extensions to the convent schools. They could not imagine that the result of all their years of hard work would soon be overtaken by events. The provincial superior, on the other hand, could see clearly that British educational legislation, with its successive Education Acts was making more and more demands on the sisters, and the cost of running fee-paying schools would soon be beyond their means. In addition, in common with all apostolic religious at the time, many young and highly qualified sisters, in a climate of new-found freedom unleashed in the wake of Vatican II, left their congregations and this put an extra strain on financial resources. The departure of these sisters meant that if they were teachers, which they invariably were, they would have to be replaced in the schools by lay teachers whose salaries would soon drain the sisters' meagre financial resources. The departing sisters did not receive a salary since all the convent money was held in common, but they had to be provided with money on their departure from the congregation in order to help them to become financially autonomous.

A number of developments can be attributed to these circumstances and this era. The Education Act of 1944 sharpened the need for Catholic schools, as we have seen. The Act gave free secondary education to all. It enjoined that children over the age of eleven years of age should be educated in separate schools instead of in the elementary or all-age schools which was the situation at that time. While new state-maintained schools were established according to the terms of the act, the Catholic Church found the financial burden so great that it was not till the nineteen sixties that these schools were provided in some areas in Wales. In some localities, the Catholic Church had found it difficult to implement these stipulations for up to fifteen to twenty years after the passing of the legislation.

The Congregation of the Daughters of the Holy Spirit was able in some small measure to help the cause of Catholic education in this area. The provincial and her council decided, in line with the demands of Vatican II for religious sisters, and also to further the cause of Catholic secondary education to close the fee-paying convent schools over a number of years, and sisters released from the convent schools were to seek employment in the new Catholic secondary schools established in the 1960s and 1970s. As we saw in the last chapter, the three schools that were run by the sisters at this time were affected by the thinking of Vatican II, and also by the falling number of sisters.

The years following the Second Vatican Council were also a time of re-structuring for the large Daughters of the Holy Spirit communities. Institutional religious life, especially of the monastic type, was becoming unpopular for apostolic religious; that is, those religious involved in teaching, nursing, and the caring services. Smaller, less institutionally structured groupings were favoured, more in keeping with the thinking of the time. The Daughters of the Holy Spirit re-structuring took place in the early nineteen sixties. Smaller communities were formed, more suited to parish life and also to the more varied ministries. For example, from the large community at Pontypool, which numbered more than twenty sisters in the immediate post-war years, the numbers were reduced to twelve by 1959. The other sisters left Pontypool, as we have already seen, either to return to France or to the retirement home, which had been opened in a former convent school at Olney in Buckinghamshire. This reduction in the number of sisters was also linked to the closure of the convent schools, where a large number of sisters had been involved in the running of the school, either as teachers, cooks, cleaners, and ancillary staff generally. Similarly, when the convent school at Abergavenny was closed, the number of sisters was reduced to half a dozen. The Abergavenny Convent Junior School continued for another eleven years, and closed in 1972. The present community of four sisters is lodged in part of the former junior school, which, as we saw earlier, was refurbished to form the residence for the sisters who live there at present. These sisters work in the local hospital, and are involved in various educational, pastoral and parish activities.

The Last Foundation in Wales: Blaenafon 1986-1995

IN LINE WITH the renewal demanded by Vatican II, a number of small communities were established in deprived areas to enable the sisters to work and witness among the poor, according to the vision of the foundress of the congregation. In returning to their founding charism, three such communities were established by the Daughters of the Holy Spirit. One of them, the last foundation in Wales, after an interval of eighty years, was established in Blaenafon. Two small parishes in the eastern valley of Gwent were amalgamated, necessitated by the growing shortage of priests. The parish priest resided in Abersychan, which left an empty presbytery in Blaenafon. It was to this presbytery **(Plate 43)** that the sisters came in January 1986.

On Saturday 9 January 1986, the two sisters arrived in Blaenavon to set up a community in the presbytery. The most significant thing about this foundation was its similarity to the early foundations established in Wales. The house did not belong to the sisters but to the diocese. In return for their work in the parish, the house was rent-free. It was a small house with three small bedrooms, a lounge, and with a dining room in the basement. It was attached to the parish church. The first entry in the Annals of the community, the source of information for this foundation (Archives, Provincial House, Northampton), echoes the experience of the earlier foundations.

> Today, after many comings and goings, with bits of furniture, crockery, etc., etc. (all second-hand), Sister Margaret Geraghty and Sister Patricia Purchase (a native of Wales) finally set up residence here. We have just got the bare necessities of life for the time being. It is rather bleak at the moment, the weather which is wet and windy did not help. Our first visitors, the Peploe family, came to borrow a screw-driver.

It should be noted, however, that these two sisters were no strangers to Blaenafon. They were both already living in the Pontypool community, and both were teaching in the locality. They did not have to face the problems of the early foundations, that is, not knowing the language, or the difficulty of having very little or no money to begin the foundation. The sisters needed no alarm to wake them each morning. Instead they were called each morning in a rather novel way. Paxo, an old cockerel, who prowled round the back of the presbytery gave a wake-up call by crowing at 5.30 am.

On the day after their arrival, the parish priest and the parishioners welcomed them to Blaenafon. A comment from the Sunday bulletin for that week, which fitted the sisters' situation, was recorded in the Annals on that day. It said:

> The Spirit of God is behind new beginnings. If we are willing to begin again, he is there to grace our new venture in faith.

One of their first acquaintances in Blaenafon was Stanley Taylor who lived across the road from the presbytery, and who was pleased to tell them that he had been taught by the French sisters who taught in the parish school, over seventy years before. Mrs Gladys Bayliss, who lived opposite the church also remembered the sisters who taught in the parish school early in the century. She said that the people of Blaenafon used to speak of the sisters as "the good ladies." It would be interesting to know whether the mother of this lady was the one who gave the sisters, who travelled from Pontypool every day to teach in the Catholic school in Blaenafon, a cup of coffee every morning and afternoon, a service for which the superior paid her each month.

Two days after their arrival in Blaenafon, the sisters made a tour of the communities of the Daughters of the Holy Spirit in the locality. They had breakfast with the Pontypool community after morning Mass, lunch with the Abergavenny community, and returned to Blaenafon for tea.

Their first weeks in this new foundation were devoted to furnishing the house and putting in place their new time-table in order to begin their ministry. The Duggan family donated a wardrobe for one of the bedrooms, and the Purchase family gave a second one. On 23 January, the two sisters went to Newport to buy necessary things for the house, like an electric kettle, a vacuum cleaner and an ironing board. Then after two months residence in their new home, there was a formal social to welcome the sisters to the parish. An entry in the Annals of the community noted:

> The atmosphere was lovely and friendly, with music and dancing. There were members of other christian demoninations present too.

At the end of the social, the sisters were touched to receive a cheque for £120, to help them in their ministry.

Since the sisters were sent to Blaenafon to be a presence in the parish and to live and work among the people, they soon organised their ministry there. They set up a prayer group in the convent and invited interested people to join them in prayer. This was in compliance with their *Rule of Life,* which says "We share in the prayer of the people among whom we live," and again: "We try to hear the Word that God speaks to us today through the scripture and through events" (Article 35).

On 28 February, some weeks after their arrival, the sisters took the children for their Sunday liturgy, Sister Margaret in Blaenafon, and Sister Patricia in Abersychan. The sisters adopted a simple life-style, and witnessed in a way that impressd the people of the town. As the *Rule of Life* says: "Our involvement in mission, is often expressed through simple human gestures. 'As you did it to one of the least of my little ones you did it to me' (St Matthew, Chap 25:40)."

Their experiment reached the ears of other congregations. On one occasion two Sisters of Charity of St Paul visited them to ask for their help to enable them to discern where they might work in a needy area of Wales.

In 1988, another sister joined the community. Sister Eileen Sammon, on her retirement from teaching in St Joseph's School, Newton Abbot, expressed the wish to be part of this new type of community. She arrived in Blaenafon in September 1988, and Sister Patricia returned to the community in Pontypool. The third sister to join the community was Sister Frances Sibeth, who arrived in September 1991 from the community at Abergavenny, where she was already involved in pastoral work. She continued her work in Abergavenny, travelling there daily from Blaenafon till it was phased out, and she then devoted her time to pastoral and social work in Blaenafon, where she became known as "the lovely lady, the angel of Blaenafon." These three sisters formed the community for the next four years till its closure **(Plate 49)**.

The sisters were always strongly involved in ecumenical activities in the town. Frequent entries in the Annals of the community point to this. The entry for 11 September 1991 reads: "Sister Margaret attends an ecumenical Bible meeting at the vicarage on the theme of evangelisation." On 19 January, there is the following entry: "Sister Margaret attends the committee meeting in Horeb Baptist Church in connection with the choosing of some suitable books to be placed in the local library." All the sisters attended the annual Christian Unity Week service every year, and were both involved in the preparation of the service and in participating during the service.

Many aspects of local, national and world issues formed part of the ministry of the sisters in Blaenafon. On 17 October 1992, they attended a Provincial Assembly of the Daughters of the Holy Spirit, which was held at the Religious Education Centre in Bedford, on the theme of Creation Spirituality. The day was facilitated by Father Frank Cama, a priest of the

Clifton diocese, and by Sister Deirdre Duffy, a sister of the Congregation of St Joseph of Peace. An entry in the community Annals has a comment on this day, and points to the sisters' involvement in ecological matters. It reads:

> Our pollution in Blaenafon is caused mainly by the open cast mines, and the vandalism in the town, with twenty boarded up shops, and all the broken windows. The weekend itself was a marvellously enriching experience on creation spirituality, which celebrates blessings and helps us to use our creativity to co-create our world rather than destroy it. It helped deepen our vision of our world and its people, the destruction that is taking place, and our part in it.

The sisters were also committed to involvement in social and political isssues. On 1 December 1992, Sister Frances and Sister Eileen went to Newport to join a coach, which would take them to London, for a national lobby of parliament at Westminster. This representation was organised on an ecumenical basis. The group met with members of parliament, whom they questioned about their policies on housing. The questions highlighted the need for housing the homeless, and the sufferings of those who had no home. They also dealt with questions on issues where changes of attitude were necessary to improve life for the deprived and the underprivileged.

In their formulation of their apostolate in Blaenafon, each sister wrote what her particulatr witness was. One sister wrote:

> My ministry is to care for the poor people that I visit and try to assist in every way possible. I undertake parish visiting, and deal with the old, the sick, with family problems, lapsed catholics, young people, children, and some little 'street friends'.

Another mentioned her ministry to school children, especially those with special needs, and her work with adults who were seeking to grow in the knowledge of God. She adds:

> In my ministry to the housebound and the lonely, I try to be the 'face' of Christ for them in bringing them some love and joy. In some cases, I feel that I am at the receiving end, but they do not realize it.

The sisters were very happy in Blaenafon. The people loved them, and life was without any of the problems that dogged some of the other foundations in Wales. However, the lack of sisters available to replace those who either had to retire or move where they were needed more urgently, brought about the closure of this Welsh foundation. The last entry in the community annals was made on 31 August 1995, and reads:

The house closed. Father Henessey thanked the sisters for all the work they had done in the parish and for their presence among the people.

The neighbours and people of the parish expressed sadness at the departure of the sisters. The community Annals end with a quotation from Psalm 90:

> Show our servants the deeds you do
> Let their children enjoy your splendour!
> May the sweetness of the Lord be upon us
> To confirm the work we have done.

The final item in the Annals of the Blaenafon community is a letter from the Most Rev John Aloysius Ward OFM Cap., Archbishop of Cardiff. He wrote to the provincial superior on 1 June 1995, and had this to say:

> Your sisters in Blaenafon have given great service in the short time they have been there, and I know they have done much to strengthen the faith of the people, not only in Blaenafon but also in neighbouring Abersychan. I know they will be greatly missed not only by our Catholic people, but by others of that area who have come to know and appreciate the value of their witness and solidarity.

New Ministries; the Growth of the Associate Movement

THE POST-VATICAN II years were also a time of spiritual formation and renewal for the sisters of the province, according to the stipulation of *Perfectae Caritatis,* which reminded religious that

> even the best contrived adaptations to the needs of our time will be of no avail unless they are animated by a spiritual renewal, which must always be assigned primary importance even in the development of the active ministry (Article 2(e)).

Almost all of the sisters were offered courses in spiritual renewal, theology, scripture and human development according to their aptitudes and ability. Some were sent as far afield as Belgium, France, the USA, and even the Holy Land, but most were sent to centres in England or Ireland. This spiritual formation was a completely new development in the post-Vatican II era. Before this, the great emphasis had been on training teachers for the convent schools. There was now a vast financial investment in this kind of formation, and houses of study were again opened, on a relatively temporary basis, to house the new 'mature' students in London, Liverpool and Maynooth in Ireland.

The post Vatican II years also saw new developments in the ministries undertaken by the Daughters of the Holy Spirit. While teaching remained the principal work of the sisters of the province, there was a move to train sisters as nurses who would be needed to staff the centre in Ireland already mentioned. Also at this time there were sisters released from their work in the convent schools who were trained as nurses destined to work in the state hospitals and nursing homes. Two sisters were trained as social workers, and this was a new ministry for the province, while others again did training in catechetics, needlework and cookery. The post-war bulge in vocations to the religious life had by the 1960s diminished. The province had opened a large noviciate at Clapham Park, Bedford in 1958, but by the end of the 1960s, the number seeking admission to the congregation had fallen so markedly that the property was used as a retreat centre.

The most significant development in the history of the Daughters of the Holy Spirit in Wales at the end of the twentieth century, and into the new millennium, has been the growth of the Associate Movement, a new branch of the congregation, which has enlarged the Daughters of the Holy Spirit family 'by extending the tent', to use a biblical term. This has, in fact, been part of the growing movement at the present time, of lay associateship in religious congregations and institutes, and it is one of the signs of the times to which we should be attentive. All charisms or gifts of the Holy Spirit belong first and foremost to the Church community, the Body of Christ as a whole (I Corinthians) and therefore cannot be claimed by anyone or any group in the church as belonging exclusively to them. All the members of the Christian community can share all charisms in some way. Religious life, a fundamental charism of the church, takes shape and becomes individualised and embodied in various congregations. Since the fundamental charism does not belong to the religious congregation but to the church at large, lay people today, in increasing numbers, are seeking to participate in this fundamental charism in its expression of spirituality and mission in the church. The sharing of the charism of the Daughters of the Holy Spirit, as indeed the charisms of all religious congregations, is to be appreciated as an enrichment of the charism and not an impoverishment or even a watering down.

The first forty-four Articles of the *Rule of Life* of the Congregation of the Daughters of the Holy Spirit dealing with charism, mission, vowed life, prayer life and ongoing formation, which was updated in 1982, constitute a remarkable and inspiring document, deeply rooted in the origins of the Congregation, in the Word of God and the realities of the world today. It is not surprising then that in the living out of the charism, lay Associates are attracted to a closer collaboration with the mission and spirituality of the Daughters of the Holy Spirit.

It was in Wales, in fact in Abergavenny, that the first group of Associates in Europe (there were already Associates in the Congregation in the USA) joined the congregation, and did their formation under the leadership of Sister Philomena White. There is a period of formation which lasts between one and two years during which the candidates study the charism, spirituality and mission of the congregation, its history and also examine more deeply their own baptismal consecration through a study of *Christifideles Laici*, an Apostolic Exhortation from the Vatican in 1985, which is a presentation of the role and mission of the lay members of Christ's faithful people. At the end of the period of formation, they decide whether they wish to make a commitment to the congregation or, as is the case in the USA, enter into a covenant with the congregation, on an annual basis.

The Associates have their own *Book of Life* containing many excerpts from the sisters' *Rule of Life*, to help them to live out their commitment. There is also a growing number of Associates in Aberystwyth, up to twenty at the time of writing. There is a group in Pontypool, which was formed before the convent in Pontypool closed in 2001. With twenty four associates and seven sisters in Wales at present, it will undoubtedly be the presence of a strong and dedicated band of Associates sharing the spirituality and mission of the congregation (the question of community is not yet clear) who will help to ensure the future of the congregation in the third millennium.

Chapter Eleven
Conclusion

THE YEAR 1902 WILL ALWAYS REMAIN A SIGNIFICANT DATE IN THE history of the Congregation of the Daughters of the Holy Spirit. It was the year, which saw the sisters driven from their native Brittany to seek asylum in more friendly territories abroad. Although persecution is never easy to live through, the sisters came to Wales where, after their difficult early years, they were happy and flourished. The common Celtic ties ensured that the warmth and friendliness of the Welsh people struck a welcome chord in the hearts of the Breton exiles.

The commitment of the sisters to ecumenism from the very beginning, at a time when ecumenism was not very developed in Wales, is one of the outstanding marks of their service to Wales. Their convent schools received pupils of all denominations and none, even though, as we saw, they always seemed to feel that their first call was to the Catholic population, as in Catholic Brittany.

It is significant that relations with the Welsh people were always cordial, and that their difficulties usually came from the church to which they themselves belonged. Occasionally, as we have seen, parish priests did not support them in the way they would have expected. Our sources tell us one side of the story, however, and this perhaps, is the limitation of the type of sources used, namely, the correspondence of the superiors of the foundations. To get the complete picture, we would need to hear the other side of the difficulties, as no doubt there was considerable misunderstanding on the part of the sisters in a strange culture, and with little knowledge of local conditions. The use of primary sources in this study, almost all of which are in French, serve to highlight aspects of the religious and social history of Wales and thus contribute to a fuller picture of the rich heritage of the nation.

The first fifty years of the sisters' presence in Wales was a time of concerted effort and struggle to build up the flourishing convent schools of which they could boast when they celebrated the Golden Jubilee, in 1952. The second half of the twentieth century saw great changes in their ministries, their structures, their dress, and life-style. Whatever the changes in what was to become an ever-changing era, they have always remained true to their origins: simplicity of life-style, ministries among the poor and deprived, and an increasing commitment to the development of their own spirituality and to sharing the same with the People of God, among those with whom they live and work.

The witness of community life has never been more urgent, living as we do in an individualistic society where hedonism, narcissisism and self-glorification have become characteristic of the age. The call to work for justice, equal rights for all and a fair distribution of the goods of this world becomes the lived expression of the sisters' own vow of poverty, since they own nothing and have all things in common, an image of the nature of the kingdom, where in primeval times man was asked to care for the earth, and be the steward of its goods. The call to an inclusive love for all peoples, whatever their race, creed or colour is the most powerful manifestation of the vow of celibacy to which the sisters have committed themselves. The growth of unlimited freedom or more accurately of unfettered licence, to do whatever one wants, as one wants, and when one wants, is countered by the witness of religious sisters who bind themselves to discern among themselves and with others, the will of God, in obedience to the congregation to which they have committed their lives. Indeed the call of the three vows can be summed up in the words of the prophet Micah when he tells the people of his time: "This is what God asks of you, only this: To act justly, to love tenderly and to walk humbly with your God" (Micah 6:8).

In the year 2002 the Daughters of the Holy Spirit celebrated the centenary of their presence in Wales. The centenary celebrations in Wales were held at Abergavenny on 1 June 2003, with a centenary Mass celebrated by the Most Rev Peter Smith, Archbishop of Cardiff, accompanied by the Bishop of Menevia, the Abbot of Belmont and other Benedictine monks. Present also were the descendants of the Honourable Mrs Herbert, who brought the sisters to Abergavenny in 1906. Mr Robin Herbert, CBE, her great grandson, who in past years has continued to support the work of the sisters in Abergavenny was the guest of honour at the celebration. His grand-daughter, Alice, the-great-great-great grand-daughter of the Honourable Mrs Herbert, read one of the lessons during the Mass. Present, too, were the Right Honourable Paul Murphy, Member of Parliament for Torfaen, and Secretary of State for Northern Ireland, and Sir Richard Hanbury-Tenison, formerly Lord-Lieutenant of Monmouthshire. After the Mass, a celebration lunch was held at St Mary's Priory Centre. The event brought together sisters from all over the Province, many of whom had worked in one of the Welsh foundations. Associates, friends, and parishioners of Our Lady and St Michael's parish, where the Mass was celebrated, joined in the celebration. It was a moment to remember, and to thank God for, those brave pioneering sisters who so courageously began a century of service in Wales, initially as exiles in a foreign land.

At present, the province is in a period of retrenchment in common with all other apostolic religious congregations in the country, and indeed in the western world. The congregation is once again at a watershed in its history, as it was when it faced dissolution during the French Revolution, and exile at the beginning of the twentieth century, because of the anti-clerical laws in France.

What of the future? It is not for us to know the times and seasons which God has planned for us. What we do know is that in 2006 the Congregation of the Daughters of the Holy Spirit will celebrate the tercentenary of its foundation in the little fishing village in Brittany, to answer a critical need of that time. That too will be an occasion to look back in gratitude for what has been; to thank God for what is, and to look forward with hope to whatever the future is to bring.

The shifting paradigms of our time, the extraordinary technological advances in every aspect of life may cause alarm. But as religious, one thing we are sure of is that God is in control of the universe and will reveal his plans for certain as and when it seems good to him to do so. Religious sisters are called to be prophets in an age of increasing confusion and increasing violence, and to witness to the eternal in the midst of the temporal. Meanwhile, wherever we are or wherever we minister as Daughters of the Holy Spirit, serving the Gospel now as we do in three continents, we realize that we are citizens of a global village which we share with six billion other human beings on our planet.

Bibliography

PRIMARY SOURCES

The primary sources used in this study, dealing with the foundations in Wales, are all in French, and are catalogued in the Archives of the Congregation of the Holy Spirit at the Mother House, Saint Brieuc, Côtes du Nord, Brittany:

File 12G-4 : St Mary's Convent, Monmouth
File 12G- 5 : File 8T-5 – St Winefride's Convent, Carmarthen
File 12G- 6 : St Joseph's Convent, Usk
File 12 G- 7 : St Margaret's Convent, Tenby
File 12G - 8, File 8T-8 : St David's Convent, Brecon
File 12G - 9, File 8T-9 : St Padarn's Convent, Aberystwyth
File 12G - 10, File 8T-10 : St Alban's Convent, Pontypool
File 12G - 11 : St Anne's Convent, Llanrwst
File 12G - 12 : St Mary's Convent, Pembroke Dock
File 12G -13 : St Joseph's Convent, Pwllheli
File 12G -14 : St Helen's Convent, Caernarfon
File 12G -16, File 8T-16 : St Michael's Convent, Abergavenny
File 8T : St Felix Presbytery, Blaenafon
File 8T-19 -Juniorate House, Monaghan, Ireland
File 8T-21: Provincial and Noviciate House, Woodbury, Farley Hill, Reading
File 1P-1 : *White Sisters* – Being a chronicle of events connected with the origin and development of the Congregation of the Daughters of the Holy Ghost, Vols 1 & 11- (Unpublished)
File 1P-1 : *Inter* –Special Edition on the Origins of the Congregation, Anne Marie Couloigner, FSE,1989.

The Constitutions and Directory of the Congregation of the Daughters of the Holy Ghost, editions of 1730, 1749, 1927 and 1960. Manuscripts, documents and records kept in the Archives of the Congregation at the Mother House, Saint Brieuc, Brittany, and in the Archives of the Province of England, Ireland and Wales, at the Provincial House of the Daughters of the Holy Spirit, Northampton.

REPORTS AND OFFICIAL PUBLICATIONS

Abbot, W. M. (ed.), *Decrees and Declarations of the Second Vatican Council 1962 – 1965* (Geoffrey Chapman, London, 1966).
Declaration on Christian Education (*Gravissimum Educationis*) 1965.
Declaration on Ecumenism (*Unitatis Reintegratio*) 1964.
Declaration on the up-to-date Renewal of Religious Life *(Perfectae Caritatis)* 1965
Declaration on Religious Liberty (*Dignitatis Humanae*) 1965
Dogmatic Constitution on the Church (*Lumen Gentium)* 1964
Pastoral Constitution on the Church in the Modern World (*Gaudium et Spes*) 1965

General Catechetical Directory: Catechesis in our Time(Catechesi Tradentae) St Paul Publications, Slough, 1979.
The Catholic School (The Sacred Congregation for Catholic Education, Vatican, 1977)
The Easter People: *A Response to the National Pastoral Congress held in Liverpool* (Episcopal Conference of England and Wales, May, 1980).
Daughters of the Holy Spirit – Rule of Life (Approved by Cardinal Pirinio for the Sacred Congregation for Religious and Secular Institutes, 9 December 1983).

SECONDARY SOURCES

Attwater D. *The Catholic Church in Modern Wales* (London, 1935).
Bank of England *The Pound, Equivalent Contemporary Values*. A Historical Series 1270-1999. (London, n.d.).
Cahen, L. & Mathieu A. *Les Lois Françaises de 1815 à Nos Jours*, (Felix Alcan, 1919).
Dale, Hilary *The Congregation of the Daughters of the Holy Ghost and the Struggle for Christian Education in France* (unpublished dissertation, University of Durham, 1963).
De la Villerbel , André du Bois – *Dom Jean Leuduger, Fondateur des Filles du Saint Esprit* (Prud'homme, Saint Brieuc, 1924).
Dwyer, John C., *Church History, Twenty Centuries of Catholic Christianity* (Paulist Press, New York, 1985).
Franciscan Missions among the Colliers and Ironworkers of Monmouthshire (author unknown, London ,1876).
Gilkey, L, *Catholicism Confronts Modernity* (Seabury Press, New York, 1975).
Konstant, D. *Signposts and Homecomings: A Report to the Bishops of England and Wales* (St Paul Publications, Slough, 1981).
Latzko, Andrea, *Lafayette* (Methuen 1936).
Lemercier, L'Abbé , *Notice sur la Congregation des Filles du Saint Esprit 1706 – 1850* (Prud'homme 1888).
Masson, Chanoine, *Les Soeurs de la Tourmente* (undated and unpublished; Archives, Saint Brieuc).
Powell, David A, *St Mary's Catholic Church, Monmouth* (St Mary's Catholic Church, Monmouth, 1993).
Prud'homme, Père, *La Révérende.Mère Saint- Georges, Douzième Superieure Générale* (Prud'homme, Saint Brieuc, 1925).
Randell Alan, *Carmarthen Mission, The Early Years* (Clive James, Narberth, 2002).
Saunders, Sister Mary Aloysia Lantern Lecture 1952 (Unpublished).
Shuster G.N. *Catholic Education in a Changing World* (Holt, Rinehart and Winston, New York, Chicago, San Francisco,1967).
Tolles DHS, Sally, *The Daughters of the Holy Spirit in the Eighteenth Century* (Unpublished dissertation, University of California, 1970).
Torlay FSE, Marie, *Marie Balevenne, 1666-1743* (unpublished ; Archives, Saint Brieuc).
Idem, Jean Leuduger, Missionaire Apostolique en Haute Bretagne (1649 – 1722), (unpublished; Archives, Saint Brieuc).
Trebaol OMI, Père: 'The White Sisters in Llanrwst', *Petites Annales (*April 1904).
Tucker, B (ed), *Catholic Education in a Secular Society* (London 1968).
Vie de Mère St Georges (author unknown, Prud'homme, St Brieuc, 1925).

List of Illustrations

Plate 1
Jean Leuduger (1649-1722) who inspired the foundation of the Congregation (p.14)

Plate 2
The first foundation of the Daughters of the Holy Spirit at Le Légué, 1712 (p.16)

Plate 3
Plérin—A wing of the school and first mother house of the congregation (p.17)

Plate 4
Mère Saint Georges, the superior-general who sent the sisters to Wales (p.33)

Plate 5
The sisters leave Brittany to go into exile (p.34)

Plate 6 (Frontispiece)
The Honourable Mrs Herbert of Llanover By permission of Llyfrgell Genedlaethol Cymru/The National Library of Wales (p.35)

Plate 7
St Mary's Convent, Monmouth (28 St Mary's Street) (p.39)

Plate 8
St Mary's RC Church, Monmouth (p.40)

Plate 9
Cartref, St James' Square, Monmouth (Became the convent in 1908) (p.43)

Plate 10
St Joseph's Convent, Usk (The first pupils of the private school) (p.49)

Plate 11
The Woodlands, Brecon, (first house of the sisters, 1903) p.55

Plate 12
The house in Glamorgan Street, Brecon, 1905 (p.58)

Plate 13
Pupils of St David's Convent, c.1905 (p.58)

Plate 14
Morganwy House, Brecon, St David's Convent in 1928 (p.63)

Plate 15
Park House, Pontypool (St Alban's Convent) (p.79)

Plate 16
Picton Villa, Carmarthen (St Winefride's Convent) (p.87)

Plate 17
Picton Terrace, Carmarthen, (St Winefride's Convent) (p.91)

Plate 18
Picton Place, Carmarthen (St Winefride's Convent) (p.91)

Plate 19
Sister Pierre Lazare "Ma Mère." (p.92)

Plate 20
St Mary's RC School, Carmarthen (p.92)

Plate 21
The Old Rectory, Tenby—St Margaret's Convent (p.97)

Plate 22
Salisbury House, Aberystwyth (St Padarn's Convent) (p.111)

Plate 23
St Michael's Vicarage, Aberystwyth (St Padarn's Convent) (p.118)

Plate 24
St Padarn's Convent—A group of pupils, 1946 (p.124)

Plate 25
St Anne's Convent, Llanrwst (p.135)

Plate 26
Grave of Sister St Félicien, Pwllheli (p.174)

Plate 27
The Small Community of Sisters, Caernarfon (p.196)

Plate 28
Pen-y-pound House, Abergavenny (St Michael's Convent) (p.203)

Plate 29
St Michael's Convent, Abergavenny—The Needlework Room (p.205)

Plate 30
Gwladys Eileen Masters, Pupil at St Michael's Convent, c.1918 (p.213)

Plate 31
St Michael's Convent, Abergavenny (The Junior Convent School) (p.226)

Plate 32
Provincial and Noviciate House, Woodbury, Reading, England (p.234)

Plate 33
Glaslough, Co Monaghan, Ireland (juniorate) (p.235)

Plate 34
Students aspiring to religious life, Apostolic School, Monaghan, Ireland (p.236)

Plate 35
Stained glass window in St Mary's Church, Carmarthen, a memorial to Sister Pierre Lazare (p.238)

Plate 36
Sister Mary Enda and her class, St Mary's School, Carmarthen (p.239)

Plate 37
A plaque unveiled in Carmarthen in tribute to the service of the sisters (p.240)

Plate 38
St Padarn's Convent School Extensions, Aberystwyth (p.241)

Plate 39
St Alban's Secondary School, Pontypool (p.246)

Plate 40
Hillgrove Convent, Pontypool (p.247)

Plate 41
St Michael's Convent School, Abergavenny. Prefects on the lawn at Glancibi Grange (p.248)

Plate 42
Sister Brendan Downing, provincial charged with re-organisation and renewal in the province (p.253)

Plate 43
Blaenafon—St Felix Presbytery 1986-95

Plate 44
The St Alban's Convent School Old Girls' Association on the steps of the entrance to Park House

Plate 45
St Alban's RC Elementary School, Pontypool—Sister Callista, "football coach" and her team

Plate 46
St Alban's Convent School, Pontypool—the school netball teams

Plate 47 (Front Endpaper)
Sister Imelda and her class at St Michael's Convent, Abergavenny

Plate 48 (Rear Endpaper)
A school outing to the seaside, St Mary's RC School, Carmarthen 1954

Plate 49
The Blaenafon community (p.258)

MADE AND PRINTED IN WALES BY
GWASG DINEFWR PRESS
LLANDYBIE FOR
THREE PEAKS PRESS
9 CROESONEN ROAD, ABERGAVENNY,
MONMOUTHSHIRE NP7 6AE